THE NEW TESTAMENT STUDENT AT WORK

Volume II of

THE NEW TESTAMENT STUDENT

JOHN H. SKILTON, *Editor*

PRESBYTERIAN AND REFORMED PUBLISHING CO.
1975

Library of Congress Catalogue Card Number 75–24949
Printed in the United States of America

To the Memory of

FRED CARL KUEHNER

1912 — 1975

Educator, Pastor, Editor, Author, Man of God

Dedication

On a plaque in Dr. Kuehner's study was inscribed the first question of the Heidelberg Catechism. In his closing days as throughout his life he rejoiced in its warm and moving expression of truths which he cherished. The English translation is:

Question 1.

What is thy only comfort in life and in death?

Answer.

That I, with body and soul, both in life and in death, am not my own, but belong to my faithful Saviour Jesus Christ, who with his precious blood has fully satisfied for all my sins, and redeemed me from all the power of the devil; and so preserves me that without the will of my Father in heaven not a hair can fall from my head; yea, that all things must work together for my salvation. Wherefore, by his Holy Spirit, he also assures me of eternal life, and makes me heartily willing and ready henceforth to live unto him.

THEOPHILUS J. HERTER

THE PILGRIM'S DEPARTURE

The Reverend Fred C. Kuehner, Th.D., D.D., to whom this volume is dedicated, served for many years as dean (the chief administrative officer) and professor of biblical languages at the Theological Seminary of the Reformed Episcopal Church, and he had agreed to serve also as one of the editors of The New Testament Student. *It is appropriate that this volume should open with the sermon which was preached at the funeral services for Dr. Kuehner, on February 3, 1975, by Bishop Theophilus J. Herter, Th.D., professor of New Testament at the Reformed Episcopal Seminary and an associate editor of this series.*

How would you refer to your own death if you knew that it was both certain and imminent? The Apostle Paul knew that his own death was an impending reality. He was in prison, awaiting execution; his death was certain and imminent. And as he waited for the day of execution he wrote a letter to his young preacher friend, Timothy. Referring to the coming execution, Paul used these words: "The time has come for my departure" (II Tim. 4:6).

In using the word "departure" Paul was sketching out a picture. The word suggests the breaking up of camp, the striking of the tent, folding it up for the next move. And who would be breaking up a camp, striking the tent for the next move? Soldiers, you say. Yes, but the biblical emphasis is on the pilgrim, the spiritual pilgrim. Christians are pictured in Scripture as pilgrims, whose earthly life is a wandering that precedes their coming home to heaven.

v

The Apostle Peter, in his first letter, addresses his Christian readers as "elect pilgrims." He exhorts them to live after the pattern of their pilgrim character by abstaining "from fleshly lusts which war against the soul" (I Pet. 2:11). They are to live as though simply passing through this world, without taking on any of its form or fashion, in expectation of arriving at their heavenly home. The believer's pilgrim character is most fully developed in the case of Abraham, described in the eleventh chapter of Hebrews. I give a summary as it is expressed in the language of the New International Version, the translation with which Fred C. Kuehner was associated:

> By faith he made his home in the promised land like a stranger in a foreign country; he lived in tents. . . . For he was looking forward to the city with foundations, whose architect and builder is God . . . they were longing for a better country—a heavenly one. Therefore God is not ashamed to be called their God, for he has prepared a city for them (Heb. 11:9-16).

From a different perspective the Apostle Paul likened the physical body to a tent, as compared to the resurrection body which would be "a building from God." "Now we know that if the earthly tent we live in is destroyed, we have a building from God, an eternal house in heaven, not built by human hands" (II Cor. 5:1). Bringing all these ideas together we have the picture of a spiritual pilgrim leaving the tent of his earthly wanderings, expecting that he will possess an eternal dwelling in the city that God has built. Thus, when Paul wrote that the time had come for his departure, the words were free from any suggestion of apprehension. In his spirit there was a quiet peace that produced a joyous anticipation.

"The time has come for my departure." We may think of this in terms of two emphases. God's sovereign control is the first emphasis, and the Christian's assured hope is the second. In saying that the time had come, Paul was voicing the truth that all time is under the control of God and that God's wise providence fashions the forms of our experiences. Chance has no part in the Christian's life. Chance may be the god of the atheist; chance may be the god of the gambler and evolutionist. But chance neither determines nor influences anything in the experience of the Christian. All things are by God's appointment, under his sovereign and gracious control, and we have the assurance of Scripture that all such things are good. Paul voiced this faith in that brief statement, assured that God's purpose for him had run its full course. The time was God's time. There was peace in his heart as he contemplated this sure fact. This leaving of the tent, this making ready to enter the building from God, this coming to the city of God was nothing to fear. This was God's own gracious way of perfecting the salvation he had so freely given.

I can imagine that when Timothy read this letter and came to the words "the time has come for my departure" the blood rushed to his face, his heart skipped a beat, and he cried in protest: No! It cannot be! But then, I also imagine that Timothy would recall the instruction he had been given from the Scriptures by his grandmother and his mother, Lois and Eunice. His mind would have turned to those Old Testament passages which speak of the godly hope of the righteous: "My times are in thy hand" (Ps. 31:15). "The steps of a good man are ordered by the Lord, and he delighteth in his way" (Ps. 37:23). We do not know whether Timothy had opportunity to read any of the Gospels, or what words of the Lord Jesus might have been recounted to him by those who had heard Christ. But we know that our Lord spoke of God's sovereign control over nature and the lives of men: "Are not two sparrows sold for a farthing? and one of them shall not fall to the ground without your Father. But the very hairs of your head are all numbered. Fear ye not, therefore, ye are of more value than many sparrows" (Matt. 10:29-31). God is ever active in savingly providing for his own.

But we must be more specific in speaking of God and sovereignty. We must recognize that the Lord Jesus himself is the sovereign God! Following his resurrection Jesus told Peter that he would serve as his witness throughout a long life that would end in martyrdom. Peter did not object. He knew that the one who had conquered death was able to control all other things. But Peter was interested in and curious about his fellow disciple, John. "And what shall this man do?" he asked. The reply of Jesus was direct and revealing: "If I will that he tarry till I come, what is that to thee? Follow thou me."

"If I will"—that is the point. Christ, the sovereign Lord, determines the span of the believer's life. He appoints the believer's service, and determines when that service comes to its end. The time is neither too soon, nor too late. All this is implied in Paul's brief and calm statement: "The time has come for my departure."

These words also suggest the Christian's assured hope. This may not be clear from the statement itself, but it is clearly expressed in the sections that precede it. In the first portion of his letter Paul had written: "Our Savior Jesus Christ . . . hath abolished death and hath brought life and immortality to light through the gospel" (II Tim. 1:10). And almost in the same breath Paul gave another assurance, "I know whom I have believed, and am persuaded that he is able to keep that which I have committed unto him against that day" (v. 12). Whom had he believed? The one whom he had proclaimed in all his preaching: The Lord from glory! The Lord who had taken on true human nature, so that in that body of flesh he might die for our sins. The Lord of glory who became sin for us that we might be made the righteousness of God in him. The Lord from glory who made reconciliation by the shedding of his blood. By his death Christ provided a full and complete ransom payment so that we might be freed from the bondage of sin. This is the Lord in whom Paul trusted, the Lord whom he proclaimed and in whose resurrection victory Paul himself would share as he came to the time of his departure. This is not only the confidence of Paul, but the assured hope of every Christian.

God had given this hope to his servants in earlier times as well, and by that godly hope they were enabled to see beyond the dark barrier of death. David said, "Thou wilt show me the path of life: in thy presence is fulness of joy; at thy right hand there are pleasures for evermore" (Ps. 16:11). And in the Psalm that follows David says, "As for me, I shall behold thy face in righteousness: I shall be satisfied when I awake with thy likeness." The same confidence is expressed in Psalm 49:15: "But God will redeem my soul from the power of the grave: for he shall receive me." And in the midst of great trouble the Psalmist found this hope a source of supporting strength: "Thou shalt guide me with thy counsel, and afterward receive me to glory" (Ps. 73:24). And nothing in the Old Testament is so boldly confident as Job's reply to his miserable comforters: "I know that my redeemer liveth and that he shall stand at the latter day upon the earth: and though after my skin worms destroy this body, yet in my flesh shall I see God: whom I shall see for myself, and mine eyes shall behold, and not another" (19:25-27).

Such are the assurances given before God's salvation had been perfected by the Lord Jesus Christ. Now that the work of redemption has been accomplished we have all these and greater assurances: "Now is Christ risen from the dead and become the first-fruits of them that slept." Through him who is the life-giving spirit we have been assured of the resurrection of the body, a resurrection unto glory. He himself assures us of this: "Because I live, ye shall live also" (John 14:19). If all these assurances and comforts are given to make us understand the meaning of death for the Christian, then surely when we individually come to the time of our own departure the Lord himself will be with us as we go through that valley of the shadow of death. If in the course of our earthly pilgrimage God is with us, then surely he will be with us at the moment we strike our earthly tent in preparation for entering the heavenly mansions. Surely this is the meaning of the Psalmist's word: "Yea, though I walk through the valley of the shadow of death, I will fear no evil: for thou art with me."

We have been thinking of Paul's brief statement: "The time has come for my departure." All that we have said might be summarized under another word of Paul's: "Christ in you, the hope of glory" (Col. 1:27). Immediately after this word of assurance Paul says, "Whom we preach, warning every man, and teaching every man in all wisdom; that we may present every man perfect in Christ Jesus." We have been speaking of the hope of the Christian. It is the hope of the one who has recognized that his sin will bring only the eternal judgment of God, and that only the Lord Jesus Christ can save him from that judgment of sin. This is the hope of the one who has fled to the Savior for refuge. And because this hope is limited to those who come to Christ in faith, Paul says that he warns every man. He warned of eternal judgment and pleaded that men would be reconciled to God through Jesus Christ.

You have come to honor a friend. You have come in recognition of a servant of God who has faithfully fulfilled his stewardship. Have you come with the faith that this servant of the Lord had? He believed the Word of God, and he loved and trusted the Lord Jesus Christ whom that Word revealed. His every intent was to honor the Lord Jesus Christ who only is our hope of glory. Are you here with that same faith? Will you be able to say at the hour of your own death, The time has come for my departure? Will you have a quiet confidence, knowing that it is the appointment of God? And will you find your soul supported by the assurances of the gospel? Let it be so with you. Acknowledge and trust the Lord Jesus as your redeemer. Be ready for the hour when the Lord will say, "The time has come."

Table of Contents

xi

Foreword

JOHN H. SKILTON

This is the second in a series of volumes devoted to the interests and needs of students of the New Testament. A special design of the series is to assist students in college, seminary, and beyond in improving their knowledge and competence in the field and in becoming productive scholars. It is hoped, however, that many who do not plan to become specialists in New Testament studies will find much in the series which will be profitable to them.

The second volume, like the first, contains articles on various New Testament subjects. Although some volumes, according to our plan, will deal with a single subject, others, like our initial issues, will be diversified in content. Indeed the diversity of the articles in the present volume makes it rather difficult to choose a suitable title for it. However, an emphasis does fall, notably in Part II, on the work and activity of the New Testament student and scholar in the study, the library, and the classroom. Therefore, the title which has been selected, *The New Testament Student at Work,* seems reasonably appropriate.

Again, as in the first volume, contributions both new and old have been included. This series will serve to give a new currency to outstanding articles which have previously been published and which may not be readily available to many of our readers; but there is no intention of providing simply an anthology of meritorious studies from the past. In this volume, for example, the greater number of the articles are being published for the first time.

Students and scholars working in the New Testament field are invited to send contributions to the editor. Articles on all aspects of New Testament study will be welcome for consideration. Of practical value to those working in the field will be suggestions by experts as to how to produce both scholarly and popular works; annotated bibliographies; discussions of teaching methods, of problems of curriculum, and of promising areas for research; surveys of literature; abstracts of theses and dissertations; and reports of work being done in various institutions and countries throughout the world. It is hoped that this series will provide an instrument which many will use for their mutual assistance and for the glory of the triune God.

Thanks are expressed to the following publishers and publications for permission to make use of the articles named: To *Themelios* ("The New Quest for the Historical Jesus" by Harvie M. Conn), to the Wm. B. Eerdmans Publishing Company ("The Virgin Birth of Christ" from *What Is Christianity?* by J. Gresham Machen), to the *Westminster Theological Journal* ("The Zero Tense in Greek" by Stephen M. Reynolds), and to the *Presbyterian Guardian* (articles on "Amillennialism in the New Testament" by Robert Strong).

Gratitude is expressed to the publisher, Mr. Charles H. Craig, for his encouragement and helpfulness, to Mr. Earl L. Powell for the excellent typesetting, to Mrs. Michael D. Knierim for preparing part of the typescript, and Professor Leslie W. Sloat for assistance in reading the proofs.

—John H. Skilton

PART I

ARTICLES ON NEW TESTAMENT THEMES

Chapter 1

W. P. ARMSTRONG

The Witness of the Gospels*

Mr. President and Gentlemen of the Board of Directors:—It is with a deep sense of its responsibilities that I have accepted your call to the Chair of New Testament Literature and Exegesis. In formally entering upon its duties I am conscious of the greatness of the work, its importance for the Church we serve and its close relation to the kingdom of our Lord and Saviour Jesus Christ. It is my earnest desire that grace may be given me to be found faithful in the administration of the high trust which you have committed to my charge. I am well aware of its difficulties. They do not, however, weaken my conviction that in loyalty to the pledge which I have taken, in loyalty to the truth as it is given me to see it, in patient and honest investigation, they will provide opportunities for a deeper insight into the manifold wisdom of God.

With a painful appreciation of my own limitations and a keen feeling of my unworthiness to follow in the footsteps of those illustrious men of God, Dr. Charles Hodge, Dr. Joseph Addison Alexander, Dr. Caspar Wistar Hodge and Dr. George Tybout

---

*Inaugural address delivered before the Board of Directors of Princeton Theological Seminary in Miller Chapel on induction into the Chair of New Testament Literature and Exegesis on Friday, September 18, 1903. [Editor's Note: This address was published in the *Princeton Theological Review* II (1904), 32-64. Its importance for the student of the history of Gospel criticism will be obvious. Despite its age it continues to furnish insights of value to New Testament students today. In the form in which it is reproduced here, a few typographical errors have been corrected and some adjustments have been made to current practice in capitalization and spelling.]

Purves, who here served their Master and are now fallen asleep, I take encouragement both from your call and from the cordial support and sympathy which the Faculty of the Seminary have given me during the four years I have spent in pleasant and grateful association with them. When I first came among them, they were the men whom as a student I had learned to love and respect. Two have now departed. One, the noble scholar, learned instructor and devoutly Christlike man, the Rev. Dr. William Henry Green, who opened to me the Scriptures of the Old Testament. Following him likewise into his rest my friend and beloved teacher whose work I am now called to continue, the Rev. Dr. George Tybout Purves. At his feet I first learned to love with enthusiasm the New Testament of our Lord, and for one brief year I enjoyed the privilege of sharing with him his plans, hopes and labors for this Chair. To his memory, which is blessed among the sons of Princeton Seminary, I gladly and from my heart pay a tribute of love and honor and gratitude, in recognition of his life of self-sacrifice and devotion and of his splendid scholarship, ever aglow with the warmth of close contact with life. His sympathies were wide, his labors unceasing, his ideals of Christian service the noblest and most unselfish, and these, with his enthusiasm for his work, springing from a strong conviction of its value, and his deep interest in men, made him a power for good to all those who knew him. He was always both a teacher and a preacher, teaching us to love truth and reverence it as the revelation of God. He knew its beauty, and might have exclaimed with the Jewish philosopher, τί δ' οὕτως ἐν βίῳ καλὸν ὡς ἀλήθεια.[1] But he knew also that its relation to life was more vital than the satisfaction of the æsthetic sentiment, touching as it does the very springs of all truly moral and rational life. In seeking truth he taught us to seek God; to cherish every revelation that through it He might make to us; but chiefly to know, revere and trust the revelation which He has been pleased to make through His written Word and in His Son, and through its intimate appropriation to gain sustenance for our spirits, that we might realize

---

1. *Philo de judice*, M. II, 346.

in ourselves His purpose to the praise of the glory of His grace. "Ye shall know the truth, and the truth shall make you free." To serve, to know, to love the truth, and thus to serve Christ and God, was the service of freedom which he taught us, and in his life he showed to us its joy. From such a memory I take inspiration as I face the possibilities of the future, thankful for the heritage which through him whom I was permitted to know has come down from the past, and cherishing the hope that the same spirit of loyal devotion to the truth as it is in Christ will continue with me during my work in Princeton Seminary.

I shall not attempt at this time to give an account of Dr. Purves' conduct of the New Testament Chair. One well qualified to speak, himself a New Testament scholar and a classmate and colleague of Dr. Purves, has, as the Faculty's representative, addressed you in commemoration of his services.[2] It is my desire, however, if only briefly, to make mention of them again. The relation which Dr. Purves sustained to Dr. Caspar Wistar Hodge is well known. For eight years (1892-1900) he strove to maintain in the Department of New Testament Studies the same high standard of excellence which Dr. Hodge had established, and in the light of the progress of scientific investigation to deepen and broaden the foundations he had laid. By the inauguration in 1893 of a professor of biblical theology his work was divided, but in 1899 its needs had again become so pressing that an instructor in the New Testament was appointed to give opportunity for the further enlargement which he planned.

To those who sat under Dr. Purves his controlling interest seemed to lie in the field of exegesis; and here he revealed careful and exact scholarship, sanity of judgment, thoroughness of method and forcefulness of presentation which made disciples of his pupils. And yet exegesis was with him always a means

---

2. An address delivered in Miller Chapel on November 26, 1901, by B. B. Warfield, D.D., LL.D. Cf. *The Bible Student,* Vol. iv, No. 6, December, 1901, pp. 310-323; Purves, *Faith and Life,* Presbyterian Board of Publication, 1902, pp. ix-xxx.

to an end. With true historical sense he sought by it to understand and interpret to his students the sources of early Christian
history, while with this was united the deeper religious interest
of one who had made his own the principles of the Protestant
Reformation. Hence, while his chief interest and work was
directed to the New Testament, he sought to study also with his
students the historical environment in which it arose. Even before
he came to this Chair, when invited to deliver the L. P. Stone
lectures, he chose as his subject *The Testimony of Justin Martyr
to Early Christianity*,[3] thus revealing an interest and an insight
into the historical problems surrounding the origin of Christianity which characterized in a marked degree his subsequent
work. To this his articles and reviews[4] bear witness, as does
also his admirable book entitled *Christianity in the Apostolic Age*.[5]
He loved exegesis and he loved it as a teacher. To it in his classroom he gave himself with compelling intensity which kindled an
abiding and commanding interest in the New Testament. Rightly
to estimate its effect one must weigh the influence which has gone
out through the lives of his students who, scattered throughout the
world, bear testimony by their work to his power as a teacher.
His work will endure, engraven as it is upon the hearts of the living,
and for it Princeton Seminary may well be deeply thankful.

It is fitting that I address you on some theme in the Department of New Testament Literature and Exegesis. For purposes
of lower criticism the New Testament falls naturally, by reason
of the nature of the materials upon which we are dependent, into
four sections: the Gospels, the Acts and Catholic Epistles, the
Pauline Epistles with Hebrews, and the Apocalypse. Equally

---

3. *The Testimony of Justin Martyr to Early Christianity*. Lectures delivered on the L. P. Stone Foundation at Princeton Theological Seminary in
March, 1888. Randolph & Co., New York, 1889.

4. Among others *The Presbyterian Review*, October, 1888, pp. 529ff.:
"The Influence of Paganism on Post-Apostolic Christianity"; *The Presby-
terian and Reformed Review*, 1895, pp. 239ff.: "The Formation of the New
Testament"; *ibid.*, 1898, pp. 23ff.: "The Witness of Apostolic Literature to
Apostolic History."

5. *Christianity in the Apostolic Age*. Charles Scribner's Sons, 1900.

natural for purposes of historical study is the twofold division by which our principal sources for the history of the Church in the days of the apostles—the Acts, Epistles and the Apocalypse—constitute, because of their close interrelation, one group; while the Gospels, the chief sources for our knowledge of the life of Christ, may be treated as forming another group. This division, of course, is a broad one, and does not obscure the fact that a very close relation subsists between the Gospels on the one hand and the Acts and the Epistles on the other. The Acts and Epistles contribute much to our knowledge of the life of Christ; while the Gospels, regarded as literary products, fall within the history of the apostolic Church. But if the epistolary literature of the New Testament be in part earlier than the Gospels, and the Gospels fall within the history of the apostolic or post-apostolic Church, there emerges for the student of New Testament literature and exegesis a problem of some importance. Has the testimony of the Gospels been deflected, distorted or discolored by the environment in which they arose, and if so, to what extent? It is my purpose to face this problem, and to consider in some of its aspects the question of the trustworthiness of our Gospels as sources of our knowledge of the life of Christ; or, more briefly stated, my subject is "The Witness of the Gospels." Such a subject may be approached from a number of viewpoints and discussed in many different ways. For my present purpose the discussion may be ordered under two principal lines of thought, namely, the character or nature of the Gospel witness, and its origin in relation to its value.

THE CHARACTER OF THE GOSPEL WITNESS

The word gospel (εὐαγγέλιον) means good news, though in Aramaic the root בְּשַׂר does not indicate so plainly as the Greek the kind of news.[6] It occurs frequently both in the Epistles and in the Gospels, where it means a message rather than a book. In the Epistles and Acts it is used of the message which the apostles

---

6. Dalman, *Die Worte Jesu*, S. 84.

proclaimed concerning Christ; in the Gospels of the message of Christ concerning the kingdom of God. The apostolic usage continued for some time, and lies at the basis of the titles given to our Gospels. The message concerning Christ was conceived as unitary, and hence the different Gospels were regarded as but different narratives by their several authors of the one Gospel. We have four such Gospels in the New Testament; and out of the differences and the agreements between them arise very intricate and difficult literary and historical problems. It is clear that the fourfold Gospel furnishes us with a twofold message concerning Christ; that of the three synoptics which, whatever be the cause, present the same general features, and that of John.

What are the chief characteristics of this twofold tradition concerning Christ? In order to ascertain them and properly to estimate it, it will be necessary to bear in mind several things. The Gospels are manifestly Christian documents. They were written to meet the needs of the Church, and like the apostolic Gospel-preaching they contain a message about Christ which is at the same time a witness to Christ. What effect this has on their value as trustworthy historical sources we shall consider later. Here it is important to note their close connection with the apostolic idea of the Gospel. In accordance with this, three characteristics of the Gospels in their twofold witness to Christ stand out distinctly: an account of the facts of Christ's life, including the environment in which He lived and the character of His teaching; a very distinct estimate of His person; the significant prominence given to His passion.

Of the synoptic Gospels only Matthew and Luke give the narrative of Christ's supernatural birth. Luke alone gives us a glimpse into the boyhood of our Saviour, and tells us of His normal development during the period previous to His entrance on His public ministry. All three agree in connecting His ministry with that of His forerunner, John the Baptist; and from this point on their representation is in broad outline the same. Matthew's arrangement, however, is topical, and Luke furnishes material not found in either Matthew or Mark. Matthew and Luke, moreover, give us a much fuller account of the teaching of Jesus. But the picture is the same in all. They represent John's work as prophetic and preparatory for the messianic work of Jesus. After the baptism of Jesus, His temptation in the wilderness and the imprisonment of John, Jesus comes into Galilee. He takes up the call of John to repentance, and adds to it the call to belief in the Gospel which was His own proclamation of the kingdom of God. We see Him moving through Galilee in a ministry of healing and teaching. He gathers about Him a band of disciples; and the people flock to hear Him, bringing their sick that He may heal them. In the midst of this popular enthusiasm we are struck by two things: the character of His teaching and His intentional avoidance of the messianic title. He is training the people and His disciples to appreciate the spiritual character of the kingdom, and His avoidance of the messianic title may have served simply a pedagogic purpose, or, as is more probable, it may have been practised by Jesus in the control which He exercised over the events of His public messianic work. It is not long, however, before opposition from the religious leaders of the people, the Pharisees, arises, and the enthusiasm of the people begins to wane. The opposition found its occasion in the neglect by Jesus and His disciples of the sabbath customs; but this only served to make clear the opposition in principle between the two forms of religious life thus brought into conflict. The legalism which had become all-pervading in the religious life of the nation found itself face to face in the person of Jesus with the denial of its *raison d'être,* and through its accredited representatives it was logically compelled to crush Him. "It was expedient that one man should die for the people."[7]

From this time Jesus began to devote Himself to the instruction of His disciples, with a view to preparing them for the issue which He foresaw. He continued to speak to the people, but He spoke in parables, while in His relations with His disciples He seems to

---

7. John xviii. 14.

have been intent upon deepening in them a clear and abiding insight into the significance of His own person for the kingdom which He had been proclaiming. The Pharisees meantime had taken counsel with the Herodians to kill Him. News of His work had reached Herod; and the feeding of the five thousand had made plain the fact that the old messianic ideal still controlled the popular mind. Jesus turns now to His disciples. At Cæsarea Philippi He calls forth by His question the confession of Peter. From this time on He seeks to make clear to them that He must suffer and after three days rise from the dead. Jerusalem is now His goal; and here, after having given His disciples further instructions regarding the future and having come into conflict with the Jewish leaders, He is crucified by order of the Roman Procurator, and on the third day rises again.

In the Gospel of John the course of the narrative is somewhat differently ordered. Just as in the synoptic Gospels, Jesus at the opening of His ministry is brought into contact with John the Baptist. Here the fourth Gospel adds the testimony of John to Jesus, and tells of a work of Jesus in Jerusalem, Galilee and Judea previous to the imprisonment of John the Baptist. Withdrawing through Samaria He comes into Galilee, but concerning the length of His stay and the nature of His work there we learn little. What strikes us at once in this account of the early ministry of Jesus is not so much the additional information which places the beginning of Christ's ministry earlier than the time mentioned by the synoptics, nor the fact that its scene lies chiefly in and about Jerusalem, but the difference in method. The messianic claim is here openly witnessed to by John. Christ Himself by cleansing the temple publicly assumes the function of the Messiah, and in His conversation with the woman of Samaria distinctly asserts His messiahship. His words in the temple[8] and His conversation with Nicodemus make it clear, moreover, that even at this early time He looked forward to His passion as involved in His messianic work. Passing over much

---

8. John ii. 19.

of the work in Galilee, the fourth Gospel tells us of the beginning of the conflict between Jesus and the rulers in Judea, the question as in the synoptics being the violation of the sabbath or the fundamental antagonism between Jesus and legalism. In the sixth chapter the fourth Gospel joins the synoptics in the narrative of the feeding of the five thousand. John tells us that Jesus walked in Galilee, for he was unwilling to walk in Judea because the Jews sought to kill Him.[9] With his interest in the ministry of Jesus at Jerusalem, John tells us of Jesus' visit to the city at the Feast of Tabernacles, and again at the Feast of Dedication. The resurrection of Lazarus constitutes a crisis in Jesus' relation to the leaders at Jerusalem, and from this time on, after the withdrawal to Ephraim, Jesus sets His face to Jerusalem and the last Passover. As in the synoptic Gospels, so in the Gospel of John, Jesus is represented as performing wonderful works of healing. In both He raises the dead. So also in regard to the teaching of Jesus. In both He is a teacher, though the character of the teaching preserved in the two traditions differs markedly both in form and content. In the synoptic Gospels the teaching of Jesus centers chiefly around the kingdom, its character and the conditions of entrance. The form for the most part is gnomic or parabolic. In the fourth Gospel the teaching of Jesus centers about His own person, His relation to God and His own significance for the kingdom which He was founding. The form is closely related to the nature of the themes discussed, and is thus more theological—informed by direct intuition of spiritual realities.

But beside the general environment in which Jesus' ministry of healing and teaching is set, the gospel witness contains also an estimate of His person. From the sketch given of the gospel witness to the character of Christ's ministry, there can be little doubt that the Gospels represent it as messianic and Christ as the Messiah. Whether Christ Himself claimed to be the Messiah has indeed been questioned, and recently denied by Wrede,[10] but, as

---

9. John vii. 1.
10. *Das Messiasgeheimnis.* 1901.

it seems to me, without good ground.[11] Here, however, we are concerned simply with the fact that the Gospels so represent Him; and for the present we may leave open the question of His own claim. In Matthew and Luke the genealogies trace Christ's line of descent through David. His birth in Bethlehem, the city of David, is significant to Matthew because of its messianic associations, while Luke connects Christ's birth there directly with the fact that Joseph was of the house of David. In fact, in both Matthew and Luke the whole infancy narrative is controlled by the thought that in this child the long-expected, prophetically proclaimed Messiah had come. The prophetic message is taken up by John the Baptist; and the baptism of Jesus, whatever else it may have meant, certainly, according to the Gospel narrative, signified for Jesus the voluntary assumption of His messianic work; while the temptation which followed this baptism is represented as a trial of the Messiah in view of His office and prospective work. In His temptation Jesus as the Messiah relates Himself specifically to His future messianic work by maintaining His loyalty to the spirit of dependence on God, of filial obedience and trust, in which He was determined to fulfill the work to which in the baptism He had just consecrated Himself. However much He may have charged secrecy on those who recognized in Him the Messiah, He nowhere disavows the title. He accepts the confession of Peter; He calls himself frequently the Son of man; He is called the Son of David, the Son of God; and by His triumphal entry into Jerusalem He most publicly proclaims His messianic dignity. In the fourth Gospel the testimony of John the Baptist to the messiahship of Jesus is given explicitly; and Jesus Himself, from the very opening of His public ministry in Jerusalem, makes definite and distinct claim to be the Messiah. This representation, in fact, lies so plainly upon the face of the Gospels that it will not be necessary to treat it in detail.

It is important, however, for our conception of this aspect of the gospel witness to notice that the character of the messianic work

---

11. Cf. O. Holtzmann, *Das Leben Jesu*, 1901, and *Zeitschrift für die Neutest. Wiss.*, 1901, S. 265; J. Weiss, *Das aelteste Evangelium*, 1903.

which Christ performed is intimately bound up with what He was, or with what He is represented by the Gospels to have been. While He came as the Messiah, He did not fulfill His work in the manner popularly expected. His work was through and through self-determined, the conscious carrying out of a purpose definitely formed. Back of His work stands the volition of a person dependent only on God. He is represented distinctly as the creator of His work, never as its product, the child of circumstance; and this is the representation in the synoptic Gospels as well as in John. It is true that we do find adjustment of His work and teaching to the changes which took place in His surroundings during His public ministry, but never a departure from His controlling purpose nor an alteration in the character of His work. It is consistently determined throughout in the interest of moral and spiritual renovation. Hence the central place of His person in His whole work and teaching. In the synoptic Gospels emphasis is laid at first on His message, but it is ever His message through which, by its very character, the dignity of His person and His authority clearly appear. In John's Gospel the determining relation which Christ sustained to His messianic work is characteristic. From this point it is now not difficult to understand the transcendent significance which the Gospels assign to the person of Christ.

In the opening chapters of the first and third Gospels we find the narratives of His supernatural birth. It is often affirmed that they belong to the secondary strata of Gospel tradition; but here again we are concerned with the representation of our Gospels as they stand; and this must be distinguished from the further questions as to how they came to give such a representation and what value, in view of its origin and character, we may allow to it in forming our view of the actual occurrence. The fact that two of the Gospels contain such narratives constitutes them a part of the gospel witness and cannot be without significance for its representation of the nature of Christ's person. As we watch the progress of His ministry in the synoptic Gospels, we are impressed by the power which He exercises in the performance of miracles, by the authority with which He speaks, by the spotless purity of His life, by a consciousness in which no trace of a sense of sin can be found, which acknowledges its dependence on God, but knows Him in intimate, unbroken communion. At the request of His disciples He teaches them to pray, embodying in their prayer the petition "forgive us our debts, as we forgive our debtors"; but in His own prayer-life He does not associate Himself with them. Twice He is represented as the recipient of direct testimony from heaven—at the baptism and on the Mount of Transfiguration. He claims that He is greater than the temple. As He stands before the high priest He not only definitely asserts His messiaship, but asserts for Himself the prerogative of a seat at the right hand of power—an assertion at once interpreted by His auditors as blasphemy.[12] Finally, on the third day, He rises from the dead, and after being seen by His disciples, He ascends to heaven. In view of this representation of the course of His ministry and characteristics of His life, there can be little doubt that underlying their representation of the messiahship of Jesus there is a deeper and more fundamental estimate of His person, which conceived of Him as by nature sustaining a unique relation to God and thus, in respect of being, the Son of God. The messianic implications of this term should not obscure to us the fact that in the Gospels there is this deeper meaning given to it which does not always appear, but which is bound up with their account of who this messianic Son of God really was.

In the fourth Gospel this view of the transcendent significance of Christ's person is not merely the view of the author of the Gospel. It is represented also as that to which Christ in His whole activity of miracle-working and teaching bears witness. The prologue of the Gospel begins with an account of the preexistent Logos, describing His relation to God as direct and immediate,[13] and His essential nature as divine. Then follows an account of

---

12. Mark xiv. 61f.
13. The preposition πρός suggesting the idea of mutual intercourse between persons (Aall, *Gesch. der Logosidee,* II, S. 111).

His activity, His incarnation and the witness of John the Baptist, together with that of the author. The identification of the Logos with Jesus Christ, concerning whom the fourth Gospel is written, is made in verse 14. Whatever be the source of the form of the Logos-doctrine—whether it came to John from Philo's doctrine of the Logos or from the Jewish Memra—John has given to it a content distinctively his own by connecting it directly with the historical person of Jesus Christ. It was, moreover, well adapted to convey his idea, for it cannot escape us that what John is here intent upon emphasizing is not simply the divine origin of the person of Jesus Christ—the description of Him as a unique preexistent divine being standing in closest relation of loving complacency to God, and in the ultimate character of His being, God; but with this also the idea of His revelation-character as the mediator of true knowledge concerning God. As between finite spirits the word performs a most important function in common intercourse, so in the revelation of God to men which John describes as light, the mediator was the word incarnate in the person of Jesus Christ—for the enlightening work of revelation made sufficient by His relation both to God and to men. Of both He had intimate knowledge, being with God in the bosom of His Father and being God—being also the agent in creation and the light of men. For this conception John had, beside the natural basis in the spiritual significance of the word as a means of communion, also the fact that the Old Testament Scriptures were to him the word of God[14]—possibly also before John wrote, the designation "word of God" (ὁ λόγος τοῦ θεοῦ) had been applied to the Gospel message[15]—while Philo, following the Greek philosophers, especially Heraclitus, gave it a prominent place in his system of thought. John, however, by identifying the eternal Logos, conceived not abstractly as wisdom or reason but personally, with the incarnate Christ, gives to it its peculiar Christian content.

---

14. Cf. x. 35, v. 38. Cf. also Heb. iv. 12; 1 Peter i. 2; James i. 18.

15. Holtzmann, *Handkommentar*, S. 32; Weizsäcker, *Das Apostolische Zeitalter*, S. 32; Harnack, *Zeitschrift für Theologie und Kirche*, 1892, S. 223[2].

For though Philo sometimes personified the Logos, it meant with
him an abstract conception without messianic associations, certainly without definite identification of the Logos with the Messiah.[16]
Whether John was the first to make this identification or not we
do not know. It has been urged that the way in which the Gospel
opens suggests that the connection of the Logos with Christ had
already been made. The Logos-doctrine was certainly current.
Hence, John does not affirm there is a Logos and this Logos is
Christ. He seems intent rather upon defining its content or fixing
the predicates which, in view of the identification which had been
made or which he proposed to introduce, could under it be made
of Christ.[17]

That the prologue of the fourth Gospel gives us the idea of its
author about Christ is rendered certain from the first Epistle
of John.[18] Is this, however, the view which obtains throughout
the Gospel? Opinions differ as to the relation of the prologue to the
rest of the Gospel. On the one hand, it is said to contain the key
to the Gospel, being a summary or the quintessence of the Gospel.
The Gospel would thus appropriately be called the Logos-Gospel,
and the Christ whom it portrays the Logos-Christ. The Gospel has,
according to this view, been constructed under the influence of an
idea, its whole narrative being controlled by and in explication of
this idea.[19] On the other hand, the prologue is said to constitute only
the introduction to the Gospel, the Logos-doctrine being dropped
after the eighteenth verse. "The prologue of the Gospel," says Harnack,[20] "is not the key to the understanding of the Gospel, but
rather prepares the Greek readers for this. It takes up a known

---

16. Aall, *Geschichte der Logosidee*, I, S. 213f.; II, S. 110, 146[2].
17. Cf. Harnack, *Zeitschrift für Theologie und Kirche*, 1892, S. 222f.
18. i. 1-4. Cf. also Apoc. xix. 13.
19. Baur, Holtzmann, Weizsäcker, and Schmiedel.
20. *Zeitschrift für Theologie und Kirche*, 1892, S. 230f.: Der Prologue
des Evangeliums ist nicht der Schlüssel zum Verständniss des Evangeliums.
Sondern er bereitet die hellenischen Leser auf dieses vor. Er knüpft an eine
bekannte Grösse, den Logos, an, bearbeitet ihn und gestaltet ihn um—
falsche Christologieen implicite bekämpfend—um ihm Jesus Christus, den

thing (Grösse), the Logos, works it over and reshapes it, attacking implicitly false Christologies, in order to substitute for it Jesus Christ, the μονογενὴς θεός, or rather to disclose it as this Jesus Christ. When this has been accomplished, from that moment on the Logos-idea is dropped. The author tells only of Jesus for the purpose of grounding the faith that He is the Messiah, the Son of God." One thing is clear: John does not place in the mouth of Jesus the *terminus technicus* of the Logos-doctrine. For though the term Logos recurs frequently in the Gospel, both in the narrative portions and in the words of Jesus, in no instance after the prologue is it used in the technical sense which it there has. From this it would appear that the author knew how to distinguish between his own thought about Jesus and the words of Jesus which he records. The two, it is true, are often very closely related, especially in respect of form, and John frequently intentionally adds to the words of Jesus words of his own.[21] It would be wrong, however, to infer from this that the prologue stood in no close relation to what follows. The dropping of the technical use of ὁ λόγος is significant, but chiefly from a formal point of view. In the prologue the term Logos is a central unifying idea, under which a number of ideas are subsumed which give it its content—ideas such as life, light, truth and the relation of the personal Logos to God and to the world. These ideas, however, recur in the subsequent description. On the other hand, the view which finds in the prologue the formative idea of which the Gospel is simply an elaboration cast in the form of history, rests on a particular theory regarding the origin of the prologue. If the prologue be the result of reflective speculation cast in the form of the Alexandrian philosophy, then the Gospel must likewise be interpreted as ideal history. This, however, unduly exalts the purely formal side and has to face the

---

μονογενής θεός, zu substituiren resp. ihn als diesen Jesus Christus zu enthüllen. Von dem Momente an, wo dies geschehen ist, ist der Logosbegriff fallen gelassen. Der Verfasser erzählt nur noch von Jesus, um den Glauben zu begründen, dass er der Messias, der Sohn Gottes sei.

21. Cf. also I Cor. xi. 26.

fact that the central and controlling idea, as technically formulated in the term ὁ λόγος, plays no part in the subsequent narrative. If we banish the background of history from the prologue, they are most logical who banish it also from the Gospel.[22] Another account of the origin of the prologue will enable us to do greater justice to the Gospel as it stands complete together with the prologue. We will seek its genesis in the history which follows—a history which had long been the cherished tradition of the Church; which had already found written expression in the synoptic Gospels, of which Matt. xi. 27f. was an integral part; and thus ultimately in the person of Jesus Himself. In the history which follows we find that Christ is identified with His gifts. He is Life and Light and Truth. As in the synoptics, He works miracles and is distinctly declared to be the Messiah. He receives the Spirit at His baptism, and bears the titles Son of man and Son of God. His heavenly origin constitutes one of the features of John's Gospel. In dependence on God, who had sent Him, and therefore making God's will the inner law of His life, He is yet conscious of unity with God —"I and the Father are one."[23] Here, then, even more clearly than in the synoptic Gospels, I think we shall find underlying the whole witness of the fourth Gospel to Christ not merely the messianic idea, but with it also the deeper conception of the real nature of Christ's person to which the prologue bears unmistakable testimony. And this not simply as the view of the author. It is represented as that to which Christ Himself bears witness in word and work.

The third characteristic of the gospel witness to which I desire to call attention is the prominence given in all our Gospels to the passion of Jesus. In itself it is so apparent as scarcely to require proof. If we take Cæsarea Philippi as marking the time when the passion-idea explicitly emerges in the synoptic Gospels, though

---

22. The one view destroys the significance of the prologue, the other destroys the significance of the rest of the Gospel.

23. John x. 30; cf. Lütgert, "Die johanneische Christologie," *Beiträge zur Förderung christlicher Theologie,* III, 1899.

there are traces of it earlier,[24] we shall find that in Matthew chapters xvi. 21-xxviii. 20, in Mark chapters viii. 31-xvi. 8, and in Luke chapters ix. 22-xxiv. 53, or about half of the synoptic Gospels, are devoted to this period; or if we take the arrival of Jesus in Bethany before the last Passover as the actual beginning of the passion-narratives, we find ourselves in the synoptic Gospels at Matt. xxvi, Mark xiv and Luke xxii; or if we begin with Jesus' entrance into Jerusalem, at Matt. xxi, Mark xi and Luke xix. 28f. In the fourth Gospel the passion idea appears at the very beginning (ii. 19), and in chapter xii Jesus is in Bethany six days before the last Passover. The details of this period in Christ's life are more numerous, and with the exception of the feeding of the five thousand, which constituted the Galilean crisis, it is the only period for which we have four parallel sources. We have already noticed how soon both in the synoptic narratives and in that of John the leaders begin to plot His death.

My purpose in calling attention to this fact is to seek from it the light which it should throw on the character of the gospel witness. Being a marked and characteristic feature, it cannot be without significance for our idea of this witness, which must in turn affect our conception of the nature of the Gospels. It will be important, therefore, to notice that the passion-narrative of the Gospels, both in its prophetic announcement and in its subsequent realization, has a twofold issue. The passion of which the Gospels tell us is suffering and death followed by resurrection. It is represented, moreover, as the passion of Him whom, in their whole narrative, they declare to have been the Messiah. The passion is accepted by Him voluntarily in the fulfillment of His messianic work, and is therefore set forth by them as an integral part, the culmination of that work. Jesus is to them the Messiah, realizing His work through suffering and crowned with victory by the resurrection. His death follows as the result of His consistent adherence throughout His public ministry to the prin-

---

24. Cf. Mark ii. 20.

ciples which determined His work and made it what it was. Hence its fundamental significance and hence the prominence which is assigned to it in the gospel witness.

But what was there in the nature of Christ's work which thus made His death an integral part of it? Was it simply that His teaching differed from that of the religious leaders of Israel, that it exhibited a fundamental opposition to their legalism, and that His death was the result of unfavorable circumstances, like that of many a reformer? Or is there a deeper reason lying in the nature of His messianic work? Such a reason is not fully formulated in the Gospels, but we may find a hint of it in their connecting of Christ's work with sin. John the Baptist, the forerunner of Jesus, preached a baptism of repentance unto the remission of sins (Mark i. 4), and proclaimed the coming of the Messiah, who should baptize with the Holy Spirit and with fire. Jesus began to preach in Galilee, saying, "Repent and believe in the Gospel," and throughout His ministry He is represented as having authority to forgive sins.[25] In Mark x. 45 we read, "For verily the Son of man came not to be ministered unto, but to minister, and to give his life a ransom for many,"[26] the idea of ransom ($\lambda\acute{u}\tau\rho\text{ov}$) being most naturally connected through that of sacrifice with sin. In the Gospel of John we find in the testimony of the Baptist to Jesus the words, "Behold the Lamb of God, that taketh away the sin of the world!"[27] In most of these instances Christ's relation to sin is represented as one of personal authority over it. To the passage in Matthew (Matt. xx. 28) which connects this with His death should be added the words uttered by Christ at the institution of the Supper on the eve of His death (Matt. xxvi. 27f.): "And he took a cup, and gave thanks, and gave to them, saying, Drink ye all of it; for this is my blood of the covenant, which is shed for many unto remission of sins."[28]

---

25. Mark ii. 5f.; cf. also Matt. i. 21, Luke i. 77, vii. 47, xxiv. 47.
26. Cf. Matt. xx. 28; John x. 11.
27. John i. 29.
28. Mark and Luke do not have εἰς ἄφεσιν ἁμαρτιῶν.

These hints are sufficient to establish the fact that Christ's messianic work had reference to sin, and that in it as thus conceived His death played an important part. If Jesus spoke of His sufferings beforehand to ears hard of understanding, the Gospels give clear evidence that His words were not forgotten in circles where the memory of the past was faithfully cherished, and that His suggestions as to the relation of His sufferings to sin were not neglected.[29]

The results of our analysis of the character of the gospel witness may be briefly summed up. It tells us of Jesus of Nazareth; how He lived and wrought and taught in Jerusalem and Galilee. It tells us that this Jesus was the Christ, the Messiah. It tells us that He sustained a unique relation to God by nature and not by His messianic work only. It tells us that He suffered and rose again. It gives to His sufferings an important place in the narrative of His work, and suggests a connection between His work and the forgiveness of sin. The period covered by this witness is chiefly that of the public ministry of Jesus; only Matthew and Luke giving glimpses of His infancy, while John gives a vision of the eternal background from which Christ came to take up His messianic work. But John, like the synoptists, is concerned to trace this work only from its official assumption by Jesus.

From these facts we may draw certain conclusions about the nature of the Gospels which contain the witness. They are manifestly not intended to be biographies or to furnish us with a scientific life of Jesus. They are rather witnesses to the life and work of Jesus, chiefly during His public ministry. What is narrated beyond this—the infancy narratives in Matthew and Luke and the prologue in John—has distinct reference to it. They are thus witnesses to the person and work of Jesus as Founder of the Christian religion, to the facts and forces which centered in the person from whom it took its origin. They were written by men who were Christians and are thus essentially Christian documents. Drawing either from their own immediate knowledge or from the

---

29. Cf. Luke xxiv. 47, and in the opening chapters of Acts.

sources which were accessible to them, these men wrote the gospel narratives primarily for the Church and for the purpose of confirming faith.[30] So far as their narratives are history, therefore, they wrote history with a religious motive or purpose. They wrote for faith, and in the interest of the faith which they shared. This faith may have been without basis in fact; but as we can scarcely charge the evangelists with intention to deceive, we must, on the hypothesis of deception, hold that they were themselves unconsciously deceived. Where, then, shall we seek the cause of this deception—in Jesus or in the evangelists? And if there be deception, to what extent has it affected their narrative? Does it extend to the narrative of fact—for much of which we have only their testimony, which in turn is part of their belief—or does it extend simply to their estimate of Christ's person, or again, does it extend only to the miraculous? If we are successfully to separate the trustworthy and the untrustworthy in their witness, we must have some sure canon of criticism to guide us. The first condition, however, of fair criticism is a fair estimate of what the Gospels are, as the only safe ground from which to estimate their value. To set up an arbitrary standard and judge them deficient because they do not conform to it is to condemn them without a hearing, and must result in an altogether unfair estimate of their real significance. Being what they are, can we trust their witness? This raises for us another line of thought which I propose to consider in one of its aspects. Since much will depend in our answer to this question on the view we take of the way in which the gospel witness came to be what it is, it is important to treat briefly the origin of this witness in relation to its value.

THE ORIGIN OF THE GOSPEL WITNESS IN ITS BEARING ON THE VALUE OF THAT WITNESS

This genetic question cannot be thoroughly discussed apart from the question of the origin of the documents in which this

---

30. Luke i. 4, John xx. 30.

witness is contained; and this in turn involves the intricate problem of their mutual relations. The neglect of this feature was one of the chief defects of the pre-Tübingen criticism of the Gospels, and, strangely enough, is characteristic likewise of the neo-Tübingen criticism of the Gospels by Prof. Schmiedel. Into the details of the origin of the Gospels it will not be possible to enter now. In general, two questions may be distinguished; the when and the how, or the time and the manner of origin. Concerning the former, I shall assume the second half of the first century as a fact sufficiently established by historical criticism and widely recognized; I shall assume also that the synoptic Gospels are earlier than the fourth Gospel. Concerning the latter, I shall be compelled to limit myself to the single problem of the influence of environment or purpose on the general product called the witness of the Gospel whose character I have just discussed.

That the witness of the Gospels purports to be historical will scarcely be denied. Opinions may differ as to the extent of its historicity. In case historicity be denied *in toto,* then some satisfactory account must be given not only of how it came into existence, but also of how it obtained such wide and early acceptance. In case varying degrees of historicity be allowed, some satisfactory canon for separating what is true from what is false in its representation must be established. The first possibility may, I think, be neglected. The Gospels reflect too plainly the political, geographical, social and religious situation of the first century for historical criticism ever successfully to deny that historical elements were woven into their very structure. Historical persons known to us from other sources appear in these pages and each in his own character and place. Hence from early times, among those who have given the subject serious consideration, critical opinion has either accepted their witness as trustworthy or, on the premise of partial historicity, sought to determine how much is historical.

The early Fathers—who are sometimes spoken of contemptuously as deceived deceivers,[31] while again the pre-Eusebian age receives high praise as being almost as familiar as we are with the higher criticism in both its forms, historical as well as literary[32] —accepted the gospel witness as trustworthy. Papias wrote a commentary on the Gospels, adding in exposition of them traditions of a trustworthy kind from disciples of the Lord. Justin Martyr made extensive use of them. His disciple, Tatian, used the four Gospels in constructing a harmony. From the time of Irenæus, Clement of Alexandria and Tertullian, they were extensively used, not only as trustworthy, but as the authoritative court of appeal in argument with opponents. But even at this time there were not wanting those who denied the complete trustworthiness of the gospel witness. Some of the Gnostic sects accepted one of the Gospels, some another (Iren., c. h. iii, 11, 7). Marcion in particular received only Luke, whose text he subjected to critical purification on the ground that it had been corrupted by the Church in the interest of its doctrine. Marcion's text thus subjectively reconstructed found favor for a time with a number of modern scholars, such as Ritschl, Baur and Schwegler, who claimed for it priority to our text; while van Manen posits for Marcion's Luke and our Luke a common source. Within the Tübingen School, however, exception to Baur's view was taken by Volkmar and Hilgenfeld; while Dr. Sanday[33] has pointed out that in those passages of Luke which are not found in Marcion's Gospels there are found the same characteristics of style and diction which mark the body of the Gospel common to Marcion and the supposed Catholic enlargement. But if the principle which underlies Marcion's attack on the text of Luke be discredited, then his rejection of the other Gospels can have little weight in our estimate of them. Among the later Fathers, Augustine and Chrysostom gave attention principally to the interrelation of the Gospels; and during the mediæval and Reformation

31. Corssen, "Monarch. Prologue," *T. u. U.*, XVII, S. 109, n. 1. Cf. Jülicher, *Göttingische gelehrte Anzeigen*, 1896, S. 841f.

32. Bacon, "The Johannine Problem," *Hibbert Journal*, 1903, p. 179.

33. *The Gospels in the Second Century*, pp. 204ff.

periods likewise the historico-genetic problem received no adequate discussion. Signs of a change began to appear in the French scholar R. Simon (+1712) and in Semler (+1791) of Halle. In 1828 Paulus sought in his *Leben Jesu* to apply the principles of rationalism to the interpretation of the Gospels, explaining the miracles as due to natural causes. Here must also be mentioned Bretschneider, who in his *Probabilia* (1820) attacked the historicity of the fourth Gospel. About this time Schleiermacher was lecturing in Berlin on the life of Christ (1819, edition 1864). But though he held the fourth Gospel to be more homogeneous than the synoptic Gospels, which were in his opinion fragmentary aggregates wanting in chronological arrangement,[34] and thus assigned to the fourth Gospel an important rôle in his constructive work, he still exercised an *a priori* criticism of the contents of the Gospels, rejecting much of the miraculous[35] and explaining the rest in a manner much akin to the rationalism of Paulus.[36] This period was brought to a close and the impetus for a new discussion of our theme was given by the appearance in 1835 of Strauss' *Leben Jesu*.

In this book Strauss sought to ground his rejection of the Gospel witness by a theory of mythical origin. The Christ of the Gospels was the creation of the imagination of the Church; the myths concerning Him, having grown during the period of oral transmission, were embodied in the Gospels. The advance made by Strauss consists in his adding to the rejection of miracle or its rationalizing explanation a theory to explain the origin of the content of the Gospels. The messianic idea furnished a starting-point, a motive, and the mythical imagination of the Church created the Christ of the Gospels. It cannot escape us that what we have in our Gospels, according to this criticism, is ideal history, or history written under the formative influence of an idea. There is thus a manifest purpose or tendency. Strauss called the product myth rather than legend, and did not attempt any careful separa-

---

34. *Leben Jesu*, S. 401.
35. The supernatural birth, S. 51, and ascension, S. 500.
36. The resurrection explained by lethargy, S. 443f.

tion of the historical minimum underlying it. His criticism of the content of the Gospels gave, however, no satisfactory account of the Gospels,[37] and though in the new edition of his *Leben Jesu*[38] he adopted the general results of the Tübingen criticism, he still showed little appreciation of or historical insight into their character and origin.

Baur and his school, though still making the impossibility of miracles an axiom of historical criticism, sought to understand the Gospels as literary products of the first two centuries. When so regarded the Gospels are seen to reflect the conditions under which they were written, thus furnishing us with an objective standard for separating the earlier elements from the perverting influence of a later time. In the application of such a standard it is manifestly of the highest importance to fix accurately the forces and characteristics of the apostolic and post-apostolic ages of the Church's history. Fundamental and determining for this, in Baur's view, was the division of the Church into two antagonistic parties—the Jewish-Christian or particularistic party, with the original apostles and James at its head, and the Pauline or universalistic party, with Paul and his followers at its head. The opposition between the two parties was at first bitter, but gradually grew less and less until, under the pressure of heresy from within and persecution from without, the two were merged into the early Catholic Church. The literary remains of the first two centuries reflect this controversy in its different stages, and hence the necessity of determining the tendency of a document in order to ascertain its date and relative historicity. In the hands of this criticism our Gospels became party documents, Matthew representing the Jewish Christian, Luke the Pauline party, Mark, according to Baur, representing a later conciliatory stage, while John brought into synthetic unity earlier elements by regarding them from a higher plane. Where the idea or tendency was not consistently carried through, traces of redaction were discovered.

---

37. Cf. Holtzmann, *Einleitung*, S. 348.
38. 1864.

Baur's results have been modified by his followers, and Ritschl, at one time a disciple of Baur, has pointed out that Baur gave to Jewish Christianity an undue significance for the development of the apostolic and post-apostolic Church, the literary evidence demanding rather the view that Gentile Christianity was its constructive and organizing factor. The Dutch school, moreover, following the eccentric results of Bruno Bauer, but by a different method, reject entirely the Hegelian conception of development by antithesis which underlies Baur's whole theory, and substitute for it that of a gradual development from the simple and homogeneous to the heterogeneous and complex; they thus invert the order of the second and third stages in Baur's theory. Wider knowledge of early Christian literature has also necessitated an earlier dating of our Gospels, thus introducing uncertainty into a system which determines this under the influence of *a priori* categories. The tendency criticism of the Gospels, which regarded them as party documents, being bound up with a particular theory of the development of the Church in the apostolic and post-apostolic ages, and having no greater stability than the theory of which it was a part, failed to supply an adequate norm for separating the trustworthy from the untrustworthy elements in the gospel witness. It was not strange, therefore, that, becoming skeptical of *a priori* systems, criticism turned its attention to the Gospels themselves, and sought by literary analysis to discover their sources. Recognizing that the Gospels were products of the apostolic age, it was seen that whatever influence the environment in which they were written may have had on them, the materials from which they were composed must have come from an earlier time. The fixity of form which, with all their variations, characterizes the synoptic Gospels could not but commend this method, and at the same time it focused attention on these Gospels as the field in which sure results might be most certainly expected. The synoptic problem, which is by no means new, thus received a new prominence at the hands, among others, of Weizsäcker, Holtzmann and B. Weiss, and more recently of Wernle. Similarly also the fourth Gospel has been subjected to a like method of treatment by Wendt.

That the evangelists were students of gospel history before they became contributors will scarcely be denied by those who admit any basis of fact in their narratives. Those, therefore, who were not eye-witnesses must have gained their information about the facts which they narrate indirectly, either through oral or through written sources. That this was the case may be seen quite clearly in the prologue to the third Gospel, where the author tells us of the status of his subject at the time of writing, mentioning the work of his predecessors, his own investigation, the standard which he has adopted, and finally speaking of his purpose in writing. We thus learn then that the author of the third Gospel had predecessors, with whose work he was most probably acquainted, but that for him, as for them, the normative source guaranteeing the trustworthiness of the narrative was the παρέδοσαν of those who from the beginning were αὐτόπται καὶ ὑπηρέται . . . . τοῦ λόγου.[39] But granting the use of sources both written and oral, the determination of these must remain very largely hypothetical. In broad outline an agreement may be reached; but with little to guide us save a comparative induction, conclusions as to details depending so largely on the personal equation will remain uncertain. Dr. Weiss' "apostolic source" impresses others as a torso without natural beginning or satisfactory ending. Holtzmann held one theory of the Urmarkus source, Weizsäcker another. Eventually Holtzmann withdrew the Urmarkus theory altogether.[40] Wernle posits an original Greek Logia source, coming from the circle of the original apostles, used by both Matthew and Luke. Before it reached Matthew, however, it had passed through the hands of a number of redactors (Q¹, Q², Q³), one of whom (Qʳ) gave to it its Judaistic tone.[41] In

---

39. Zahn's inference that the prologue excludes the knowledge on Luke's part of a Gospel written by an apostle seems to me justified (*Einleitung*, II, S. 364).

40. *Einleitung*, S. 350.

41. *Die syn. Frage*, S. 231.

the fourth Gospel, where we have no comparative results to direct us, the separation of its sources is even more problematical; while the manifest unity in diction and style leaves such an analysis without formal support in the Gospel.

If, however, such an analytic study of the Gospels should not only discover for us the fact that there are sources lying back of and imbedded in our Gospels, but should also, in a measure, determine what they are in general and their history, the problem of separating the trustworthy from the untrustworthy in the gospel witness will have been pushed but one step further back. The deflecting influence may have been introduced by the evangelists, and if so, we shall have solved the problem when we have identified and set aside so much of their contribution as served this end. Or the deflecting influence may have found its way into the sources before they reached the evangelists, and if so, it must be eliminated. Then the residuum will constitute the gospel witness in its purity. Such a separation cannot, however, be carried through, either in the Gospels or in their sources, without some principle of discrimination. This may be sought either objectively, after the manner of Baur, in the history of which the Gospels form a part; or subjectively, in some idea which shall furnish us with the key to the problem. Faith in a particular solution of the synoptic problem underlies the one form, skepticism in regard to any solution of it the other.

Weizsäcker, who has contributed materially to the study of the synoptic Gospels in his advocacy of the two-document hypothesis, conceives of the sources of these Gospels as products of the early Jerusalem Church. In this environment, the center of living tradition about the life and teaching of Christ, the sources of the Gospels grew, and, before the destruction of Jerusalem, had taken on so fixed a form that the authors of the Gospels introduced very few changes into them, the composition of the Gospels falling after the creative period in the history of the gospel tradition. To understand the Gospels we must understand the growth of their sources, and this must be studied in the environment from which they came, the early Jerusalem Church. Such a study will, moreover, serve a twofold purpose. Not only will it disclose to us how the gospel tradition grew; it will shed light also on the Jerusalem Church by recovering for us documents which were formed in accordance with her needs, and upon which these needs in some instances exercised a creative influence. Following on the oral tradition, the sources of the Gospels began to take on a fixed or written form with the spread of missionary activity from Jerusalem into the diaspora. First the words of Jesus were collected and organized into groups, then came a narrative collection likewise organized into definite groups. The two sources of the synoptic Gospels thus grew to meet the needs of believers who required the information about Jesus which was current in the Jerusalem Church. In these two sources as used in the Gospels different strata may be discovered by bearing in mind their Jerusalem origin. In the Logia as preserved by Matthew, prominence is given to Christ's opposition to the Pharisees and scribes, and to their piety, reflecting the separation of the Jerusalem Church from Judaism and its authorities. In the Logia of Luke, however, prominence is given to the poor, reflecting a later time in the life of the Church. The gospel sources are, however, not only reflections of the condition of the Jerusalem Church—emphasizing in the teaching of Jesus what was valuable for her life in its different stages— they are in some instances the direct result of her creative activity, as in the parable of the tares.[42] Significant is the following statement: "From the beginning the tradition consisted not in mere repetition, but in repetition combined with creative activity."[43] Similarly also in the narrative sources. Written in Jerusalem with a practical purpose, little attention was given to chronological arrangement, and as the events are localized principally in Galilee, there was of necessity an ideal projection which resulted in generalities, such as the mountain, the sea, the city and the desert. Here also different strata in the tradition appear. The narratives

---

42. *Das apostolische Zeitalter,* S. 384.
43. S. 393, English translation, II, p. 62.

of the first stratum show Jesus in His regular activity—in the work of His calling, in His intercourse with all sorts of men. The later stratum is characterized by symbolical representation or allegory, and is best seen in such narratives as the feeding of the five and four thousand and the transfiguration. The faith which created these narratives used them as the means of expressing what it had in Jesus. Jesus had become the subject of teaching (Lehre), so that this form of teaching was intended not as history but as the symbolical representation of His nature. Conservation and free development went hand in hand in the narrative as in the Logia source, revealing a development which as compared with other lines, such as the Ebionite, has the merit of being consistent.[44]

Such a view is manifestly less burdened than was Baur's with a particular theory of the development of apostolic history. It gains in consistency by limiting both locally and temporally the formative influences which produced the synoptic Gospels. It has the merit of seeking to understand the Gospels in relation to their environment, and it commands our assent in fixing upon the Jerusalem Church before the year seventy for the origin of the material which underlies their common tradition. In regard to the nature and extent of this influence Weizsäcker's view seems less objective. Of fundamental importance in his theory is the distinction between reproductive and creative tradition. If this be established by evidence, he will have discovered the principle of separation which, on the theory of partial trustworthiness, is needed in order to account for the Gospels and their witness. Among the instances of creative tradition Weizsäcker cites the fact that Luke omits the cursing of the fig tree and replaces it by the parable of the fig tree.[45] From the fact that Peter and John were still active when the narrative of the transfiguration took on fixed form in Jerusalem, he infers its symbolical or allegorical character.[46] Such inferences

---

44. *Das apostolische Zeitalter,* 369ff.
45. S. 396.
46. S. 397.

may seem possible to some, but they furnish at best but an uncertain basis for so far-reaching a principle.

Schmiedel has less faith in the solution of the synoptic problem. He says: "The great danger of any hypothesis lies in this, that it sets up a number of quite general propositions on the basis of a limited number of observations, and thus has to find these propositions justified, come what may."[47] Or again: "We have to reckon with an immense range of possibilities, and thus security of judgment is lost."[48] Manifestly some other course must be followed. "On the one hand, we must set on one side everything which for any reason, arising either from the substance or from considerations of literary criticism, has to be regarded as doubtful or as wrong; on the other hand, we must make search for all such data as, from the nature of their contents, cannot possibly on any account be regarded as inventions."[49] Such is the principle proposed for determining the credibility of the Gospels, quite independently of "the determination of a problem so difficult and perhaps insoluble as the synoptical is." The method recommended is a simple twofold procedure: Reject the wrong, or the false; accept the true. The principle to guide us in detecting the false is any reason arising from the substance or from considerations of literary criticism which necessitates such a judgment. The principle for discovering the true is even more simple. The true is that which cannot be false, and that which cannot be false is that which cannot possibly on any account be regarded as an invention. In the application of this method to the Gospels the first principle discovers in the chronological framework, the order of the narrative, the occasions of the utterances of Jesus, the places and persons, the supposed indications of the conditions of a later time, the miracle narratives and the resurrection so large an element of the false or wrong as "to raise a doubt whether any credible elements" are "to be found in the Gospels at

---

47. *Ency. Bib.*, s.v. Gospels, vol. II, col. 1868.
48. c. 1869.
49. c. 1872.

all." With this feature of Schmiedel's criticism we are brought to the point of passing over from the theory of partial trustworthiness to that of the entire untrustworthiness of the gospel witness. By his second principle, however, a few fragments are saved from the general wreckage, and to these the high quality of absolute trustworthiness is attributed. If one principle brings the Gospels to the verge of destruction, the other exalts what it saves to a region beyond the sphere of doubt, very much as Steck comforts us for the loss of the four major epistles of Paul with the words: "If everything is ungenuine, then nothing is any longer ungenuine."[50] It will be clear that the passages saved by this principle will receive from it no greater credibility than the principle itself possesses. Since then it is supposed to furnish us with the criterion of absolute credibility, we cannot be wrong in regarding it as the fundamental principle in Schmiedel's criticism. If it commend itself as satisfactory and adequate, then it will have given us what we have been seeking in the theories of partial trustworthiness—a safe and sure principle of separation. The identification and removal of the great mass of the untrustworthy will not greatly concern us if we have in our hands a sure instrument for determining the trustworthy.

The real nature of the principle will appear in its application to the Gospels. The Gospels were written by worshipers of Jesus. They must therefore be estimated as a profane historian would estimate an historical document which testified to the worship of a hero unknown to other sources. First and foremost importance will be attracted to those features which cannot be deduced merely from the fact of this worship, for they would not be found in the document unless the author had met with them as fixed data of tradition.[51] The grounds of this reverence for Jesus are the two

---

50. *Der Galaterbrief*, S. 385: "Ist alles unecht so ist nichts mehr unecht. Die ganze Frage hört dann auf. Man streitet sich nicht mehr über Echtheit oder Unechtheit der neutestamentlichen Schriften, sondern man sucht eine jede aus ihrem Inhalt zu verstehen und in die Geschichte des Urchristentums an der Stelle einzureihen wo sie diesem nach hingehört."

51. c. 1872.

great facts that Jesus had compassion for the multitude and that He preached with power, not as the scribes.[52] Briefly stated, the Gospel authors wrote for the glorification of Jesus;[53] anything not in accord with this purpose still preserved in their narratives must therefore have come to them in a fixed tradition, since their purpose bars the possibility of their having created it.[54] Reduced to its lowest terms, this principle may be formulated somewhat as follows: Incongruity with manifest tendency is the test of historicity. Contravention of an author's purpose is the ground of absolute credibility. The result of the application of this principle to the Gospels is the separation of five absolutely credible passages which, along with four others, might be called the foundation pillars of a truly scientific life of Jesus.[55] Of these passages Mark x. 17ff. will serve best for illustration. Jesus is represented as saying, "Why callest thou me good? None is good save one, even God." This must be absolutely authentic, because the author of the Gospel, in view of his purpose, could not have invented it. An interesting parallel to this, supported by a similar principle of criticism, is the passage in the Gospel to the Hebrews:[56] "Behold, the mother of the Lord and his brothers said to him, John the Baptist baptizes unto the remission of sins. Let us go and be baptized of him. But he said to them, In what have I sinned, that I should go and be baptized of him, unless perchance this very thing that I have said is ignorance?" Such a word, says Oscar Holtzmann, would never have found entrance into a Gospel did it not come from the mouth of Jesus Himself.[57]

The comparison of this principle with that of Weizsäcker is

---

52. c. 1873.

53. c. 1874.

54. That the inference from contradiction of purpose to origin in fixed tradition does not follow necessarily may be seen in Wrede's discussion of such contradictions in Mark's Gospel (*Das Messiasgeheimnis*, S. 124-129). When the purpose is made sufficiently flexible, the contradictions of it may be subsumed under it.

55. c. 1881.

56. Nestle, *Nov. Testament. Graeci Supplementum*, pp. 76f.

57. *Leben Jesu*, S. 36.

instructive. Both Schmiedel and Weizsäcker seek to separate
the simply reproductive or trustworthy elements in the gospel
tradition from the creative or untrustworthy elements. Weizsäcker, however, seeks to ground objectively his judgment in
respect to the latter by tracing the influence of its environment in the gospel tradition. Schmiedel's principle is subjective, resting on the idea that only what cannot possibly be regarded as creative is reproductive. It may thus dispense
with any objective historical grounds, but whether because
of its subjectivity it can be regarded as a surer canon of historicity, the principle of absolute credibility, is open to question.
We have already seen the insufficiency of a tendency criticism
organized in accordance with an *a priori* system which yet sought
justification for its results in historical evidence. A tendency
criticism, therefore, which neglects such a justification from history,
where its results may most readily be brought to the test of fact,
may escape the fate which Baur's theory suffered from historical
criticism, but only by seeking the solution of an historical problem
outside the field of historical criticism.

Yet however subjective the principle, the results of its application to historical documents must submit to the judgment
of historical criticism. Let us grant that the Gospels are written
with a purpose, that they are tendency writings: does this destroy their historical value except in so far as they contain
elements which are not in harmony with this purpose? In the
first place, it should be observed that the presence of these
very elements speaks favorably for the honesty of the men who,
writing with a purpose, did not remove them. Moreover, it is
perfectly clear that the Gospels, being written by worshipers of
Jesus, were written for the purpose of narrating the facts upon
which that worship was based, primarily for Christians, and with
the intention of thus strengthening and deepening their faith.
This faith was centered in the person of Christ, and the Gospel
writers gave what they believed to be a faithful account of His life
and work, in so far as they possessed information concerning it.

In this they may have been lamentably wrong; the very purpose, which they do not conceal, serving as their sentence of condemnation. For suppose we grant the truthfulness of their representation, then under this principle of criticism, in order to secure for it absolute credibility, they must have sought to represent the facts as they were not and retained as incongruous with their purposed representation those elements which would convey the truth to us. This is, of course, impossible, since they could not have done this without conscious intention or purpose. The question is thus forced upon us, Would it have been possible under this principle for the authors of the Gospels to have written the truth on the supposition that their narratives are true? If, however, we suppose their narratives almost entirely vitiated by their purpose, we have still to face the problem of the origin of their faith. According to the witness of the Gospel, and we may add of the whole New Testament, the creative force of the Christian faith is traced to the person of Jesus Christ. Is it historically probable, as this principle necessitates, that the order must be reversed and the Christ of the Gospels made the product of Christian faith?

Here we find ourselves again in a situation very similar to that in which Strauss left gospel criticism. In both the Christ of the Gospels is the creation of subsequent Christianity—in the one case, of Christian faith; in the other, of Christian imagination. In both an idea plays the all-determining part. In the one case the purpose of faith to represent Jesus in accord with its idea of him produced the Christ of the Gospels; in the other, the idea of Jesus as the Messiah resulted, under the mythical elaboration of faith, in the Christ of the Gospels. Since, then, we cannot have an effect without an adequate cause, this principle in its application to the Gospels must face the judgment of history based on the fundamental principle of sufficient reason in answer to the question, Did the Christ of the Gospels create the faith of Christianity, or did this faith create the Christ of the Gospels? However plausible this principle of criticism may at first appear, it fails to appreciate the nature of the Gospels, and by setting up a standard of historicity to which they cannot conform, judges them very largely untrustworthy as sources of historical information. No one will deny that the Gospels were written with a purpose, but before we condemn them on this ground we must inquire whether the purpose which they manifest be of a kind to justify such a judgment.

But, it is said, the authors of the Gospels were worshipers of Jesus. This fact will also be admitted. How shall we account for this worship? The Gospels ground it in the whole life and work of Jesus, by which was made manifest to His disciples the real nature of His being. When Thomas bows in worship before his Master he cries, "My Lord and my God!" It must also be borne in mind that the basis of the gospel tradition comes to us from Jews whose ideas about the true object of worship had been formed under the influence of the Old Testament. Schmiedel, however, tells us that the grounds of this worship were two great facts—the compassion of Jesus for the multitudes and the character of His preaching.[58] These we learn from the gospel account of His activity, but just why these two elements are given such fundamental significance we are not informed. Is it because they could not possibly, on any account, be regarded as inventions? And yet it can scarcely be maintained that they are so out of accord with the purpose of the Gospels as to secure for them the judgment of absolute credibility. But were this the case and were we justified in giving them this significance, it may still be questioned whether in themselves alone they constitute a sufficient basis for the worship whose genesis they are used to explain. Discovery of purpose cannot justify the judgment of historical untrustworthiness apart from the determination of the kind of purpose, neither can the discovery of a religious purpose be so conceived apart from an investigation of its nature; and finally, if the effort of faith to give an account of itself be rejected, some satisfactory explanation must be offered in its place. Such considerations make it difficult to believe that in

58. c. 1873.

Schmiedel's principle of criticism we have at last the sure standard by which to separate creative from reproductive faith or the norm of absolute credibility.

The question of the origin and character of the fourth Gospel in their bearing on the witness of this Gospel to Christ carries us back to patristic days. With the exception of a small sect called by Epiphanius the Alogi, its Johannine origin was not seriously questioned until the appearance of Bretschneider's *Probabilia* (1820). Modern discussion of the problem has been abundant, with wide divergence of opinion, but still very generally within the limits of the theory of partial trustworthiness. In its more recent aspects there is observable, I think, a tendency to connect the fourth Gospel either directly or indirectly with the apostle John by means of Ephesus, Jerusalem, or the presbyter John, and to recognize in the narrative-sections many authentic elements. An interesting example of this may be found in the two editions of Jülicher's *Einleitung in das Neue Testament,* published in 1894 and 1901. According to the first edition, the value of the fourth Gospel consisted in the witness which it gave, not to Christ, but to the idea of Christ as conceived by a great thinker of the third Christian generation. Its connection with the apostle John, together with the residence of the apostle in Asia Minor, were rejected. In the second edition the origin of the Gospel indirectly from John in Asia Minor is affirmed, the author being an enthusiastic disciple of the apostle. Schmiedel,[59] it is true, sees in it only ideal history, and Kreyenbühl discovers in it the work of the Gnostic Menander;[60] while Zahn upholds its Johannine authorship.[61]

Taking its place among the Gospels, and yet with a grandeur of its own bearing its witness to Christ, the fourth Gospel, by reason of the characteristics which separate it from the synoptic Gospels,

59. *Ency. Bib.,* s.v. John, vol. II, c. 2518ff.
60. *Evangelium der Wahrheit,* I, S. 368.
61. Cf. *Theo. Rundschau,* 1899; A. Meyer, *Die Behandlung der joh. Frage* and *Theo. Litteraturblatt,* 1903; Hausleiter, *Der Kampf um das Joh. Ev.*

raises its own distinctive problems. Among these, for the question we are considering, the problem of authorship plays an important part. In a measure, it takes the place in the discussion of the fourth Gospel which the problem of the sources takes in the discussion of the synoptic Gospels. If it came from the apostle John, we shall have in his authorship the guarantee of its trustworthy character. If it came from him only indirectly, then we must seek what elements he has contributed, determine whether they have in any way suffered change in transmission and reconstruct their original form. We must also ascertain whether the author had any other sources of information and, if he had, their quality; from this we must separate what he himself has contributed and estimate its value. For this process, however, the theories which deny the direct Johannine authorship of the Gospel and affirm its partial trustworthiness offer only very general criteria, suggested chiefly by the divergence both in form and content of the fourth Gospel from the synoptic Gospels.

If the two be really inconsistent, then, on the theory that the synoptic Gospels are trustworthy or at least partially trustworthy, the credibility of the fourth Gospel will, of course, be correspondingly limited. Then some satisfactory explanation must be offered of how such an inconsistent account came into existence at a time when the synoptic Gospels were not only written, but widely used and known in the circles where the fourth Gospel originated. For it is clear from indications in the fourth Gospel that knowledge of the synoptic tradition of Christ's life is presupposed on the part of the readers for whom it was written. To have secured the reception that it gained in Christian circles at the time when it was written, it must, on this theory of its relation to the synoptic Gospels, have had back of it a person whose authority was clearly recognized. But since this authority cannot have been ignorant of the synoptic Gospels, we must suppose that he was either unconscious of contradicting their account or, being conscious of it, he has left this to be inferred from his narrative, without himself having introduced into it a single distinct intimation of such an intention; and yet the author of the fourth Gospel speaks elsewhere quite plainly of the purpose which he had in view in writing and which is stamped clearly upon the face of his narrative. This view, therefore, of the relation of the fourth Gospel to the synoptics may be a hasty inference from their differences, for it leaves the origin of the fourth Gospel obscure. It must thus be judged unwise to accept such an inference as supplying a sure basis for our estimate of this Gospel. That there are striking differences has been admitted; but that they necessitate a theory of the relation of the fourth Gospel to the synoptics which is largely destructive of the trustworthiness of the former, can be maintained only when on this theory a rational account of the origin and character of this Gospel is given. More consistent with the phenomena of the fourth Gospel is the theory which conceives of its relation to the synoptic Gospels as supplementary, and which seeks the explanation of the differences in the time when it was written, the needs of those for whom it was written and the source from which it came.

The genetic problem is thus seen to have fundamental significance for any theory regarding the credibility of the Gospel witness. In order, however, to determine its origin, its character must be rightly apprehended. For its character throws an indispensable light on the nature of the Gospels in which the witness is contained. Having determined its character, our judgment regarding its credibility may take an *a priori* form: being what it is, the gospel witness may be judged trustworthy or untrustworthy on the ground of its content. Or our judgment may take the historical form: in view of the origin of the Gospels which contain this witness, it may be judged trustworthy or untrustworthy.

In regard to the former, the judgment of trustworthiness finds support in the consistency of the gospel witness with the whole apostolic testimony to Christ as found in the New Testament. The close connection of this witness with the apostolic conception of the Gospels has been mentioned. The gospel witness presents in historical form just those facts which underlie the apostolic preaching, together with an estimate of Christ's person and work, which, if not elaborated in doctrinal form, is congruous with the doctrinal elaboration that we find in the Epistles. That it is the witness of faith cannot invalidate this judgment, unless it be shown that faith has created a witness without basis in fact.

In regard to the latter, the historical question of value in the light of origin, the judgment of trustworthiness may be justified. The form of the gospel witness, however close its relation in respect of content to the apostolic preaching and doctrinal teaching, makes it impossible to explain this witness as the product rather than the source of this teaching. Thus we do not find in the Gospels the formal statement of the doctrine of justification by faith or of the atonement. But we do find there a prominence given to the passion of Christ which lays a basis in fact for the central and determining significance given to these doctrines by Paul. "Christianity was from its beginning a religion of redemption. It was not first made so by Paul."[62]

We cannot, however, estimate fairly the origin of the gospel witness apart from the origin of the Gospels. To estimate the latter, historical criticism must ascertain and seek to understand the environment in which the Gospels were written and the source or sources from which they came. For its guidance it will find traces in the Gospels themselves which reveal something of the time and purpose of each. The opinion of the early Church about their origin will also be of service. It will be clear from such a study that the Gospels, like the Epistles, were concretely motived and written to supply some need in the life of the Church. Each Gospel, moreover, with dependence on a common tradition or departure from it, has its own portrait of Christ which the author sought to produce from the materials at his command. To the understanding of all this, the study of origin cannot but contribute materially. But when the environment has been ascertained and its influence traced in the Gospels thus produced, we desire to know the nature of this

---

62. Feine, *Jesus Christus und Paulus*, S. XII. Cf. also Loofs, *Herzog Realency.*, 3. A., B. iv, s.v. Christologie, S. 17, 1. 30.

influence; and this must be judged in the light of its effect. Has the pure Gospel tradition been discolored? And if so, how may it be restored to its former purity?

The review we have taken of the attempts which have been made to secure this end by a critical separation of the reproductive from the creative elements in the genesis of the Gospels and the gospel tradition has discovered to us no principle to guide us safely through such a process. That there is a trustworthy reproductive element is generally admitted. The failure to identify the creative or untrustworthy element must lead us to question its existence, since it owes its existence to a particular theory of the relation of the Gospels to the environment in which they arose. Such a theory cannot be accepted as solving the problems raised by its conception of this relation, until the more fundamental problem into which these are merged has found a satisfactory solution in the separation required. The facts, however, do not necessitate such a theory, since they are capable of explanation on another view of this relation. This view, while recognizing that our Gospels are historical documents, whose origin in space and time constitutes a proper theme for historical investigation, yet holds that the influence upon them of their environment has not destroyed their trustworthiness; recognizing also that their content is grounded in historical fact, it finds the creative influence, as distinguished from the reproductive, not in the later environment and embedded in the Gospels, but underlying the Gospels and centered in the person and work of Jesus Christ, to whom they bear witness. Such a view is ready to trust the witness of the Gospels, making confession with it of Jesus Christ as Lord and God.

Chapter 2

HARVIE M. CONN

The New Quest for the Historical Jesus*

In 1953 Dr. Ernst Käsemann, professor of New Testament at Tübingen University, Germany, presented a paper to a meeting of former students and disciples of Rudolf Bultmann. His topic was, "The Problem of the Historical Jesus."[1] The occasion was to indicate something of a shift in the direction of New Testament studies. Into the sixties, the shift was often regarded as of radical importance by those in sympathy with it and by those strongly opposed to it. James M. Robinson claimed the paper inaugurated the post-Bultmannian "new quest of the historical Jesus."[2] Werner G. Kümmel, who has served as president of Studiorum Novi Testamenti Societas, was said to trace the death knell of the Bultmannian school to the paper.[3] From the opposite side of the theological spectrum, Carl

---

1. Ernst Käsemann, *Essays on New Testament Themes* (London: SCM Press, 1964), pp. 15-47.
2. James M. Robinson, *A New Quest of the Historical Jesus* (London: SCM Press, 1959). This book is a classic statement of the factors leading to the decline of the old quest and the rise of the so-called "new quest." Another useful summary is found in Heinz Zahrnt, *The Historical Jesus* (New York: Harper and Row, 1963).
3. Carl F. H. Henry, *Frontiers in Modern Theology* (Chicago: Moody Press, 1966), p. 15.

*This study has been developed from an article with the same title by Professor Conn in *Themelios* 6(1969), 25-40. Permission has been granted by *Themelios* for use of that article here. Mr. Conn is associate professor of missions and apologetics at Westminster Theological Seminary.

F. H. Henry focused on the moment as symptomatic of a third major reconstruction of European theology since the beginning of the twentieth century.[4]

The years since then have not altogether supported the lavishness of these judgments. The debate itself has produced no epoch-scale work on a par with Käsemann's original paper. Käsemann himself "has also moved in a new direction. He has turned his attention to the history of Christian thought."[5] And this new direction on his part has so disenchanted the original supporters of the "new quest" that Käsemann himself is now accused of "once more converting the kerygma into a mythology."[6] Bultmann has not died and the "new quest" has not created so much a new direction in studies as an alternative group, weakened by the loss of its original leadership. In the meantime, a new school of thought has arisen around the writings of Wolfhart Pannenberg, a school of considerably more strength and impact in current discussions. Even the topic of discussion has shifted. The redaction school of criticism seems to have succeeded in shifting the limelight of New Testament studies from the relation of Jesus Christ to history to the evangelists as theologians.

Nevertheless, the 1953 paper does provide a historical dateline to assess a historical trend taken by New Testament studies. Though the diminution of a movement to a trend hardly allows us to speak of "major reconstruction" or "the death of Bultmann's theology," we can certainly regard it as a return to a question which was laid aside by many scholars for several decades. What can be known about Jesus of Nazareth by means of the scientific methods of the historian? What can be recovered of historical, factual value concerning the life and thoughts of Jesus?

---

4. *Ibid.*, pp. 9ff.

5. Reginald H. Fuller, "The New Testament in Current Study," *Perspectives in Religious Studies* I(1974), 104. Compare Ernst Käsemann, *New Testament Questions of Today* (London: SCM Press, 1969), pp. 23-65.

6. Fuller, *loc. cit.*

Background for the New Quest

Several streams make up the sources behind the debate of the "new quest." The term itself is an expression first used as the English title of Albert Schweitzer's turn-of-the-century title, *Von Reimarus zu Wrede* (1906). That book itself is an important part of the background for this "new quest." It carried as its title the names of the two terminal points of the life-of-Jesus era: Hermann Samuel Reimarus (1694-1768) and Wilhelm Wrede (1859-1906).[7] It was a comprehensive and masterly survey of German scholarship's investigation of the relationship of Jesus Christ and history. It was a history which presupposed a division between the Jesus of history and the Jesus of the Bible. It assumed that the Christ presented in the kerygma of the New Testament was not, in fact, the Jesus of Nazareth who actually lived in first-century Palestine.[8] It saw the whole history of nineteenth- and twentieth-century New Testament scholarship as an effort to separate the so-called "true Jesus of history" from the doctrinal formulations of Him in Bible, creed, and church.

Its conclusions were strongly negative.

> Those who are fond of talking about negative theology can find their account here. There is nothing more negative than the result of the critical study of the Life of Jesus.

> The Jesus of Nazareth who came forward publicly as the Messiah, who preached the ethic of the Kingdom of God, who founded the Kingdom of Heaven upon earth, and died to give His work its final consecration, never had any existence. He is a figure designed by rationalism, endowed with life by liberalism, and clothed by modern theology in an historical garb.[9]

Schweitzer's own attempt in a concluding chapter of this book to make good the deficiency and to depict Jesus as an apocalyptic visionary, the deluded victim of a fixed eschatological phobia which

---

7. 1970 saw the appearance in English translation at last of Wrede's classic work, *Kyrios Christos,* John E. Steely, tr. (Nashville: Abingdon Press, 1970).

8. Albert Schweitzer, *The Quest of the Historical Jesus* (New York: The Macmillan Company, 1910), pp. 1-12.

9. *Ibid.,* p. 396.

finally destroyed Him, did not escape the same verdict.

Schweitzer's book marked the end of an era. As Robinson has indicated, it did not cause the end of the old quest. But it most certainly marked "a temporary suspension of the quest."[10] Schweitzer had devastated the old liberal picture of Jesus which minimized or eradicated the eschatological element in Jesus' life and teaching sufficiently to "deliver the funeral oration" of the old liberal quest. But he had succeeded only in damaging the results of the old quest. Inasmuch as he himself shared the same presuppositions of the old "seekers" regarding the infallibility of the Bible, he could not destroy the liberals' method of critical study. And insofar as the methodology remained basically rooted in an Enlightenment rejection of the supernatural character of revelation,[11] the old quest was bound to reappear one day. Schweitzer had shown the results of the old quest to be bankrupt. But he had not sought to show that the methodology of the old quest was equally bankrupt.

In the years from 1906 to 1953, a new voice increasingly dominated New Testament studies—Rudolf Bultmann (b. 1884). His work, *The History of the Synoptic Tradition*, which appeared in 1921, marked him as a founding father of the Form Critical School. It was Bultmann's skepticism with regard to the quest of the historical Jesus that now underlined the moratorium declared by Schweitzer's earlier work. His distinctive approach to the Gospels, regarded as sources for the knowledge of Christ, and his estimate of the theological message of the New Testament and of the person and work of Jesus Christ became a new focal point for the study of the New Testament. His orientation emphasized the futility with which Schweitzer had also concluded. According to Bultmann, "the historical Jesus is so to speak hidden. We can know nothing of His personality or inner development."[12]

---

10. Robinson, *op. cit.*, p. 32.

11. For a defense of this position, see C. Van Til, *The New Hermeneutic* (Presbyterian and Reformed Publishing Co., 1974), pp. 54ff.; S. U. Zuidema, *Van Bultmann naar Fuchs* (Franeker: T. Wever, n.d.).

12. Edgar Krentz, *Biblical Studies Today* (St. Louis: Concordia Publishing House, 1966), p. 43.

In 1926, Bultmann's frustration regarding the historical Jesus was expressed in his only full-length contribution to the life-of-Jesus literature, *Jesus* (an English translation, *Jesus and the Word*, appearing in 1934). More recently, Ralph P. Martin of Fuller Theological Seminary has summarized the book's thrust as a twofold negative premise:

> (A) *Form critically,* it is impossible, Bultmann avers, to recapture Jesus as He moved in Galilee and to know "precisely what took place" in A.D. 27-30. The Gospels do not give scientific biography. They show no interest in Jesus' personality. They offer no psychological study. There is no fascination with Jesus' charm, no window into His "inner life." . . .
>
> (B) *Theologically,* also, a negative verdict must be returned to the question of whether we can know the Jesus of history as a figure of the past. Even if it were possible to learn of the Jesus of history, it is illegitimate so to inquire, for faith can never be at the mercy of historical criticism and suspend its activity while the historians debate the issue. The person in whom Christian faith confides is the risen Christ, living in the Church, having ascended (as it was once facetiously put) into the kerygma and now mediated by the morning sermon of the Lutheran rector in his pulpit![13]

Bultmann's study helps explain both the further retrenchment into the irrelevancy of another quest of the historical Jesus and its eventual reappearance. Contradictory though it may seem, the skepticism of Bultmann's conclusions reinforced earlier skepticism and also provided the principles from which his disciples took a new direction in 1953.

It is not hard to see how Bultmann's argument could corroborate the view that life-of-Jesus research is impossible and illegitimate. According to Bultmann, nothing of significance concerning the "Christ event" need be known except that He once lived, taught, and died.[14] That alone (what Bultmann calls the *Das,* the fact that

13. Ralph P. Martin, "The New Quest of the Historical Jesus," *Jesus of Nazareth: Saviour and Lord,* Carl F. H. Henry, ed. (Grand Rapids: William B. Eerdmans Publishing Company, 1966), pp. 29-30.

14. Rudolf Bultmann, *Jesus and the Word* (New York: Scribners, 1958), pp. 3-15.

He once existed) is sufficient. As to the character of Jesus (the *Wie,* how He acted) and the content of His message (the *Was,* what He said in Palestine 1900 years ago), these are beyond recovery and unnecessary to faith anyway. What Martin Kähler had urged in the nineteenth century had now, through Bultmann, become standard. To seek for the historical Jesus was denounced as tying faith to the shifting results of historical criticism.[15] Under Bultmann, the object of faith became, not the historical Jesus, but the kerygma, the Word preached by the apostles, and continued in the church. The history of Jesus was irrelevant for faith.

It is here that we must note also the relevance of these same remarks for the reappearance of the quest for the historical Jesus. For while Bultmann denounces the quest as impossible and illegitimate, his basic methodology continues to be accepted and used by those who have followed him and are demanding the new quest. And insofar as the methodology retains its continuity with the liberal past, it will demand further consideration of the same problems that plagued the old liberalism. In other words, as long as any particular school continues to separate Christ from history, to disregard the Bible's own presuppositions regarding itself, and to reject the factuality of the biblical record, the quest cannot help but continue. Inevitably, the cause for the reawakened interest in the historical Jesus lies within the Kantian presuppositions of the seekers themselves.[16]

Generally speaking, this emphasis on the continuity of the old quest and the new quest is not part of the apology for the current trends in study. The major focus of Robinson's study, for example, is on the contrast between nineteenth- and twentieth-century studies. Nineteenth-century historians "assumed the general historical relia-

---

15. Martin Kähler, *The So-called Historical Jesus and the Historic, Biblical Christ* (Philadelphia: Fortress Press, 1964). Kähler's part in the quest is summarized in Carl Braaten's symposium, *The Historical Jesus and the Kerygmatic Christ* (Nashville: Abingdon Press, 1964), pp. 79-105.

16. These presuppositions are given some attention in Robert D. Knudsen, "Roots of the New Theology," *Scripture and Confession,* John H. Skilton, ed. (Nutley, N. J.: Presbyterian and Reformed Publishing Co., 1973), pp. 247ff.

bility of the Gospels and eliminated only such elements as they felt were blatant cases of doctrinal embellishments. . . . Now the kerygmatic nature of the Gospels is assumed, and historical credibility is assured only when the details 'cannot be explained in terms of the life of the Church.' "[17] The nineteenth-century quest attempted "to avoid the risk of faith by supplying objectively verified proof for its 'faith.' " The twentieth-century quest "calls for existential commitment to the meaning of Jesus."[18] These deep roots in existentialism and the new emphasis on the kerygmatic nature of the Gospels are said by Robinson to demand an evaluation of the new quest "as completely different from the original quest."[19] Modern views of history and the self make the new quest not only possible but legitimate.

To be sure, these differences between old and new exist. But they cannot diminish the homogeneity of old and new in that rationalistic framework by which the Enlightenment, and particularly the formulations of Immanuel Kant, have structured the modern understanding of the relation of history and faith. Enlightenment thought had proposed a criterion of historical judgments predicated on a closed universe, in which all historical facts occur within discoverable cause-and-effect relationships.[20] Lessing in 1778 saw this criterion as creating "the ugly ditch which I cannot get across," a gap between accidental truths of history and necessary truths of reason. Nineteenth-century theologians presupposed that gap by calling into question the historicity of the biblical records in areas

17. Charles C. Anderson, *Critical Quests of Jesus* (Grand Rapids: William B. Eerdmans Publishing Company, 1969), p. 158.

18. Robinson, *op. cit.*, p. 44.

19. Anderson, *op. cit.*, p. 162.

20. *The Nature and Extent of Biblical Authority* (Grand Rapids: Board of Publications of the Christian Reformed Church, 1972), p. 30. This study committee report presented to the Synod of 1972 of the Christian Reformed Church contains a helpful analysis of the Enlightenment concept of "the historical method" with an attempt to differentiate it from a use of the method within the framework of biblical presupposition. In words that could be applied to the new quest, it notes that "the historical-critical method as employed in contemporary theology often betrays fundamental religious presuppositions which compromise a wholehearted confession of the full authority of Scripture" (p. 56).

of "doctrinal embellishments." The twentieth-century new quest, borrowing heavily from Kierkegaard's leap of faith, has continued to presuppose it by its appeal to the existentialist kerygma, isolated from historical realities.

Robinson himself, though supporting the necessity of the new quest, does not escape these presuppositions either. He questions the legitimacy of any attempt to equate the Jesus of history with the Christ of kerygma. The statement "Christian faith is not interested in the historical Jesus" is, he holds, "to a considerable extent true."[21] Yet, at the same time he argues that "man's quest for meaningful existence is his highest stimulus to scholarly enquiry; consequently, a serious quest of the historical Jesus must have meaning in terms of man's quest for meaningful existence."[22] Robinson's understanding of existential selfhood becomes the bridge by which he seeks to cross Lessing's ditch between history's Jesus and the kerygma's Jesus. He will not discard an Enlightenment concept of the historical-critical method,[23] nor will he see Bultmann's focus on the kerygma as anything less than "the impetus leading to a new quest of the historical Jesus."[24] He fears a concept of kerygma which sees itself as the proclamation of mythical ideas. Yet, with Bultmann, he admits that the kerygma makes use of mythological concepts in getting its message across, "the existential meaningfulness of a historical person." It is in his concession that "the *kerygma* consists in the meaning of a certain historical event"[25] that he claims departure from Bultmann. But even with all these strictures and differences, Robinson's effort still focuses around the central theological problem raised by Enlightenment presuppositions, that is to say, how is the certainty of faith to be related to the uncertainties of historical research?

---

21. Robinson, *op. cit.*, p. 32.
22. *Ibid.*, p. 75.
23. *Ibid.*, pp. 95-100.
24. *Ibid.*, p. 80.
25. *Ibid.*, p. 90.

The History of the New Quest

The history of the new quest still remains largely associated with former pupils and disciples of Bultmann, at least in terms of its most vigorous results. Karl Barth has disclaimed any interest in it with these words, ". . . to my amazement [the New Testament men] have armed themselves with swords and staves and once again undertaken the search for 'the historical Jesus'—a search in which I now as before prefer not to participate."[26] With the possible exception of the noted Barthian Hermann Diem,[27] the quest remains largely a revolt within the Bultmannian school.

Nonetheless, the historical Jesus has become an increasing concern in that school. Not all have engaged in the debate with the same enthusiasm or the same purpose as others. Ernst Fuchs of Marburg, Gerhard Ebeling of Zürich, Günther Bornkamm of Heidelberg have entered into the discussion with major contributions and increasing historical interest. A former Bultmann student like Hans Conzelmann had produced an article, "Jesus Christus," in the German encyclopedia, *Die Religion in Geschichte und Gegenwart,* which extends from column 619 to column 653 of volume III.[28] Yet his interest has obviously waned to the point of conscious withdrawal, and he is more easily classified today as a formative participant in the emergent Redaction School *(Redaktionsgeschichte).* A minority of Bultmann students like Philipp Vielhauer of Bonn and Manfred Metzger of Mainz seem to be resisting this historical interest. James M. Robinson has been listed among this minority, although his 1959 book has played a leading role in the understanding of the question. Perhaps the best way to do justice to these divergencies in the debate is to single out several men for individual attention before we outline

---

26. Karl Barth, "How My Mind Has Changed," *The Christian Century* LXXVII, No. 3 (January 20, 1960), 75.

27. Daniel Fuller, *Easter Faith and History* (Grand Rapids: William B. Eerdmans Publishing Company, 1965), pp. 136ff.

28. Hans Conzelmann, "Jesus Christus," *Die Religion in Geschichte und Gegenwart,* 3rd ed. (Tübingen: J. C. B. Mohr, 1957), III, 619-653.

the composite picture which emerges from their efforts.[29] Three men especially will receive our attention here because of their unique or representative efforts.

Ernst Käsemann (b. 1906)

Since Käsemann is credited with inaugurating the debate by his 1953 paper, his lecture may provide some useful light as to the beginning of the renewed search. Earlier regarded as "the most disaffected member of the Bultmann school,"[30] Käsemann has moved further away from the debate.

And yet, however disaffected Käsemann may seem to be, his essay must not be regarded as radical revolt from the Bultmann camp. Though he seeks to find an appraisal of Jesus which will be more positive than Bultmann's estimate, he does so as a disciple of Bultmann who still largely shares Bultmann's general theological

---

29. Several excellent surveys have sketched all or part of this history: James M. Robinson, "The Recent Debate on the New Quest," *Journal of Bible and Religion* XXX (1962); James M. Robinson, "Basic Shifts in German Theology," *Interpretation* XVI (1962), 76-97; Schubert Ogden, "Bultmann and the 'New Quest,' " *Journal of Bible and Religion* XXX (1962), 209-218; Günther Bornkamm, "Die Theologie Rudolf Bultmanns in der neueren Diskussion; zum Problem der Entmythologisierung und Hermeneutik," *Theologische Rundschau* XXIX (1963), 33-141; J. B. Bederbaugh, "The First Decade of the New Quest for the Historical Jesus," *The Lutheran Quarterly* XVI, no. 3 (August, 1964), 239-267; Raymond E. Brown, "After Bultmann, What?—An Introduction to the Post-Bultmannians," *Catholic Biblical Quarterly* XXVI (1964), 1-30; P. J. Cahill, "Rudolf Bultmann and Post-Bultmann Tendencies," *Catholic Biblical Quarterly* XXVI (1964), 153-178; Harvey K. McArthur, "Basic Issues: A Survey of Recent Gospel Research," *Interpretation* XVIII, no. 1 (1964), 39-55; R. S. Barbour, "Theologians of Our Time: Ernst Käsemann and Günther Bornkamm," *Expository Times* LXXVI (1965), 379-383; J. D. Godsey, "Some Observations on German Protestant Theology," *Drew Gateway*, XXXVI (1965–1966), 1-21; J. H. Elliott, "The Historical Jesus, the Kerygmatic Christ, and the Eschatological Community," *Concordia Theological Monthly* XXXVII (1966), 470-491; W. G. Kümmel, "Jesusforschung seit 1950," *Theologische Rundschau* XXXI (1966), 15-46; W. E. Hull, "The New Quest of the Historical Jesus," *Review and Expositor* LXIV (1967), 323-339; G. G. O'Collins, "Reality as Language: Ernst Fuchs's Theology of Revelation," *Theological Studies*, XXVIII (1967), 76-93; Harvey K. McArthur, "From the Historical Jesus to Christology," *Interpretation* XXIII (1969), 190-206.

30. Henry, *op. cit.*, p. 16.

viewpoint as well as his basic approach to the Gospels. That approach continues to be controlled by the Form Critical view that biography and the revealing of traits of personality are not found there. Like Bultmann, he continues to separate radically the Christ of the early church kerygma and the Jesus of history. Like Bultmann, he recognizes that the Gospels were written by those who had faith in the Christ of kerygma. Like Bultmann, he also realizes that "it was difficult to get back through that faith to see Jesus as he really was."[31] And like Bultmann, he grants that it is not possible to construct a life of Jesus containing exact chronological data.[32]

Where then lies the uniqueness of Käsemann's challenge? Part of the answer lies in Käsemann's fear that Bultmann's deemphasis on history will lead the church back into first century Docetism. He is unwilling to admit "a disengagement of interest from the earthly Jesus."[33] He continues, "If this were to happen, we should either be failing to grasp the nature of the primitive Christian concern with the identity between the exalted and the humiliated Lord: or else we should be emptying that concern of any real content, as did the Docetists."[34]

In other words, for Käsemann, there is indicated in the Gospels a connection between the early church kerygma and history, however tenuous he sees it to be. The very concern of the early church to distinguish between the exalted Lord and the humiliated Lord is a recognition of distinction in history. One does not write four gospels if there is as little interest in history as Bultmann claims. The very fact that the Gospels were written indicates that the early church wished to make its faith in Christ consistent with Jesus as a person of history.[35]

What points does Käsemann find in the Gospel records which he is willing to regard as historical? Obviously his Bultmannian presuppositions forbid his accepting the records as they are. What

31. Fuller, *op. cit.*, p. 118.
32. Käsemann, *op. cit.*, p. 45.
33. *Ibid.*, p. 46.
34. *Ibid.*
35. *Ibid.*, pp. 24-25.

elements can be regarded as historical in any sense? And how does one determine such a choice?

Käsemann centers on the preaching of Jesus as the distinctive element in the Gospels. Jesus' other activities and His destiny itself must be interpreted in the light of this preaching.[36] Certain selected sayings of Jesus may be regarded as unmistakably authentic.

How do we select these sayings? "The only way this can be done is to look for certain things in the gospels which cannot be explained by any parallels found in the faith and practice of the early church of that time or in Judaism and Hellenism from which particular parts of the church borrowed ideas."[37]

If a saying stands in sharp contrast to anything in the Jewish surroundings of Jesus' day, if a saying seems already to have been unable to be understood by them, we may reasonably conclude these sayings are authentic.

What then emerges from the application of such criteria? What may we know about the historical elements in the recorded sayings of Jesus? Those passages where the absolute authority of Jesus is found can be given some credence. The declaration of Jesus that His authority was greater than that of the Mosaic law, His contempt for the separation of the holy and the profane, His freedom in dealing with the sabbath rules, His dealing with demoniacs, His avowed relationship to John the Baptist—these elements may reasonably be trusted.[38] To be sure, Käsemann doubts any messianic self-consciousness of Jesus.[39] Unlike Bultmann, he contends that in Jesus the kingdom arrived and was not simply regarded as proximate.

Käsemann's conclusions remained slim and skeptical. But they did indeed constitute something of a breakthrough. Now others began to explore the question he had initiated. "Who shall forbid us to ask the question concerning the historical Jesus? This defeatism has

---

36. *Ibid.*, p. 44.
37. Fuller, *op. cit.*, p. 118.
38. Käsemann, *op. cit.*, pp. 37-45.
39. *Ibid.*, p. 38.

no justification . . . ," cried Gerhard Ebeling. Bultmann had once written, "We may not go behind the kerygma, using it as a source . . . to reconstruct an 'historical Jesus.' " Now men like Günther Bornkamm began to challenge that word. "How could faith of all things be content with mere tradition, even though that be contained in the gospels? It must break through it and seek behind it. . . ."[40] Käsemann had raised the issue.

Ernst Fuchs (b. 1903)

In 1956, Käsemann's proposal of a new quest was supported in a guest lecture at the University of Zürich by Ernst Fuchs, at that time professor of New Testament at the Church Academy, Berlin.

Whereas Käsemann regarded certain elements in the *teaching* of Jesus as historical and relevant for faith, Fuchs concentrated upon an aspect of Jesus' *conduct* as the real context of His preaching. The specific act he singled out is Jesus' readiness to eat and have fellowship with tax collectors and sinners. According to Fuchs, the post-Easter church would have been much less likely to tamper with any tradition regarding Jesus' conduct than a tradition regarding His teaching. Hence, this theme was less likely to be a product of Easter faith than Jesus' teaching, as Käsemann had argued.

This act of table fellowship with sinners was no simple illustration of sociability or condescension. It is an eschatological act by which Jesus determined to begin "here on earth with the work of God visible only in heaven." The conduct of Jesus "is neither that of a prophet nor of a teacher of wisdom, but that of a man who dares to act in God's stead, and who . . . draws to himself sinners who, but for him, would have to flee from God."[41] Because this conduct by implication claimed to be divine conduct, it led to open opposition and Jesus' eventual death, according to Fuchs.

In his formulation, Fuchs has departed from Bultmann at several points. Unlike Bultmann, he has made some attempt to explore

---

40. Zahrt, *op. cit.*, pp. 95-96.
41. Ernst Fuchs, *Studies of the Historical Jesus* (Naperville, Ill.: Alec R. Allenson, 1964), p. 22.

the psychological makeup of Jesus. This departure is particularly apparent in Fuchs's treatment of the relation of Jesus to John the Baptist. According to Fuchs, John's death had some psychological significance for Jesus. Jesus had seen what had happened to John the Baptist, who had also acted as God's representative and proclaimed the coming of the kingdom. John had been put to death and Jesus knew that, should He continue John's message, He would die also. In conscious decision, He willed to follow the path of John. He had found in John's death a personal, psychological significance for His own life and destiny.

Fuchs also departs from Bultmann in a more open willingness to associate the message Jesus preached and the kerygma of the early church. Jesus has chosen to appear as the one in whose work can be seen the redemptive work of God. This implicit declaration by conduct of His own self-understanding as One who assumed the role of God's representative has been made explicit in the post-Easter proclamation of the early church. Inspired by Jesus, who had dared to demonstrate God's grace as God's true will for men, the church repeated the significance of His conduct in the myth of the resurrection of Christ.[42] In the message and action of Jesus an eschatological understanding of His person is implicit, which becomes explicit in the kerygma of the primitive church.

Fuchs's position has drawn sharp criticism from Bultmann. The teacher attacks his errant disciple's explanation as a "relapse into the historical-psychological interpretation" in which Jesus' attitude becomes a "phenomenon perceptible to the objectifying historian."[43] But, regardless of Bultmann's sharp words, as we saw with Käsemann, Fuchs continues to share with his teacher too much common ground to be radically distinguished from any critical point of view. Like Bultmann, Fuchs conducts his exegesis with the benefit of existentialist philosophy. It is the existential truth of the resurrection that Fuchs promotes, not the genuinely historical fact. In some ways, Fuchs draws the Jesus of history closer to the Christ of faith.

---

42. *Ibid.*, pp. 26-31.
43. Braaten, *op. cit.*, p. 32.

But, in a fuller sense, there is still a great chasm between the two in his mind.

Günther Bornkamm (b. 1905)

In 1956, the preliminary work of Käsemann and Fuchs was superseded by the first full-length book on the historical Jesus to appear from the Bultmann school since Bultmann's own *Jesus and the Word* thirty years earlier. Unlike Käsemann's or Fuchs's essays, Bornkamm's book, *Jesus of Nazareth,* was a rather full presentation (239 pages in the English edition)[44] of the new quest for the historical Jesus and therefore deserves more attention than either Käsemann or Fuchs's earlier work.[45]

Like his predecessors, Bornkamm also, though still a disciple of Bultmann, and though still largely sharing Bultmann's general theological viewpoint as well as his basic approach to the Gospels, has presented an appraisal of Jesus which remains, in important respects, more positive than the work of Bultmann. Ned B. Stonehouse, late professor of New Testament at Westminster Theological Seminary, has assessed this positiveness in three areas. "First of all in a more constructive estimate of the witness of the gospel as against Bultmann's extreme agnosticism. Secondly, in a fresh interest in recovering a knowledge of the Jesus of history in contrast to Bultmann's radical indifference. . . . And finally in the recognition of significant continuity between the Jesus of this reconstruction and the kerygma of the Christian church. . . ."[46]

Nevertheless, these positive features are far from marking a return to traditional or orthodox views. Rather they point to the conclusion that this new quest for the historical Jesus is, as to its basic thrust, a resurgence of liberal perspectives and spirit. As such, it

44. Günther Bornkamm, *Jesus of Nazareth* (New York: Harper and Row, 1960).

45. It is rather surprising, in this connection, that the otherwise excellent article by Ralph Martin, mentioned earlier, treats Bornkamm's title in only one brief paragraph (Martin, *op. cit.,* p. 33).

46. Ned B. Stonehouse, review of Bornkamm's *Jesus of Nazareth,* in the *Westminster Theological Journal* XXIII, no. 2 (1961), 181ff.

does not appear to involve any significant weakening of Bultmann's authority in present-day theology but simply what Stonehouse called "a corrective or readjustment which is viewed as necessary in order to commend more effectively the essentially Bultmannian preferred answer to the intellectual despisers of the gospel in our day."[47]

Several examples could easily illustrate the radical skepticism of Bornkamm's judgments. Like Strauss and Bultmann, he regards the Gospels as primarily products of the faith of the Christian community rather than trustworthy records of the apostolic witness to Jesus as He actually lived before the resurrection. Accordingly the birth narratives "are too much overgrown by legends and by Jewish as well as Christian messianic conceptions to be used for historical assertions."[48] The miracle stories, particularly the nature miracles, "have taken on legendary traits and legends have been added."[49] In spite of all the evidence to the contrary, Jesus, he argues, never claimed to be the Messiah.[50] The narratives of the suffering and death of Christ, while containing elements of history, are so fully written from the viewpoint of the post-Easter faith of the Christian community that "we have little certain knowledge in the proper historical sense about the last chapter of the life of Jesus."[51] The resurrection narratives are said either to exclude any possibility of an actual bodily resurrection or, at the least, not to allow for any certainty as to what precisely happened.[52]

In the face of all these skeptical judgments regarding the life and testimony of Jesus, how can Bornkamm reach any conclusions more positive than those of Bultmann? Precisely where does Bornkamm's Jesus differ from Bultmann's Jesus?

---

47. *Ibid.*, p. 182. In this connection, it is most misleading to note the emphasis of Carl F. H. Henry on Bornkamm's study as a signal of "an impending breakup of the total Bultmannian empire" (Carl F. H. Henry, *op. cit.*, pp. 3-9). Henry's judgment does not seem to this writer to treat adequately the common presuppositions shared by both Bultmann and Bornkamm.

48. Bornkamm, *op. cit.*, p. 53.

49. *Ibid.*, pp. 131, 208.

50. *Ibid.*, pp. 169ff., 228ff.

51. *Ibid.*, p. 157; cf. pp. 153ff.

52. *Ibid.*, p. 184; cf. pp. 179ff.

It is the authority of Jesus as the "unmediated presence" *(unmittelbare Gegenwart)* that pervades every aspect of the Gospels and demands our historical credence. And it is this "unmediated presence" that is "distinguished by an authenticity, a freshness, and a distinctiveness not in any way effaced by the Church's Easter faith. These features point us directly to the earthly figure of Jesus."[53]

This "unmediated presence" is manifest in many areas. Though He was a rabbi, He did not, like the rabbis, base His authority on the Scriptures. There was nothing in contemporary Judaism that corresponded with the immediacy with which He taught. Though He was a prophet of the coming kingdom of God, He does not find it necessary to produce His credentials. His authority was not derived. Rather, it was immediately in His person and was fulfilled in Him. In His encounters with people, He displays an "astounding sovereignty." Even the simplicity of Jesus' preaching is said to echo this theme of "unmediated presence." The material for His parables came from the everyday life of the particular group to which He was speaking. Thus, even in the materials that illustrated the message of God, Jesus confronted the people with God as an immediate fact.

Bornkamm is willing to admit that Jesus actually awakened messianic expectations by His coming and by His ministry.[54] But one should not confuse this awakening with any actual claims made by Jesus himself. Though Bornkamm is willing to speak of "the Messianic character of his being" as contained *"in* his words and deeds and *in* the unmediateness of his historic appearance," he also refuses to acknowledge that Jesus actually claimed to be Messiah. He explains Peter's confession at Caesarea Philippi of Jesus' messiahship as simply the believing interpretation of the post-Easter church. Jesus' life cannot, in any sense, be regarded as messianic. Those sayings regarding the Son of man which can be retained as authentic are said to be Jesus' references to a coming figure other

---

53. *Ibid.,* p. 24.
54. *Ibid.,* p. 172.

than Himself.[55] The messianic elements in the Gospels are said to be reflections of the church's post-Easter faith tradition, awakened by the resurrection.

Similar to this method of treatment is Bornkamm's handling of the resurrection. Like the "unmediated presence" of Jesus, the resurrection message of the early church also pervades every part of the Gospels. Hence, one cannot dismiss the resurrection narrative as simply a product of the believing community, as Bultmann has done. "Certainly the form in which it comes down to us is stamped with this faith. But it is just as certain that the appearances of the risen Christ and the word of his witnesses have in the first place given rise to this faith."[56] Similarly, Bornkamm refuses to say the origin of the resurrection faith is purely psychological.

But none of this means that Bornkamm has moved toward a biblical estimate of the resurrection. He quickly concedes that this resurrection faith of the early church is not bound up with "the theory of the resurrected Christ walking the earth for a time and only subsequently ascending into Heaven."[57] It is not to be pinned down to a calendar date.

What precisely does Bornkamm mean by this? Stonehouse comments that "in dealing with the resurrection of Jesus, it must be said, Bornkamm leaves the reader in greater doubt as to his precise meaning than is customarily true of his exposition as a whole. Exactly what happened to produce the Easter faith, and in particular how Jesus himself is understood as bringing it about, is not made clear. If Bornkamm holds to the 'objective vision' theory, as he would seem to have to if he were to credit Jesus with decisive action in producing faith, he might have been expected to make that clear. On the other hand, if his viewpoint is that of the 'subjective visions' theory, as one might be inclined to suppose in view of his general critical position, he leaves unexplained what he means by the appearances of the risen Christ as the cause of this faith. But this lack of

---

55. *Ibid.*, pp. 169ff.
56. *Ibid.*, p. 183.
57. *Ibid.*

clarity evidently stems from the very feature in Bornkamm's general construction which is offered as providing the key to the understanding of the history and person of Jesus to which attention was drawn above: the fluidity of the line between the history of Jesus and that of the church. . . ."[58]

Bornkamm's conclusions place him alongside Käsemann and Fuchs in finding in history some relevance for an already existent Easter faith. But, like these men also, his conclusions are far short of identifying the historical Jesus with the Jesus of the early church.

The Emerging Christ of the New Quest

In 1959, in the face of growing discontent and rebellion within his camp, Rudolf Bultmann reflected again on his approach to the life and ministry of Jesus. Willing cautiously to affirm the factuality of Jesus' person, he summarized what he felt can be known concerning Jesus' activity: "Characteristic for him are exorcisms, the breach of the Sabbath commandment, the abandonment of ritual purifications, polemic against Jewish legalism, fellowship with outcasts such as publicans and harlots, sympathy for women and children; it can also be seen that Jesus was not an ascetic like John the Baptist, but gladly ate and drank a glass of wine. Perhaps we may add that he called disciples and assembled about himself a small company of followers—men and women."[59] Unfortunately, says Bultmann, "we cannot know how Jesus understood his end, his death."[60] It is conceivable (Bultmann imagines) that Jesus died in utter bewilderment and abject despair, a frustrated and rejected prophet of God.

May one legitimately contrast this Jesus of Bultmann with the emerging portrait of Jesus being fashioned by the writers of the new quest? How new is the new Jesus of the post-Bultmannian period? To answer that question, we propose to erect a composite picture of the Jesus of the new quest by combining several

---

58. Stonehouse, *op. cit.,* pp. 186-187.
59. Rudolf Bultmann, "The Primitive Christian Kerygma and the Historical Jesus," in Braaten, *op. cit.,* p. 22. There is a useful summation of Bultmann's reactions in Cahill, *op. cit.,* pp. 166-170.
60. Braaten, *op. cit.,* p. 23.

of the features already discerned in our study of the individual scholars' contributions. We grant that such a procedure does injustice to the differences between the various scholars on this issue.

One is struck immediately by the lack of biographical information supplied by the post-Bultmannian scholars. Like Bultmann, they share a profound lack of interest in this area. Bornkamm has most certainly pushed beyond Bultmann by dealing in his book with the "historically indisputable traits" of Jesus of Nazareth.[61] But what do these amount to? His childhood and adolescence are obscure. He belonged to Galilee. His native town was Nazareth. He was a Jew, a son of Joseph the carpenter. He had brothers and sisters. His mother tongue was Galilean Aramaic. Small towns like Bethsaida, Chorazin, Capernaum were the scene of His activity. We do not know exactly how long His ministry lasted. At last He went up to Jerusalem to His death on the cross. Fuchs adds to these data what he feels to be the outstanding trait of Jesus' ministry—His readiness to consort with tax-collectors and sinners and to share meals with them. Käsemann underlines Jesus' dealing with demoniacs and His freedom in dealing with the sabbath rules and ceremonial prescriptions for purity and diet. But when we are through, the biographical information seems no fuller than what Bultmann himself is willing to concede.

It is in the area of the preaching of Jesus that the post-Bultmannians more clearly seem to diverge from Bultmann. And yet here too the divergence is not so sharply marked. It is in the fullness of the treatment that the followers of the new quest stand out most sharply from Bultmann. Whereas Bultmann wrote thirty pages on Jesus in his *Theology of the New Testament,* relegating Him to the "presuppositions" for the kerygma,[62] Bornkamm deals, in the main body of his work, with Jesus' message of the dawn of the kingdom of God, the will of God, and discipleship. In strongly existentialist language, he develops the theme that all men "now stand in the

---

61. Bornkamm, *op. cit.,* pp. 53-63.
62. Rudolf Bultmann, *Theology of the New Testament* I (New York: Scribners, 1951), 3-32.

sudden flash of light of the coming God, in the light of his reality and presence."[63]

In confronting men, Jesus is said to proclaim the kingdom of God. This reign, says Hans Conzelmann, "while future, was effectively engaging men already in the present in the word of Jesus himself. It demands decision, response, acceptance of the challenge. It is making itself felt in advance in the words and works of Jesus, so that men's lives here and now are 'decisively qualified' in the present by the future Reign of God."[64] His words and actions revealed a claim higher than that of the rabbis, for He placed Himself over the decalogue, the sabbath and demons (Käsemann). "Jesus dared to make God's will as relevant as if he stood in God's place . . . his manner was that of a man who dared to act in God's stead in that he . . . drew sinners close to him, who would have had to flee from God without him" (Ernst Fuchs).

Jesus' use of "amen" is said to point in this same direction of authority calling for obedience. Whereas the Jew concluded his prayer to God with amen, thus expressing his faith that God would act, Jesus introduces His words with amen, "thus denoting that prior to his utterance there is his total engagement to the act of God, of which his words thus become the channel" (Ebeling).[65]

Is this authority of Jesus, this "immediate presence," to be interpreted as messianic? Did Jesus claim to be Messiah? Did He possess a "messianic consciousness"?

Bultmann and Form Criticism with him had rejected any messianic elements in the gospel tradition as unhistorical. Peter's confession at Caesarea Philippi, Jesus' claim to Sonship in Matthew 11:27—all such texts are said to reflect merely the post-Easter faith of the early church. And again, within the radius of post-Bultmannian research, one does not find any significant changes from this position. Bornkamm, for example, repudiates a text like Matthew 11:27

---

63. Bornkamm, *op. cit.*, p. 63.
64. Reginald H. Fuller, *The New Testament in Current Study* (New York: Scribners, 1962), p. 34.
65. *Ibid.*, p. 35.

by saying that, since it makes such exalted claims and uses such exalted titles about Jesus, it necessarily reflects the greatest impact of the church's myth-making formulations and confessions. It is least likely therefore to represent the actual words of Jesus.[66] The post-Bultmannian scholars have made little change here except possibly in the severity of their conclusions.

Within the context of the elimination of the messianic consciousness of Jesus, reference is made to the question of the meaning of the titles of Jesus. And here there seems to be a difference of sizeable proportions within the group.

Some, like Käsemann, Conzelmann, and Vielhauer, hold that Jesus never used the term "Son of man" regarding Himself. All occurrences of the term are said to be due to the creations of the early church theology. Since the Gospels do not place the words, "Lord," "Son of God," or "Messiah" into Jesus' mouth, these terms also are evidence of the theology of the early church, but not the theology of Jesus.[67] In particular, Conzelmann and Vielhauer "are so impressed by the immediacy and finality of God's presence in Jesus that there can be no room for a second soteriological figure between Jesus and the coming Kingdom, as Bultmann . . . had postulated" regarding the Son of man.[68]

Others in this same orbit take a more positive position regarding the titles of Christ. Bornkamm in this instance is closer to Bultmann in being more willing to accept as authentic those sayings about the coming Son of man. However, like Bultmann, he distinguishes sharply between Jesus and the Son of man, insisting that Jesus never identified Himself as the Son. More recently, this position has been supported in the studies of Heinz E. Tödt.[69]

---

66. Bornkamm, *op. cit.*, p. 128.
67. Krentz, *op. cit.*, p. 48.
68. R. Fuller, *op. cit.*, p. 39.
69. Heinz E. Tödt, *The Son of Man in the Synoptic Tradition* (Philadelphia: Westminster Press, 1965). One will find a useful summary of the problem of messiahship in the post-Bultmannian debate in Hugh Anderson, *Jesus and Christian Origins* (New York: Oxford University Press, 1964), pp. 160-165.

For our purposes, it is best simply to remember that none of this controversy has changed the basic approach of either "wing" towards a more biblical estimate of the titles of Jesus. Both sides in the argument presuppose the elimination of the redemptive, divine, messianic consciousness of Jesus and work from that foundation. The research into the titles of Jesus is intended merely to recover the faith of the early church, not the faith of Jesus Himself.

In this light, one cannot expect to find a more biblically oriented picture of the death of Christ among these men. Bornkamm, to be sure, includes a chapter in his book on Jesus' journey to Jerusalem, His suffering and His death. And he is much more willing than Bultmann to regard these events as essential and ascertainable parts of Jesus' history. However, he refuses to admit that Jesus deliberately went up to Jerusalem to die. That, he says, would be tantamount to suicide. The final journey to Jerusalem was deliberate, but its purpose was "to confront Judaism at its very center with the challenge of his eschatological message. But with the fate of John the Baptist before him he could very well have known that death was a possible, and indeed probable, outcome of this challenge."[70] Any redemptive significance in the death of Christ is absent in Bornkamm as well as in Bultmann.

Critique of the New Quest

Reaction to the new quest for the historical Jesus has come from many quarters. Karl Barth has bluntly refused to have anything to do with the trend, as we have noted earlier. Rudolf Bultmann has also remained unmoved by the appeals. He has discussed the movement and seems willing to acknowledge that a number of things about the historical Jesus can be known. But he still continues to insist that the only Jesus we can know from the New Testament is the Jesus of the early church faith. And this kerygma remains basically uninterested in history.

Enthusiasm for the "new quest" had excited great interest in Germany in the 1950s. But even then, there were many skeptical

---

70. Fuller, *op. cit.*, p. 44.

voices, even among those who do not credit the Bible with infallibility. Joachim Jeremias, for example, has never acknowledged the
futility of the "old quest," and has continued to preserve an interest
in the Jesus of history. Sharply critical of Bultmann, Jeremias maintains that by careful historical research, we can recover the very
words of Jesus and thus be placed before God Himself. He deplores
the Bultmannian reduction of Jesus to an existentialist Docetist,
and the tone of his work towards the post-Bultmannian period
seems more of surprise than agreement. For Jeremias, the post-
Bultmannian seekers raise no new issues. The issue remains the
same. ". . . study of the historical Jesus and his message is no
peripheral task of New Testament scholarship, a study of one particular historical problem among many others. It is *the* central
task of New Testament scholarship."[71]

In the late 1950s and particularly from 1962, the rise of a new
school of thought in Germany has increasingly drained that enthusiasm on the continent. Bearing the name of its central figure,
Wolfhart Pannenberg of Mainz, the school's emphasis on a recovery
of the dimensions of history for faith has provided even sharper
criticism of Bultmann's kerygma without history as "a meaningless
noise."[72] Both Bultmann and the New Questers are castigated as
attempting to flee into some suprahistorical harbor supposedly safe
from the critical historical flood tide. Though it is not accurate in
view of Pannenberg's sharing of Enlightenment concepts of history
to call the movement "a mediating position in the debate of New
Questers and Kerygmatists,"[73] it is certainly accurate to say that the
Pannenberg school's emphasis on universal history as the exclusive
medium for revelation forced German theology in the 1960s to
abandon temporarily its re-investigation of kerygma for a look at
history as a hermeneutic. American evangelicals have welcomed
this shift with what appears to be undue exuberance, giving slight

71. Joachim Jeremias, *The Problem of the Historical Jesus* (Philadelphia: Fortress Press, 1964), p. 21.

72. Carl Braaten, *History and Hermeneutics* (Philadelphia: Westminster Press, 1966), p. 26.

73. R. Fuller, *Perspectives in Religious Studies*, p. 104.

attention to the dialectic in Pannenberg which can insist that revelation is objective in the form of historical events (against Barth) but not objective in the form of concepts (against Calvin).[74] It would seem that the focus has shifted, but the factors for internal disintegration remain.

In the English-speaking world, the earlier debate has apparently "intensified research that had never really died down. British scholars have generally shown more skepticism over against the results and values of form criticism (with the exception, perhaps, of Robert H. Lightfoot) and more faith in the historical framework of Mark's gospel. Vincent Taylor, for example, had been preparing for a life of Christ some years before Käsemann's article appeared. The new quest served to sharpen the differences in approach between British and continental scholars."[75]

North American scholarship, suffering from the usual translation time-lag that separates German theology from the English-speaking world, has felt much less the impact of the questions raised by the "old Marburgers." An avant-garde minority led by James Robinson had drawn the attention of the American scene to the debate. And, for a while, there was some feeling that the discussion might flourish. However, the shift in German theological circles to the question of the new hermeneutic and history, coupled with America's long-standing support on the theological frontiers of a more Bultmannian stance,[76] has placed the question of the new hermeneutic much more in the central focus of American thought in recent years.[77] As in

---

74. Carl F. H. Henry had welcomed Pannenberg as the way out of the "chaos in European theology" (*Christianity Today*, October 9, 1964, 19). For a similar evaluation, see Daniel Fuller, *op. cit.*, pp. 176-197, 251-253. A much more accurate appraisal of Pannenberg's presuppositions will be found in C. Van Til, *The Great Debate Today* (Nutley, N. J.: Presbyterian and Reformed Publishing Co., 1971), pp. 201-202.

75. Krentz, *op. cit.*, pp. 49-50. For an analysis of the "British viewpoint," consult Harvey K. McArthur, *The Quest Through the Centuries* (Philadelphia: Fortress Press, 1966), pp. 124-126.

76. Henry, *Frontiers in Modern Theology*, p. 133.

77. James Robinson himself has taken a leading role in this shift. Cf. James M. Robinson and John Cobb, Jr., eds., *Theology as History* (New York: Harper and Row, 1967), pp. 62ff.

Germany also, the rise of support for the Pannenberg school has affected the debate. The saddest part of the American scene is the almost complete silence of evangelical scholarship on this issue.

A similar impression characterizes the sophisticated theological discussions of Asia. Isolated essays give proof of awareness of the debate in Japan[78] and Korea.[79] But the interest of both countries in the question of the indigenization of theology has narrowed their concern to the question of hermeneutic rather than the new quest.[80] In addition, the broadly conservative theology of the Korean church remains generally inimical to the radical thinking of either Bultmann or his students, thus braking any far-reaching impact of the European discussion. The liberal theological world in both Korea and Japan is more Barthian than Bultmannian.

What then shall we say about the quest?

Any evaluation of the post-Bultmannian movement must recognize some of its salutary emphases. As Stonehouse has indicated, the trend represents an appraisal of Jesus which, in many respects, is far more positive than the radical skepticism of Bultmann. And, in that sense, we may regard the study as producing some positive contributions.

The discussions represent an attempt to move away from the radical skepticism of Bultmann in the question of the historical Jesus. These men are no longer content with merely fixing their attention on their act of faith. They are asking the question, "Does

---

78. Tamotsu Hirano comes strikingly close to the "British viewpoint" in "The Problem of the Historical Jesus," *Northeast Asia Journal of Theology* II (1969), 1-16.

79. Kim Yong-ok, "Challenges to the Theology of Rudolf Bultmann," *Theology and Modern Times* II (1966), 63-102 (Korean language); Kim Yong-ok, "The Question of the 'Historical Jesus,'" *Kidokyo Sasang* (December, 1968), 27-35 (Korean language). An unfortunate feature of these essays from both Japan and Korea is their lack of treatment of the theological debate in their own countries. This pattern is rather typical.

80. Rhee Jong-sung, "Trends and Issues in Recent Theology," *Theology and Modern Times* I (1964), 59-91 (Korean language). Dr. Rhee, president of the Presbyterian Theological Seminary, Seoul, and neo-orthodox in his convictions, deals with post-Bultmannian studies, but strictly around the question of hermeneutic (68-76).

not a context of actual historical events stand as the actual basis of faith? What is that context? Can we continue to ignore these events?" They are not satisfied with merely an excessively loose connection to the historical Jesus.

There is also in this search a fresh recognition of a significant area of continuity between the historical Jesus and the Christ of faith. Bultmann makes a radical disjuncture between "(1) the prophet and rabbi Jesus, whose message as reconstructed by Bultmann . . . supposedly had contemporaneous validity and (2) the Son of God of the *kerygma*, which is judged to be mythological and obsolete and yet allows of a demythologizing which supposedly preserves the Christian proclamation."[81] The leaders of the new quest are much less willing to recognize that juxtaposition and much more willing to seek continuity between Jesus' preaching and that of the early church.

But having said this, we must also note that all those positive features are far from marking a return to biblical or traditionally orthodox views. "Rather they point up the conclusion that this movement of thought and criticism, while to be sure not simply a return to the older Liberalism is, as to its basic thrust, indicative of a resurgence of Liberal perspectives and spirit."[82] As such, the program does not represent, as Carl Henry's early enthusiasm suggests, any significant weakening of the form-critical methods of Bultmann, but is simply "a corrective or readjustment." Just how new is the "new quest of the historical Jesus"?

1. Though there is recognition of the necessity for a relationship between the kerygma and history, the post-Bultmannians retain Bultmann's essential rejection of the New Testament as an accurate historical record of the historical Jesus. With Bultmann, they retain the notion that the New Testament cannot provide us with an infallible picture of the historical Jesus or of the faith of the early church. For Bultmann's pupils, the important thing is not the *exact* continuity between the historical Jesus and the kerygmatic Christ,

---

81. Stonehouse, *op. cit.*, p. 181.
82. *Ibid.*, pp. 181-182.

but merely *some* continuity. Perhaps parallelism, rather than continuity, would express that relationship more adequately. To the extent that they fail to recognize the apostolic tradition that draws together the Christ of the early church and true history, they fail in precisely the same area that Bultmann has failed.

James M. Robinson asserts that the "old quest of the historical Jesus," the great monument of Protestant liberal theology in the nineteenth century, was impossible, among other reasons, because it relied on a "positivistic nineteenth-century historiography."[83] However, it is our contention that the "new quest" is equally impossible because it is basically dependent upon a historiography equally committed to a closed world of brute facts. As long as the Enlightenment problematic of the tensions of faith and history continues to be the unseen presupposition of New Testament scholarship, one can continue to choose between an "old quest" "wedded to a Cartesian hermeneutic which viewed the interpreter as an investigating object intent on gaining intellectual mastery over the object of his inquiry" or a "new quest" wedded to an existentialist hermeneutic which viewed the interpreter as an investigating subject intent on gaining ontological mastery through self-awareness in dialogue with the text.[84] But ultimately one has merely selected one pole of the built-in dialectic that is inherently self-destructive. It is not enough to say that in this new quest "the center of gravity is shifted"[85] unless we also admit that this dialectic is the center of gravity. So too, the judgment that "the historiography involved in the new quest reflects a too one-sided existentialist preoccupation"[86] presumes the answer lies in balance against over-breeding, rather than total rejection of a dichotomy built into New Testament study from the days of Reimarus. Until the debate recognizes that a philosophy of history must be

---

83. Robinson, *A New Quest of the Historical Jesus*, pp. 35-38.
84. Hull, *op. cit.*, p. 334, partly uses this language in his contention that the new quest "attempts to offer an escape from the futility of 'objectivity' . . ." (p. 333).
85. *Ibid.*, p. 334.
86. Brown, *op. cit.*, p. 25.

drawn from the Scripture with the same care we draw our faith, until it sees that a proper approach to the Jesus of the kerygma is possible only on the basis of a biblical philosophy of history, this "new quest" will continue to fail. One may on a chronological level be happy, as Reginald Fuller is, that there seems to be "a growing consensus that the historical Jesus is both necessary and relevant to the kerygma."[87] But, on the deeper metaphysical level to which we now are drawing attention, there will continue to be no hope for solving what Fuller also recognizes as "the first major unresolved problem . . . the place of the historical Jesus in the kerygma."[88] The problem remains not kerygma without history or even kerygma in relative continuity with history, but the very necessity for such a dichotomy.

2. Though there is a recognition of continuity in some measure between the historical Jesus and the kerygmatic Christ, it is not sufficient to overcome the inherent defects of Bultmann's plunge into Docetism. Insofar as the post-Bultmannians share Bultmann's methodological approach to the gospel records, they share also the danger of evaporating Jesus of Nazareth into "a cipher, a symbol, a formula, or an idea." Insofar as they continue to repudiate large parts of the New Testament record as mythology and attempt to cut out all supernaturalism from the fabric of that record, they continue to repudiate the Jesus of the early church and the Jesus of history. For both, according to the New Testament, are one. And when one has succeeded in paring away supernatural "myth" from the Jesus of the gospel records, one has succeeded in paring away the Jesus of history. The historical Jesus can be recovered only by a "full rehabilitation of the historical realities of the gospel."

Here again, we are arguing contrary to the contentions of someone like James Robinson. He insists that the old quest was illegitimate because it failed to recognize the kerygma as the center of the Gospels. And precisely because the new quest speaks of any historical elements of the kerygma as "valid only as an impressive way

---

87. R. Fuller, *op. cit.*, p. 113.
88. *Ibid.*, p. 114.

of witnessing to this kerygmatic message," it can succeed where the old quest failed.[89]

We agree with Robinson that the old quest was illegitimate. But it was not illegitimate because it had not grasped the significance of the kerygma in the Gospels.[90] It was illegitimate because it failed to grasp the foundation of the kerygma in history. The kerygma was not a philosophy, as Robinson is inclined to make it. ". . . It was not a set of directions for escape from the misery of the world; it was not an account of what had always been true. On the contrary, it was an account of something that had happened. . . ."[91] It was founded on certain known events of history—the events we find recorded in the gospel records. And it is precisely here that the new quest must also be denounced as illegitimate, for it continues to make the same mistake that nineteenth-century theology has made. It is content with the narrowest kind of parallelism between Jesus and the kerygma. In terms of the New Testament documents, if it is content with anything less than equation, it is proportionately a failure.

3. One must also protest the narrow criteria established by the new quest in its search for authenticity in the words and work of Christ. The general presupposition of the various participants seems to be that, by the use of critical methods and the application of certain criteria, "one can expose a residuum of authentic sayings of Jesus which betray His understanding of His existence. Such an examination excludes all elements in the Gospels which are kerygmatic or confessional, all material which can be paralleled in apoca-

---

89. Robinson, op. cit., pp. 38ff.

90. Van A. Harvey and Schubert Ogden claim, in this connection, that Robinson "greatly overstates" the difference between Bultmann and the new questers by not seeing that for Bultmann "there is some kind of recognizable continuity between the message of the historical Jesus and the proclamation of the church" (Carl Braaten, The Historical Jesus and the Kerygmatic Christ, p. 207). The point has some validity as a corrective to Robinson, but it operates with the same ultimate presuppositions as Bultmann and Robinson.

91. J. Gresham Machen, The Origin of Paul's Religion (Grand Rapids: William B. Eerdmans Publishing Company, 1947), p. 316.

lyptic or rabbinic contemporary Judaism, and all possibly doubtful Aramaic *logia* which could be considered on other grounds as the inauthentic creation of the early church in Palestine."[92]

The results of such a skeptical attitude towards the gospel records cannot help but be negative. So "Bornkamm's list of the indisputable historical facts concerning Jesus is pitiably short and relatively incidental to his book. Fuchs assures us that the authenticity of Jesus' words is not as vital a question as we might suppose since a particular saying may be a model of faith true to Jesus even if he never uttered it. Bornkamm reflects the same attitude when he tells us that Jesus' every word and deed betrayed the secret of his being, even if he did not use the titles attributed to him in the Gospels."[93] The meagerness of the conclusions are intimately related to the assumption of Form Criticism that one of the main creative tasks of the early church was the putting back of its ideas and beliefs into the mouth of Jesus. As others have well indicated, such a position does rank injustice to the nature of the apostles as transmitters and witnesses of the Christian gospel and their writings as accurately conveying that witness.[94] There is less fluidity in that transmission of the gospel than the form critics generally maintain.

4. The leaders of the new quest continue, like Bultmann, to be deeply molded by an existentialist interpretation of the Gospels. The only continuity they basically seek between the Jesus of history and the Christ of kerygma is ultimately an existential continuity. Like Bultmann, they continue to adhere rigidly to existentialist presuppositions in their exegesis. Oscar Cullmann has drawn attention to this recently. For these scholars, he says, "the historical Jesus, like the kerygmatic Christ of the Church, is considered only in the light of his address to our self-understanding. So from the outset one could not expect that the constant would be seen in anything other than 'the call of Jesus to decision' (Bultmann), 'Jesus' faith' (Ebeling) or

---

92. Martin, *op. cit.,* pp. 35-36, 42-43.
93. Brown, *op. cit.*
94. Ned B. Stonehouse, *Origin of the Synoptic Gospels* (Grand Rapids: William B. Eerdmans Publishing Company, 1963), pp. 113-131.

in 'Jesus' behaviour' [existentially interpreted] (Fuchs). Basically, the Bultmann pupils hardly go beyond their teacher at all."[95]

Bornkamm's title, *Jesus of Nazareth,* meets this same criticism elsewhere. "The standpoint adopted by him then is so 'kerygmatic,' so 'existentialist,' so overwhelmingly concerned with existentialist interpretation of the message of Jesus, that we begin to wonder how far he really has pushed beyond Bultmann and to what extent the title of his book is not a misnomer."[96]

The end results of their efforts, therefore, cannot hope to be any more successful than those of Bultmann. Nor does it help to see this existentialist structuring as Fuller does, "the growing understanding of exegesis as involving not simply what the text meant but what it means."[97] It is rather an effort to seek to interpret the God-centered character of New Testament revelation with man-centered existentialism. The new quest seeks to demythologize supernatural theology into natural anthropology. As Bultmann has indicated elsewhere, exegesis without presuppositions is impossible.[98] But the presuppositions must be those which the New Testament itself supplies. It cannot be a superimposed existentialism. At this point, there is a radical need for the demythologization of demythology.

5. What Jesus is left after the new quest has concluded its studies? Robinson has deplored the uselessness af the old quest of those who, some generations ago, saw in Jesus a good nineteenth-century liberal humanist with a simple faith in a paternal deity. But is not the Jesus of Robinson's construction equally faulty? The Jesus of Robinson and Bornkamm talks suspiciously like a modern existentialist of the early Heidelberg stripe. Robinson, building on his existentialist *a priori,* has constructed his own image of Jesus, a first-century pre-

---

95. Oscar Cullmann, *Salvation in History* (London: SCM Press, 1967), p. 53.
96. Anderson, *op. cit.,* p. 82.
97. R. Fuller, *op. cit.,* p. 114.
98. Rudolf Bultmann, *Existence and Faith* (New York: Meridian Books, 1960), pp. 289ff.

existent Heidegger.[99] How really "new" is the new Jesus of the new quest?

Here is perhaps the greatest tragedy of "the new quest of the historical Jesus." "They have taken away my Lord and I know not where they have laid him" (John 20:13). The center of the New Testament is a glorious fact of history: Jesus Christ, the promised Messiah, has come, and inaugurated His reign of salvation and judgment. Because of His coming, a whole new face has been put on history. Because of His coming, the final reality of eternal life is guaranteed to us. The kerygma of the church is the proclamation of salvation, freedom from the curse and bondage of sin in Christ.

All this is swept away by the new quest. The Jesus of the new quest has no place in history. His entire meaning must be sought largely outside of history, in authentic existence, in existential reality. Docetism remains to plague the new quest. In spite of the umbilical cord that a hyperskeptical approach has created to tie the historical Jesus to the Christ of the kerygma, Jesus Christ has been allowed a place in history through the mini-theology of mini-men. We are left with nothing but a mini-Jesus.

99. W. D. Davies, ed., *The Background of the New Testament and Its Eschatology* (Cambridge: Cambridge University Press, 1956), p. 220.

Chapter 3

J. GRESHAM MACHEN

The Virgin Birth of Christ*

According to the belief of all the historic branches of the Christian Church, Jesus of Nazareth was born without human father, being conceived by the Holy Ghost and born of the virgin Mary. In the present lecture we shall consider very briefly the origin of this belief. The belief of the Christian Church in the virgin birth of Christ is a fact of history which requires an explanation. And two kinds of explanation are possible. In the first place the belief may be explained as being based upon fact. It may be held that the Church came to believe in the virgin birth because as a matter of fact Jesus was born of a virgin. Or in the second place it may be held that the belief arose in some other way. The task of the historian is to balance these two kinds of explanation against each other. Is it easier to explain the belief of the Church in the virgin birth on the hypothesis that it originated in fact or on the hypothesis that it arose in some other way?

We shall first examine the former hypothesis—that the belief in the virgin birth is based upon fact. Of course, the most obvious thing to say is that this belief appears in the New Testament in the clearest possible terms. And most of our time will be taken up in examining the New Testament evidence. But before we come

---

*This address was originally published in *The Bible Today* and later in *What Is Christianity? and Other Addresses,* by J. Gresham Machen, ed. Ned B. Stonehouse (Grand Rapids: Wm. B. Eerdmans Publishing Company, 1951). It is included here by permission of the Eerdmans Company. For a fuller treatment of the subject, see Dr. Machen's *The Virgin Birth of Christ* (New York: Harper & Brothers, 1930).

to examine the New Testament evidence it may be well to glance at the later Christian literature.

At the close of the second century, when the Christian literature outside of the New Testament becomes abundant, when we have full information about the belief of the Church at Alexandria, in Asia Minor, at Rome and in the West, we find that everywhere the virgin birth was accepted as a matter of course as one of the essential things in the Christian view of Christ. But this same kind of belief appears also at an earlier time; for example, in the old Roman baptismal confession which was the basis of our Apostles' Creed, in Justin Martyr at the middle of the second century, and in Ignatius, bishop of Antioch, at the beginning of the century. There were, it is true, denials of the virgin birth not only by opponents of Christianity but also by some who professed a kind of Christian faith. But all of these denials look far more as though they were due to philosophical prepossession than to any genuine historical tradition. The plain fact is that the virgin birth appears just as firmly fixed at the beginning of the second century as at the end of it; it is quite impossible to detect any gradual establishment of the doctrine as though it had to make its way against opposition. Particularly the testimony of Ignatius · and of the Apostles' Creed shows not only that the virgin birth was accepted at a very early time, but that it was accepted as a matter of course and as one of the facts singled out for inclusion even in the briefest summaries of the most important things which the Christian needed to know about Christ. Even this evidence from outside the New Testament would suffice to show that a firm belief in the virgin birth existed in the Christian Church well before the close of the first century.

But still more important is the New Testament evidence, and to that evidence we now turn.

The virgin birth is attested in two of the New Testament books, the Gospel according to Matthew and the Gospel according to Luke. The value which will be attributed to this testimony depends of course to a considerable extent upon the view which one holds of each of these two Gospels as a whole. Obviously it will not be possible to discuss these questions here; it would carry us too far afield to discuss the evidence for the early date and high historical value of the two Gospels in which the virgin birth appears. But one remark at least may be made in passing: it may at least be observed that the credit of the great double work, Luke-Acts, has been steadily rising in recent years even in circles which were formerly most hostile. The extraordinary strength of the literary evidence has led even men like Professor Harnack of Berlin, Professor C. C. Torrey of Yale, and the distinguished historian Professor Eduard Meyer, despite their rejection of the whole supernatural content of the book, to accept the traditional view that Luke-Acts was actually written by Luke the physician, a companion of Paul. It will not be possible here to review that literary evidence in detail; but surely the evidence must be very strong if it has been able to convince even those whose presuppositions render hypothesis of Lucan authorship so extremely uncomfortable.

But if the third Gospel was really written by Luke, its testimony as to events in Palestine must surely be received with the greatest possible respect. According to the information derived from the use of the first person plural in the book of Acts, Luke had been in contact with James, the Lord's own brother, and with many other members of the primitive Jerusalem Church. Moreover he was in Palestine in A.D. 58 and appears there again two years later; so that presumably he was in the country during the interval. Obviously such a man had the fullest possible opportunity for acquainting himself, not only with events concerning the Gentile mission of Paul but also with events in the life of our Lord in Palestine. It is therefore a matter of no small importance that the virgin birth is narrated in the third Gospel.

But the virgin birth is not merely narrated in the third Gospel; it is narrated in a very peculiar part of that Gospel. The first two chapters of the Gospel are possessed of very remarkable literary characteristics. The hand of the author of the whole book has indeed been at work in these chapters, as the elaborate researches of Harnack and others have clearly shown; but the author's hand has not been allowed to destroy the underlying literary character of the narrative. And that underlying character is very strongly marked. The truth is that the first two chapters of Luke, with the exception of the typical Greek sentence in Luke 1:1-4, are in spirit and style nothing in the world but a bit of the Old Testament embedded in the midst of the New Testament. Nowhere is there a narrative more transparently Jewish and Palestinian than this. It is another question how the Palestinian character of the narrative is to be explained. Some have supposed that Luke used a written Palestinian source, which had already been translated into Greek or which he himself translated; others have supposed that without written sources he has simply caught the truly Semitic flavor of the oral information that came to him in Palestine. At any rate, however the Palestinian character of the narrative is to be explained, that Palestinian character itself is perfectly plain; in the first two chapters of Luke we are evidently dealing with a narrative that came from Palestinian soil.

That fact is of great importance for the question of the virgin birth. It shows that the virgin birth was narrated not merely in Gentile Christian documents but also in the country which was the scene of the narrated event. But there is still another reason why the Palestinian character of the narrative is important. We shall observe in the latter part of the lecture that the great majority of these modern scholars who reject the fact of the virgin birth suppose that the *idea* of the virgin birth was derived from pagan sources. But if that hypothesis be accepted, the question arises how a pagan idea came to be attested just by the most transparently Jewish and Palestinian portion of the whole New Testament. The Palestinian Judaism of the first century was passionately opposed to pagan influences, especially that loyal type of Palestinian Judaism which appears with such beautiful clearness in Luke 1 and 2. How could a pagan idea possibly find a place in such a narrative?

The question is really unanswerable; and in order to attempt to answer it, many modern scholars have had recourse to a truly desperate expedient—they have maintained that the virgin birth was not originally contained in the Palestinian narrative found in the first two chapters of Luke but has been later inserted into that narrative by interpolation. This interpolation theory has been held in two forms. According to the more radical form the virgin birth has been interpolated into the completed Gospel. This hypothesis is opposed by the great weight of manuscript attestation, there being not the slightest evidence among the many hundreds of manuscripts containing the Gospel of Luke that there ever was a form of that Gospel without the verses narrating the virgin birth. A more cautious form of the interpolation theory has therefore sometimes been preferred. According to that more cautious form, although the words attesting the virgin birth formed an original part of the third Gospel they did not form an original part of the Palestinian source which the author of the Gospel was using in the first two chapters, but were interpolated by the author himself into the source which elsewhere he was closely following.

What shall be said of this interpolation theory? Very often the best and only refutation of an interpolation theory is the refutation which Dr. Francis L. Patton is once said to have applied to theosophy. A lady is reported to have asked Dr. Patton after one of his lectures to give her the strongest argument against theosophy. "Madam," said Dr. Patton, "the strongest argument against theosophy is that there is no argument in its favor." Similarly it may be said that the burden of proof is clearly against those who advance an interpolation hypothesis; if no clear evidence can be adduced in its favor the hypothesis must be rejected, and the narrative must be taken as it stands. Even such a consideration would be decisive against the interpolation theory regarding the virgin birth in the infancy narrative of the third Gospel. The advocates of the theory have signally failed to prove their point. The virgin birth is not merely narrated with great clearness in Luke 1:34, 35, but is implied in several other verses;

and no reason at all adequate for supposing that these portions of the narrative have been tampered with has yet been adduced. But as a matter of fact we are in the present case by no means limited to such a merely negative method of defense. The truth is that in the present case we can do far more than disprove the arguments for the interpolation hypothesis; we can also actually prove positively that that hypothesis is false. A careful examination shows clearly that the virgin birth, far from being an addition to the narrative in the first chapter of Luke is the thing for which the whole narrative exists. There is a clear parallelism between the account of the birth of John and that of the birth of Jesus. Even the birth of John was wonderful, since his parents were old. But the birth of Jesus was more wonderful still, and clearly it is the intention of the narrator to show that it was more wonderful. Are we to suppose that while narrating the wonderful birth of John the narrator simply mentioned an ordinary, nonmiraculous birth of Jesus? The supposition is quite contrary to the entire manner in which the narrative is constructed. The truth is that if the virgin birth be removed from the first chapter of Luke the whole point is removed, and the narrative becomes quite meaningless. Never was an interpolation hypothesis more clearly false.

But personally I am very glad that the interpolation hypothesis has been proposed, because it indicates the desperate expedients to which those who deny the virgin birth are reduced. The great majority of these who reject the virgin birth of Christ suppose that the idea arose on pagan ground, and admit that other derivations of the idea are inadequate. But in order to hold this view they are simply forced to hold the interpolation theory regarding the first chapter of Luke; for only so can they explain how a pagan idea came to find a place in so transparently Jewish a narrative. But the interpolation theory being demonstrably false, the whole modern way of explaining the idea of the virgin birth of Christ results in signal failure. The naturalistic historians in other words are forced by their theory to hold the interpolation hypothesis; they stake their all upon that hypothesis. But that hypothesis is clearly false; hence the entire construction falls to the ground.

So much then for the account of the virgin birth in Luke. Let us now turn to the Gospel according to Matthew. Here the virgin birth is narrated with a plainness which leaves nothing to be desired. Some men used to say that the first two chapters of the Gospel are a later addition, but this hypothesis has now been almost universally abandoned.

The value of this testimony depends of course upon the view that is held of the Gospel as a whole. But it is generally admitted by scholars of the most diverse points of view that the Gospel was written especially for Jews, and the Jewish character of the infancy narrative in the first two chapters is particularly plain.

If this lecture were being delivered under the conditions that prevailed some years ago it might be thought necessary for us to enter at length into the question of Matthew 1:16. Some time ago the textual question regarding this verse was discussed even in the newspapers and created a good deal of excitement. It was maintained by some persons that an ancient manuscript of the Gospels which was discovered in the monastery of St. Catherine on Mount Sinai provided a testimony against the virgin birth. The manuscript referred to is the so-called Sinaitic Syriac, a manuscript of an ancient translation of the Gospels into the Syriac language. This manuscript is not, as has sometimes been falsely asserted, the most ancient New Testament manuscript; since it is later than the two greatest manuscripts, the Codex Vaticanus and the Codex Sinaiticus, which also have the inestimable advantage of being manuscripts of the original Greek, not of a mere Syriac translation. But the Sinaitic Syriac is a very ancient manuscript, having been produced at about A.D. 400, and despite the fact that the extravagant claims made for it have now for the most part been abandoned, a few words about it may still be in place.

The Sinaitic Syriac has a curious reading at Matthew 1:16. But the importance of this witness must not be exaggerated. In order to accept the witness of the Sinaitic Syriac against all other documents one must suppose (1) that this manuscript has correctly reproduced at the point in question the ancient Syriac translation from which it is descended by a process of transmission, (2) that this ancient Syriac translation (which was probably produced in the latter part of the second century) correctly represents at this point the Greek manuscript from which the translation was made, and (3) that that Greek manuscript correctly represented at this point the autograph of the Gospel from which it was descended by a process of transmission. All of this is exceedingly uncertain in view of the overwhelming mass of evidence on the other side. To accept one witness against all the other witnesses is a very precarious kind of textual criticism where the evidence is so exceedingly abundant as it is in the case of the New Testament.

But as a matter of fact the Sinaitic Syriac does not deny the virgin birth at all. It attests the virgin birth in Matthew 1:18-25 just as clearly as do the other manuscripts, and it implies it even in Matthew 1:16. The reading of the Sinaitic Syriac which has given rise to the discussion is as follows: "Jacob begat Joseph; Joseph, to whom was betrothed Mary the virgin, begat Jesus that is called the Messiah." That would be self-contradictory if the word "begat" meant what it means in English. But as a matter of fact the scribe of the Sinaitic Syriac, if he thought of what he was doing and was not simply making a careless mistake, clearly used the word "begat" in the sense, "had as a legal descendant." It is interesting to note that Professor F. C. Burkitt, the greatest British authority on the Syriac manuscripts, who certainly is far from being prejudiced in favor of the virgin birth, holds that even if the original text were simply "Joseph begat Jesus" (which as a matter of fact appears in no manuscript) it would be absolutely without significance as a testimony against the virgin birth; for it would only mean that Joseph had Jesus as his legal heir. The author of the first Gospel is interested in two things, in one of them just as much as in the other. He is interested in showing (1) that Jesus was the heir of David through Joseph and (2) that He was a gift of God to the house of David in a more wonderful way than would have been the case if He had been descended from David by ordinary generation.

Thus even if the Sinaitic Syriac did represent the original text, it would not deny the virgin birth. But as a matter of fact it does not represent the original text at all. The original text of Matthew 1:16 is exactly the text that we are familiar with in our Bibles.

Accordingly we have an unequivocal double witness to the virgin birth of Christ in the Gospel according to Matthew and in the Gospel according to Luke. These two witnesses are clearly independent. If one thing is clear to modern scholars—and to every common-sense reader—it is that Matthew has not used Luke and Luke has not used Matthew. The very difficulty of fitting the two infancy narratives together is, to the believer in the virgin birth, a blessing in disguise; for it demonstrates at least the complete independence of the two accounts. The unanimity of these two independent witnesses constitutes the very strongest possible testimony to the central fact about which they are perfectly and obviously agreed.

But at this point an objection is often made. The rest of the New Testament, we are told, says nothing about the virgin birth; Paul says nothing about it, neither does Mark. Hence the testimony in favor of it is often said to be weak; men are often impressed with this argument from silence.

But the argument from silence needs to be used with a great deal of caution. The silence of a writer about any detail is without significance unless it has been shown that if the writer in question had known and accepted that detail he would have been obliged to mention it.

But that is just exactly what cannot be shown in the case of the silence about the virgin birth. Paul, for example, does not mention the virgin birth, and much has been made of his silence. "What is good enough for Paul," we are told in effect, "is good enough for us; if he got along without the virgin birth we can get along without it too." It is rather surprising, indeed, to find the Modernists of today advancing that particular argument; it is rather surprising to find them laying down the principle that what is good enough for Paul is good enough for them, and that things which are not found in Paul cannot be essential to Christianity. For the center of their religion is found in the ethical teaching of Jesus, especially in the Golden Rule. But where does Paul say anything about the Golden Rule, and where does he quote at any length the ethical teachings of Jesus? We do not mean at all that the silence about such things in the Epistles shows that Paul did not know or care about the words and example of our Lord in the days of His flesh. On the contrary there are clear intimations that the reason why the Apostle does not tell more about what Jesus did and said in Palestine is not that these things were to him unimportant but that they were so important that instruction about them had been given at the very beginning in the churches and so did not need to be repeated in the Epistles, which are addressed to special needs. And where Paul does give details about Jesus, the incidental way in which he does so shows clearly that there is a great deal else which he would have told if he had found occasion. The all-important passage in I Corinthians 15:3-8 provides a striking example. In that passage Paul gives a list of appearances of the risen Christ. He would not have done so if it had not been for the chance (humanly speaking) of certain misunderstandings that had arisen in Corinth. Yet if he had not done so, it is appalling to think of the inferences which would have been drawn from his silence by modern scholars. And yet, even if the occasion for mentioning the list of appearances had not happened to arise in the Epistles it would still have remained true that that list of apearances was one of the absolutely fundamental elements of teaching which Paul gave to the churches at the very beginning.

That example should make us extremely cautious about drawing inferences from the silence of Paul. In the Epistles Paul mentions very few things about the earthly life of Jesus; yet clearly he knew far more than he has found occasion to tell in the Epistles. It does not at all follow therefore that because he does not mention a thing in the Epistles he did not know about it. Hence the fact that he does not mention the virgin birth does not prove that the virgin birth was to him unknown.

Moreover, although Paul does not mention the virgin birth the entire account which he gives of Jesus as an entirely new beginning in humanity, as the second Adam, is profoundly congruous with the virgin birth and profoundly incongruous with the view that makes Jesus the son, by ordinary generation, of Joseph and Mary. The entire Christology of Paul is a powerful witness to the same event that is narrated in Matthew and Luke; the religion of Paul presupposes a Jesus who was conceived by the Holy Ghost and born of the virgin Mary.

The silence of Mark is of just as little importance as the silence of Paul. The Gospel according to Mark was preeminently the missionary Gospel; it was not intended to give all the facts about Jesus, but simply those which needed to be given first to those who had not already been won to Christ. Reading the second Gospel, you stand in astonishment like those who were in the synagogue at Capernaum in the scene described in the first chapter. You see the wonderful works of Jesus; you stand afar off looking at Him; you are not introduced to Him with the intimacy of detail which one finds in Matthew and Luke. The fact that Mark does not narrate the virgin birth does not prove that he does not believe in the virgin birth or that it is to him less important than other facts; but shows merely that the narration of the birth of Jesus in any form is quite contrary to the plan of his Gospel, which begins with the public ministry. The most important things that need to be said are not always the first things; and Mark is concerned with the first things that would make an impression even upon those who had not already been won to Christ.

The New Testament does indeed imply that the contemporaries of Jesus in Palestine were unaware of the story of the virgin birth, and perhaps it also makes probable that the virgin birth formed no part of the earliest missionary preaching of the apostles in Jerusalem. But all that is just what could be expected even if the virgin birth were a fact. The virgin birth was a holy mystery which was capable of the grossest misunderstanding; certainly it would not be spoken of by a person like Mary, whose meditative character is so delicately and so vividly depicted in the first two chapters of Luke. It would not be spoken of to the hostile multitude, and least of all would it be spoken of to the brothers of Jesus. Also it would certainly not be mentioned in the earliest public missionary preaching before the crowds in Jerusalem. Only at some time after the resurrection, when the miracle of the virgin birth had at last been vindicated by the resurrection and exaltation of Jesus, would Mary breathe the mystery of Jesus' birth to sympathetic ears. Hence it found its way into the wonderful narrative preserved by Luke and from there into the hearts of Christians of all the ages.

Such is the course of events which would be expected if the virgin birth were a fact. And the attestation of the event in the New Testament is just exactly what is suited to these antecedent probabilities. The attestation in the very nature of the case could not be equal to that of an event like the resurrection, of which there were many eye-witnesses; but it is just what it would naturally be if the event really occurred in the manner in which it is said to have occurred in Matthew and Luke.

But the full force of the New Testament evidence can be appreciated only if the accounts are allowed to speak for themselves. These narratives are wonderfully self-evidencing; they certainly do not read as though they were based on fiction; and they are profoundly congruous with that entire account of Jesus without which the origin of the Christian religion is an insoluble puzzle.

If this testimony is to be rejected, what is to be put in its place? If the belief of the Christian Church in the virgin birth was not founded upon fact, how did it actually originate? The consideration of this question constitutes the second main division of our subject. If the virgin birth is not a fact, how did the idea find a place in the New Testament and at the center of the Church's belief? If Jesus was really born of Joseph and Mary, how shall we explain the fact that in the New Testament we have this strange false account of His birth?

The first explanation which has been proposed is that the false idea arose in Jewish-Christian ground. We have observed that the New Testament narratives of the virgin birth are strikingly Jewish in character; it is natural then to find the origin of the idea among the Jews. Some scholars therefore have supposed that the virgin birth was attributed to Jesus because devout Jewish Christians desired to find a fulfillment for the prophecy of Isaiah 7:14, "Behold the virgin shall conceive." But this method of explaining the origin of New Testament narratives has come into general disfavor in recent years; and such disfavor is particularly well deserved with regard to Isaiah 7:14. There is not the slightest evidence for supposing that verse was ever interpreted by the pre-Christian Jews as indicating a virgin birth of the Messiah. We do not mean that Isaiah 7:14 is not a true prophecy; on the contrary we regard it as a very precious prophecy of the virgin birth of the Lord. But it is one thing to understand such a prophecy after the event and quite a different thing to understand the prophecy before the event. In general, adherents of the mythical theory about the New Testament have become much less confident than they formerly were about supposing that the myths arose in order to show fulfillment of Old Testament prophecies. Usually it is admitted to be clearly the other way around; only after certain things came to be believed about Jesus on independent grounds, were the Old Testament prophecies interpreted as referring to Him.

But the advocates of the Jewish derivation of the idea of the virgin birth also point to the wonderful birth of heroes like Isaac. Isaac, it is said, was born by a kind of miracle after his parents were old; it was therefore only a slight step to suppose that there was an even greater miracle in the case of one who was greater than Isaac; and thus in the case of Jesus the human father was excluded altogether. This explanation ignores the characteristic Jewish attitude toward marriage and the begetting of children. There was among the Jews not the slightest tendency toward asceticism; and far from being only a slight step in advance, the exclusion of the human father makes the birth of Jesus totally different from that of Isaac. The very point of the narrative about Isaac is that Abraham actually was in a physical sense his father; it is just the paternity of Abraham which the narrative stresses. There is nothing in the story of Isaac therefore which could have caused the development of the story of the virgin birth among the Jews. It is no wonder then that most modern scholars are inclined to agree with Adalbert Merx in saying that the idea of the virgin birth is "as un-Jewish as possible."

If then the Jewish derivation of the supposed myth of the virgin birth is impossible, recourse is often had to pagan influences. Sometimes, it is true, attention has been called to the philosophic Judaism of Philo of Alexandria, who combined a strange allegorical interpretation of the Old Testament with acceptance of the doctrines of Greek philosophy. But there is not to be found in the works of Philo any real parallel to the virgin birth of Christ, the apparent parallels being due to the fact that in his treatment of Old Testament characters such as Abraham and Isaac Philo has often lost sight of the literal significance of the history and is thinking only of the allegorical interpretation in accordance with which these characters represent only spiritual qualities or the like. Moreover the whole atmosphere of Philo is as remote as anything could possibly be from the Palestinian atmosphere that appears with such wonderful clearness in the infancy narratives of Matthew and Luke. It is no wonder then, in view of the obvious insufficiency of the Jewish derivation of the idea of the virgin birth, that the majority of modern scholars who have denied the fact have had recourse, for the explanation of the origin of the idea, to purely pagan sources.

But at this point a double protest must be raised. How could a pagan idea find a place in primitive Christianity? Against the entrance of such an idea there was a twofold barrier. In the first place there was the barrier that separated all of primitive Christianity from the pagan world. Christianity at its inception involved a tremendous protest against paganism, and nothing would have been more abhorrent to the early Christians than the introduction into their thought about Jesus of the crassly pagan idea of the begetting of men by the gods, an idea which belonged not merely to paganism but to paganism in its most revolting and immoral aspects. That was the first barrier that needed to be surmounted before a pagan idea could find a place in the infancy narratives of Matthew and Luke. This barrier has been rightly and very ably insisted upon by Professor Harnack, though in the interests not of a defense of the virgin birth but of a derivation of the idea from Jewish sources.

But even if this barrier were surmounted another question would still remain. Even if the supposed pagan idea could have attained a place in the belief of the early Church, how could it ever have entered, not into Gentile Christian documents, but into the most clearly Jewish and Palestinian narratives in the whole New Testament, particularly into the infancy narrative of Luke? This question constitutes an insuperable objection, at the start, to the whole hypothesis of pagan influence, unless the interpolation theory regarding Luke 1 and 2 be correct. The hypothesis of pagan influence is absolutely bound up with the interpolation theory. But that interpolation theory, as we have already observed, is clearly false. The virgin birth is an integral part of the narrative in Luke, to say nothing of its place in Matthew. But in reading the infancy narrative in Luke we are simply breathing the atmosphere of Palestine, and are separated by whole worlds from the life of the Gentiles. Every word breathes the spirit of the Jewish expectation of the Messiah, and of Jewish life, and thought. And yet it is supposed that a crassly pagan idea has found a place in such a narrative!

Thus the double barrier remains against the entrance of a pagan idea into the infancy narratives: first, the barrier that separated the whole of primitive Christianity, whether Jewish or Gentile, from pagan ideas; and, second, the barrier that separated Palestinian Judaism from the Gentile world. In view of these initial objections, it is only for the sake of the argument that we examine the alleged pagan parallels at all. And as a matter of fact the parallels upon examination all break down.

The Modernist preachers of the day, in their attack upon the New Testament account of our Lord, sometimes speak of "virgin births" in pagan mythology as though they were the commonest things in the world. But as a matter of fact, in Greek mythology at least, there is no such thing as a virgin birth at all. Certain heroes were regarded as having been born without human father, but that means not that they were born of virgin mothers, but that the Greek gods were conceived of in a thoroughly anthropomorphic way as possessing human passions and as falling into very human sins. The children begotten of certain women by Zeus, in the course of his numerous amours, were certainly not virgin-born. The same notion was transferred to certain historical characters such as Plato and Alexander the Great and the emperor Augustus. Whether seriously or not, these characters by a form of flattery were sometimes said to have been begotten, like the demigods of old, by some god, who took the place of the human father. But such a conception was possible only because of the grossly anthropomorphic way in which the Greek gods were conceived.

But in the infancy narratives in Matthew and Luke we find ourselves in an entirely different circle of ideas. In these narratives Jesus is represented as conceived by the Holy Ghost. But certainly the divine Spirit is not regarded in any anthropomorphic way. Indeed, as has often been observed, the word for "Spirit" in Hebrew is not of masculine but of feminine gender. And what is more important still is the character of the narrative as a whole. In these chapters the lofty spiritual monotheism of the Old Testament prophets is preserved to the very full; and the conception of our Lord in the womb of the virgin Mary is regarded not in any anthropomorphic way but as a creative act of the same divine Spirit who was active in the first creation in accordance with the majestic narrative of Genesis. It is inconceivable that such a narrative should be the product of invention; but it is still more inconceivable that it should have been derived from the most degraded and immoral parts of Greek mythology.

But one more explanation for the origin of the idea of our Lord's virgin birth has been proposed in recent years. Certain scholars belonging to the most "advanced" school of comparative religion, having detected the impossibility of the hypotheses which we have just considered, have advanced a new hypothesis of their own. They have recognized the fact that the idea of the virgin birth is "as un-Jewish as possible," and so have rejected the derivation of the supposed virgin-birth myth on Jewish ground. On the other hand they have recognized the integrity of the narrative in Luke I and have rejected the interpolation hypothesis which makes the virgin birth a later insertion. A pagan idea—that of the virgin birth—does stand, therefore, they hold, in a Jewish narrative. But, they suppose, this curious fact was possible because even before the time of Christ the Jews had, under the influence of oriental paganism, already come to believe in a virgin birth of the coming Messiah. Thus in the New Testament the virgin birth appears in a Jewish narrative; but that means, it is supposed, not that the idea was originally Jewish, but only that a pagan idea had become so well naturalized among the pre-Christian Jews that in the first century its pagan origin had been forgotten.

This hypothesis is an interesting testimony to the defects of the alternative theories. But in itself it is improbable in the extreme. What evidence is there that late pre-Christian Judaism had come to expect a virgin birth for the Messiah? There is really no evidence whatever. We do know something of the late pre-Christian Jewish doctrine of the Messiah, and what we know not only contains no mention of a virgin birth but is rather contrary to any such idea. Surely it is quite inadmissible to posit such an idea without any positive evidence and simply in the interests of a theory regarding the Christine doctrine of the virgin birth of Jesus.

Thus all of the modern theories regarding the origin of the idea of the virgin birth supposing it not to have been founded on fact have been tried and found wanting. And it is interesting to observe how the advocates of one theory are often the best critics of the others. Thus Harnack, in the interests of his Jewish derivation of the idea, does excellent service in showing the impossibility of the entrance of such an idea from pagan sources; advocates of the pagan derivation have well demonstrated the insufficiency of the Jewish derivation; and finally the most recent school of comparative religion has triumphantly and quite correctly insisted upon the falsity of the interpolation theory regarding Luke I upon which the ordinary hypothesis of pagan derivation is based. The truth is that if the belief in the virgin birth of Christ be not founded upon fact no other satisfactory way of explaining the origin of the belief and its inclusion in Matthew and Luke has yet been proposed.

Shall we then simply accept the attestation of the virgin birth, which we have seen is very strong and very early? We should probably not be able to do so, despite all that has been said, if the virgin birth stood absolutely alone, if it were a question simply of a virgin birth of a man of the first century about whom we knew nothing. For the virgin birth is a stupendous miracle, and if it stood alone there would be a tremendous burden of proof against it. But as a matter of fact it does not stand alone, but is supported by a great mass of other facts; it is not a question simply of a virgin birth of some man of the first century about whom we know nothing, but it is a question of the virgin birth of one about whom we know a great deal, namely, Jesus of Nazareth. If the New Testament picture of Jesus is false as a whole, then of course we shall not accept the virgin birth; but if Jesus was really in general what the New Testament represents

Him as being, then we shall believe with the utmost firmness, on the basis of abundant evidence, that He was conceived by the Holy Ghost and born of the virgin Mary.

But what is the importance of the matter? That question has loomed large in recent discussion, and some have held that although they accept the virgin birth of Christ themselves they can make common cause in Christian service with those who do not accept it. But this indifferentist position is really almost worse from the Christian point of view than any doctrinaire denial could be. As a matter of fact the virgin birth is of central importance for Christian faith.

In the first place, it is important because of its bearing upon the question of the authority of the Bible. No one denies that the attestation of the virgin birth forms an integral part of the Bible; it is not a question whether the Bible teaches the virgin birth but whether, teaching the virgin birth as it admittedly does, the Bible is true or false. We must therefore face the question frankly. If the Bible has allowed myth to enter at this point into the representation not of something on the periphery but of Christ Himself, then Scripture authority is gone, and some different basis must be sought for Christian doctrine and Christian life. Deny the virgin birth of Christ, and you must relinquish the authority of the Bible; accept the virgin birth and you may continue to regard the Bible as the very Word of God.

In the second place, the virgin birth is a test as to the view which a man holds in general, about Christ. Two opposite views of Jesus of Nazareth are struggling for the ascendancy in the Church today. According to one view He was a teacher who initiated a new type of religious life, who founded Christianity by being the first Christian; according to the other view He was the eternal Son of God who came voluntarily into this world from outside the world and who founded Christianity by redeeming men from the guilt and power of sin. The conflict between these two views is the conflict between naturalism and supernaturalism; and that is a conflict not between two varieties of Christianity, but between two mutually exclusive religions. But how can we tell which view any individual holds? Conceivably one might ask him whether he believes in the deity of Christ. But unfortunately the word "deity" or the word "god" has been degraded so low in Modernist parlance that when the Modernist says that "Jesus is God" he means something even far more remote from Christian belief than the Unitarian meant when he said that "Jesus is not God." Or it may conceivably be asked whether the individual in question believes in the resurrection. But here again the answer may mean nothing; since the word resurrection is often interpreted (quite absurdly, it is true) to mean simply the continued existence of Jesus or His continued influence, and not to involve the miracle of the emergence of His body from the tomb. But, over against all such ambiguities, when a man says that he believes Jesus to have had no human father, one can tell pretty clearly where he stands.

The impression is indeed often produced that many men who reject the virgin birth maintain in general the New Testament account of our Lord. But that impression is entirely false. There have been, it is true, a few men in the history of the modern Church who have rejected the virgin birth and yet have accepted the supernatural Christ and have believed in His true resurrection from the dead. But these men have been few and far between; and it would probably be impossible to name a single one of any prominence who is living today. Particularly false is the notion that many men who deny the virgin birth yet accept the incarnation; for the men who deny the virgin birth usually mean by "incarnation" almost the exact opposite of what Christians mean by that term. The truth is that the conflict about the virgin birth is only one phase of the great religious conflict of the day. And that conflict is a conflict between the Christian religion and a naturalistic or agnostic Modernism which is anti-Christian to the core.

In the third place, the virgin birth is important in itself—even aside from its importance as being connected with the question of the authority of Scripture and as being a test for the differentiating of naturalism from supernaturalism. The Christian world, in other words, has a clearer and better conception of Christ than it would have had if God had never told us of the virgin birth and had allowed us to think that Jesus was the son, by ordinary generation, of Joseph and Mary. Conceivably indeed we might have been Christians even if God had never told us of the virgin birth. Certainly never to have heard of the virgin birth would have been a much less serious thing than it is to reject it now that we have heard of it. But it is easy to see the errors which might then have arisen, or which would have attained additional momentum, if God had never told us of the virgin birth of our Lord. What the knowledge of the virgin birth does is to fix with inescapable clearness the supernaturalism of the life of Jesus from the very beginning; the virgin birth, for example, intensifies the impossibility of holding that our Lord only grew up gradually into His divinity, or of holding in gnostic fashion that the Son of God descended upon a man Jesus at the baptism. All such errors are excluded by many things in the New Testament. But they are excluded with special clearness in the precious narrative of the virgin birth. That narrative represents our Lord clearly as no product of sinful humanity but as one who came into the world by a mighty creative act of God. And that representation is at the very center and core of the Christian faith.

No doubt the virgin birth is not the point at which one should begin in trying to convince a man who has not yet come to Christian faith. No doubt one should begin rather with the resurrection, in which the direct testimony is, and must be in the very nature of the case, vastly more abundant. But when a man has once been convinced that Jesus is truly the risen and ascended Lord and when he has once accepted Him as Saviour, then his faith will be unstable and incomplete unless he goes forward to accept the precious testimony of Matthew and Luke as to our Lord's entrance into the world.

The truth is that the New Testament account of Christ is a

wonderfully unitary thing, and an integral part of it is the virgin birth. Believe that Jesus is simply the fairest flower of humanity, and the infancy narrative of the Gospels, despite its marvelous beauty, will be to you abhorrent; but accept the dear Lord and Saviour presented to you in the Word of God, and you will believe and confess, with a heart full of gratitude and love and joy, that He was "conceived by the Holy Ghost, born of the virgin Mary."

Chapter 4

STEPHEN M. REYNOLDS*

The Zero Tense in Greek

A Critical Note

Karl Theodor Rodemeyer in a study of Herodotus and Thucydides[1] advanced the proposition that the historical present in these writers indicates that an event took place at the same time as, or immediately after, a point of time already given.

Slight attention has been paid by grammarians of New Testament Greek to Rodemeyer's work, and the impression has remained with most New Testament scholars that the historical present in the Greek text is used for vividness and dramatic effect.

Paul Kiparsky has recently written an article, "Tense and Mood in Indo-European Syntax," in which he maintains that it is a characteristic of early forms of Indo-European languages, including Greek, to reduce the past tense to a zero tense in continuous narrative, after establishing that the event occurred in the past. He writes, "Schematically the sequence . . . Past . . . and . . . Past . . . is reduced to . . . Past . . . zero . . . , and since it is the present which is the zero tense, the reduced structure . . . Past . . . and . . . zero . . . is realized morphologically as . . . Past . . . and . . . Present. . . ."[2]

---

1. *Das Praesens historicum bei Herodot und Thukydides* (Basel: Buch-druckerei M. Werner Riehm, 1889).

2. *Foundations of Language* IV (1968), 35.

*Dr. Reynolds is librarian and member of the faculty at Faith Theological Seminary, Philadelphia. This article is reproduced with the permission of the *Westminster Theological Journal*. It appeared in that *Journal* XXXIII (1969–1970), 68-72.

Although some modern languages, such as Icelandic and perhaps Albanian have retained this reduction, Kiparsky says: "In general, however, conjunction of past and historical present is quite untypical of modern languages. Conversely, the sustained use of the historical present in long passages of narrative which is natural in these, is conspicuously absent in earlier Indo-European. In this respect the two systems are completely reversed."[3]

In discussing the properties of the present tense in a past situation in classical Greek, Kiparsky writes of "the impossibility of adequately characterizing the so-called historical present on a semantic basis alone. Rather, a syntactic solution is called for. It is beginning to look as if the historical present in early Indo-European is a present tense only in its superficial form. It functions syntactically as a past tense, as shown by sequence of tenses, it is semantically indistinguishable from the past tenses, and it alternates with these in conjoined structures.

"Everything points to its being an underlying past tense, and its conversion into the present tense in the surface structure must be governed by a syntactic rule, evidently some form of conjunction reduction, which optionally reduces repeated occurrences of the same tense to the present. Such a rule not only accounts for the historical present, but at the same time for the alternation of aorist and present in modal contexts, and also for the alternation of future and present, which in the traditional theory remain separate and unexplained facts."[4]

As neither Rodemeyer nor Kiparsky addressed himself specifically to the New Testament use of the historical present, it is our purpose in the rest of this note to indicate to a limited extent how the argument advanced by Kiparsky, if correct, would contribute to the understanding of New Testament usage.

When the time element is established by the context, the use of the future is optional in both New Testament Greek and modern English. It therefore creates no problem when the Greek of Matt. 26:2, in

3. *Ibid.*, p. 32.
4. *Ibid.*, pp. 33-34.

which a present tense is used, is translated with the present tense of the Greek carried over into English. Thus the King James Version has it, "after two days is *the feast of* the passover." The meaning is not changed if we change the verb to the future tense as some versions do, and say, "after two days the Passover Feast will take place." This illustrates a rule in New Testament Greek and modern English that when an action is known to be in the future the present tense may be substituted for the future tense. The present tense thus becomes semantically a "zero" tense, taking a future meaning from the context.

In English we may say, "Christmas comes next year on Thursday." We may not say, "Christmas comes last year on Monday." We have to say, "came." In classical and New Testament Greek the situation is somewhat different from English usage with regard to the past. In Kiparsky's opinion, *if the context determined that the time of the action was in the past, the present tense could be substituted for the past tense* (usually aorist).

The way the present tense is used in certain past situations in the Greek New Testament and the Septuagint would seem to follow such a pattern. It is obvious that if the narrator for vividness intended to give the impression that he was relating the events as he saw them, he would continue to use the present tense and not break the illusion by introducing a past tense. The New Testament writers make no effort to maintain an illusion of this sort. On the contrary, they frequently revert to the aorist. There are so many examples, especially in the Gospels of Mark and John, that the reader may easily find them and satisfy himself that the generally accepted explanation is entirely unsatisfactory.

When in a given passage in the New Testament there are many changes back and forth from aorist to present, it would seem that there is no forgetting of time for vividness, but that the present is considered the equivalent of the aorist in the context.

Take Mark 5:35–42 for example. Here in a continuous narrative set in the past we have the following sequence: present, present, aorist, present, present, present, imperfect, present, present, present, aorist, imperfect, imperfect, and aorist. The passage, with the verbs in question underlined, is as follows: Ἔτι αὐτοῦ λαλοῦντος ἔρχονται ἀπὸ τοῦ ἀρχισυναγώγου λέγοντες ὅτι Ἡ θυγάτηρ σου ἀπέθανεν· τί ἔτι σκύλλεις τὸν διδάσκαλον; ὁ δὲ Ἰησοῦς παρακούσας τὸν λόγον λαλούμενον λέγει τῷ ἀρχισυναγώγῳ, Μὴ φοβοῦ, μόνον πίστευε. καὶ οὐκ ἀφῆκεν οὐδένα μετ' αὐτοῦ συνακολουθῆσαι, εἰ μὴ τὸν Πέτρον καὶ Ἰάκωβον καὶ Ἰωάννην τὸν ἀδελφὸν Ἰακώβου. καὶ ἔρχονται εἰς τὸν οἶκον τοῦ ἀρχισυναγώγου, καὶ θεωρεῖ θόρυβον καὶ κλαίοντας καὶ ἀλαλάζοντας πολλά, καὶ εἰσελθὼν λέγει αὐτοῖς, Τί θορυβεῖσθε καὶ κλαίετε; τὸ παιδίον οὐκ ἀπέθανεν ἀλλὰ καθεύδει. καὶ κατεγέλων αὐτοῦ. αὐτὸς δὲ ἐκβαλὼν πάντας παραλαμβάνει τὸν πατέρα τοῦ παιδίου καὶ πὴν μητέρα καὶ τοὺς μετ' αὐτοῦ, καὶ εἰσπορεύεται ὅπου ἦν τὸ παιδίον· καὶ κρατήσας τῆς χειρὸς τοῦ παιδίου λέγει αὐτῇ, Ταλιθα κουμ, ὅ ἐστιν μεθερμηνευόμενον Τὸ κοράσιον, σοὶ λέγω, ἔγειρε. καὶ εὐθὺς ἀνέστη τὸ κοράσιον καὶ περιεπάτει, ἦν γὰρ ἐτῶν δώδεκα. καὶ ἐξέστησαν εὐθὺς ἐκστάσει μεγάλη.[5]

I believe that no idea of the illusion of actually being present, or of special vividness for certain words can be consistently maintained to explain this interspersing of aorist and imperfect tense forms with the present tense. I do not believe that any explanation saying that verbs of primary importance are put in one tense and verbs of secondary importance in another can be advanced successfully. The only plausible explanation is that the present tenses here are the equivalent of the past tense forms.

In the *New American Standard Version* of the New Testament published by the Lockman Foundation the translators assume that the historical present is used for "heightened vividness." At the same time they are aware that "in some contexts the present tense seems more unexpected and unjustified to the English reader than a past tense would have been." To preserve what they assume to be the nuance of tense in the Greek they have devised a system in which asterisks are placed before verbs translated as past which are present tense in Greek. Thus the reader is distracted by forms like "*impelled, *went, *spoke." If the thesis advanced in this note is correct,

5. *The Greek New Testament*, ed. Kurt Aland, Matthew Black, Bruce M. Metzger, Allen Wikgren (American Bible Society, 1966).

this cumbersome device is unnecessary, as in changing from Greek present to English past tense the translators are not destroying an attempt at vividness, but are merely using the proper tense to express the same idea.

Some implications of the observation made in this note which readily come to mind are that it shows grammatical terminology to be inadequate, that it has a bearing on translation, and that it is significant with regard to the synoptic problem.

1. As for grammatical terminology, it appears that the term "historical present" is really a misnomer when the present is used as a routine substitute for a past tense. The term *zero tense* more accurately suits this situation.

When, however, the present is really used for vividness as frequently in modern languages,[6] the term suggested by Otto Jesperson,[7] "dramatic present," is highly appropriate.

Another type of "historical present" is where a past action has a present reference, as, for example, "Shakespeare writes. . . ." This is similar to the Greek perfect tense, and it should have a distinctive name in English grammar.

2. The bearing on translation of this observation is to suggest caution about rendering a Greek present by an English present when the situation is in the past. In the writer's judgment it is unlikely that a genuine "dramatic present" can be proved to occur in the Greek New Testament. Translators have sensed that they should usually not translate what they called "historical present" with the English present tense, but not understanding the semantic significance of the present as "zero" tense, they have lapsed occasionally into awkward English present tense forms. This happened even with those master translators, the makers of the King James Version.

3. The observation made in this note may have a bearing on the synoptic problem inasmuch as, if it is true, it can no longer be argued

---

6. Although we think it does not occur, it is not our intention to make the sweeping statement that the historical present in the sense of the "dramatic present" is never found in classical or Koine Greek.

7. *Essentials of English Grammar* (New York: Henry Holt and Co., 1933), p. 239.

convincingly that a writer who tends to avoid the present as "zero" tense is necessarily eliminating what he considers a vulgarism in an earlier Gospel. Conversely, a writer who uses it freely may not be accused of committing a vulgarism. He may have been motivated by a desire to improve his style by avoiding the monotony of an overuse of past tenses. If accused of using a vulgarism, he could have defended his style by referring his critics to classical writers such as Herodotus and Thucydides. It is more likely that the present as "zero" tense was understood perfectly by all first-century readers of the Gospels and that no one then ever raised the question of vulgarism. Thus comparative frequency or infrequency of the present tense in past situations may have nothing to do with earliness or lateness of a Gospel passage, and attempts which have been made to use this as a criterion should be abandoned.

Chapter 5

JOHN H. SKILTON

Romans 9:5 in Modern English Versions: A Study in Syntax and Doctrine

One of the key texts which a student of Bible versions likes to check in his survey of a translation is Romans 9:5. The way in which a translator handles this verse can disclose much about his grammatical competence and his theological viewpoint. In the King James Version it reads: "Whose *are* the fathers, and of whom as concerning the flesh Christ *came*, who is over all, God blessed for ever. Amen." This verse, it will be remembered, occurs in a passage in which Paul expresses his great sorrow that his kinsmen according to the flesh, despite all their privileges, have not believed the gospel. In the first four verses of the chapter he has said: "I say the truth in Christ, I lie not, my conscience also bearing me witness in the Holy Ghost, that I have great heaviness and continual sorrow in my heart. For I could wish that myself were accursed from Christ for my brethren, my kinsmen according to the flesh: who are Israelites; to whom *pertaineth* the adoption, and the glory, and the covenants, and the giving of the law, and the service *of God,* and the promises"; and then our verse follows: ". . . whose *are* the fathers, and of whom as concerning the flesh Christ *came,* who is over all, God blessed for ever. Amen."

According to this translation of verse five, Paul affirms that Christ is over all and that He is "God blessed for ever." In this understanding of Paul's meaning, KJV was no innovator. Distinguished predecessors among English versions had taken the text in the same way. The Middle English version of Paul's Epistles in MS. Parker 32, the Wycliffite Versions, Tyndale, Coverdale, Matthew, Taverner, the Great Bible, the Geneva Version, the Bishops' Bible, and the Rhemish New Testament had all found here a witness to the deity of Christ. This interpretation had also been supported by early and later versions of the New Testament in various languages. Likewise, significant endorsement had been provided by many patristic writers from the second century on, and the Reformers had contributed their discerning testimony.[1] However, since the time of KJV not all English translations have agreed with this great company of witnesses. Today, for example, such widely read versions as RSV, NEB, and *Good News for Modern Man* have indicated at least a preference for another type of interpretation. RSV, although it gives as an alternative construction a reading of the KJV type, chooses for its text: ". . . to them belong the patriarchs, and of their race, according to the flesh is the Christ. God who is over all be blessed forever. Amen." In this rendering the deity of Christ is not affirmed; instead, a period is placed after "Christ," and the concluding words are taken as a separate sentence containing a doxology to God.

When confronted by these sharp differences in the interpretation of Romans 9:5 in our English versions, one naturally asks whether any help can be obtained from the Greek text in settling the questions in dispute. Regrettably, in regard to the problem of punctuation, the Greek texts which have come down to us do not provide real assistance. A number of uncial manuscripts and a larger company of minuscules do have a mark of punctuation after the word σάρχα in our text; but it is not easy to ascertain the intention of the scribes. Not much reliance can be placed on the punctuation of our earliest Greek manuscripts, for it is not systematic. Bruce M. Metzger has said that "the presence of marks of punctuation in early manuscripts of the New Testament is so sporadic and hap-

---

1. Cf. Bruce M. Metzger, "The Punctuation of Rom. 9:5," in *Christ and Spirit in the New Testament*, ed. Barnabas Lindars and Stephen S. Smalley (Cambridge: University Press, 1973), pp. 100-103.

hazard that one cannot infer with confidence the construction given by the punctuator to the passage."[2]

The Greek text of Romans 9:5 reads, without punctuation, as follows:

ὧν οἱ πατέρες καὶ ἐξ ὧν ὁ Χριστὸς τὸ κατὰ σάρκα ὁ ὢν ἐπὶ πάντων θεὸς εὐλογητὸς εἰς τοὺς αἰῶνας ἀμήν

Ezra Abbot held that grammatically the verse could be punctuated and interpreted in at least seven ways, and Metzger finds at least eight different possibilities for punctuating the latter part of the verse.[3] To these might be added a conjectural emendation which would substitute ὧν ὁ for ὁ ὤν.[4]

Of the various theoretically possible constructions there are two which have received and which merit chief consideration:

(1) ὧν οἱ πατέρες, καὶ ἐξ ὧν ὁ Χριστὸς τὸ κατὰ σάρκα, ὁ ὢν ἐπὶ πάντων θεὸς εὐλογητὸς εἰς τοὺς αἰῶνας, ἀμήν.

The most important feature of this construction is that it places only a comma after σάρκα, and accordingly takes ὁ ὢν ἐπὶ πάντων θεός as referring to Christ. The text of KJV, as we have noticed, is of this type.

(2) The second leading interpretation would place either a colon or a period after σάρκα. The text of RSV belongs to this category. A variety of this interpretation would put a comma after σάρκα and a colon or a period after πάντων. On either of these constructions θεὸς εὐλογητός would not necessarily be referred to Christ. In certain versions it may be very clear that such a reference

---

2. See Bruce M. Metzger, *A Textual Commentary on the Greek New Testament* (London and New York: United Bible Societies, copyright 1971), pp. 520, 521; see also *idem, The Text of the New Testament,* 2nd ed. (New York and Oxford: Oxford University Press, 1968), pp. 26-27, and "The Punctuation of Rom. 9:5," pp. 97-99.

3. Ezra Abbott, "On the Construction of Romans ix.5.," *Journal of the Society of Biblical Literature and Exegesis* I (1881): 89-90; Bruce M. Metzger, "The Punctuation of Rom. 9:5," pp. 95-96.

4. See C. H. Dodd, *The Epistle of Paul to the Romans* (London: Hodder and Stoughton, 1932), pp. 152-53; and Metzger, *Textual Commentary,* pp. 522-23, the note by W. L. Lorimer to which he refers, *New Testament Studies* xiii (1966-67): 385-86, and "Punctuation," pp. 99-100.

is not intended; but in others there may be ambiguity or there may actually appear to be a reference to Christ.

An effort has been made in this present study to determine whether modern English versions have agreed in the main with the first or the second of these two chief interpretations; in other words, whether they favor the construction of Romans 9:5 adopted by KJV or that preferred by RSV. By "modern" in this context is meant versions published from 1881 to the present. 1881 has been chosen to mark the beginning of this period because it was the year in which the New Testament in the English Revised Version appeared. Since then there has been a virtually unceasing torrent of English versions of the entire New Testament or of parts of it. For this study about one hundred translations of Romans which have been published between 1881 and 1973 have been consulted. Some of the versions included are ancillary to commentaries and a few are paraphrases. The translations considered number more than one a year for the period under review, and it is believed that they will furnish an adequate sampling of the preferences of modern translators.

At the start it is appropriate to alert the reader to some of the limitations of the present phase of our investigation. We should remember that certain versions are the work of committees and others are the work of an individual. Obviously there is a difference between the number of versions and the number of translators in the modern period. Furthermore, a quantitative observation should not be mistaken for a qualitative judgment. In a later phase of our study we shall be drawn into an evaluation of the merits of the principal interpretations of Romans 9:5. However, at no point will we go into the question of the circulation of versions and the extent of their influence.

It has been claimed that the greater number of modern commentators favor interpreting Romans 9:5 in a way similar to the preference of RSV. One may doubt that any accurate census has been taken to justify this assertion. But whatever may be the position of commentators, such an assertion cannot rightly be made about English versions. Of the approximately one hundred versions considered, only about twenty-seven can be counted on the RSV side, and a few of them inform the reader of an alternative reading of the KJV type.

The versions are here very briefly designated and the date either of first publication or copyright is usually furnished. Additional bibliographical information will be found in the appended list of versions.

The following may be counted on the RSV side: Weekes (1897), Way (1901), Moffatt (1901, Historical New Testament; and 1913, New Translation), Ballantine (1923), Goodspeed (1923), Wade (1934), Greber (1937), RSV (1946), Griffith (1949), New World (1950), C. K. Williams (1952), Schonfield (1955), Laubach (1956), Barrett (1957), Hudson (1958), Green [various issues with little variation at Romans 9:5: Children's N.T. (1960); Children's Bible (1962); Teen-Age (1962); King James II (1971)], NEB (1961), Today's English Version (1966), Jordan (Cotton Patch Version, 1968), Barclay (1969), New American Bible (1970), Translator's New Testament (1973). The total so far, counting Green's issues as one, is twenty-three.

There are, however, a number of versions with unusual or ambiguous renderings, some of which properly belong in the RSV group. Thus Fenton (1895 or 1896) has "from amongst whom the Messiah who is above all became incarnate, thank God, for ever." But it should be mentioned that in another issue of Fenton's New Testament the rendering is quite different and is ambiguous: "and from among whom the Messiah became incarnate; He who is God over all, most certainly blessed through eternity!" Likewise ambiguous is Godbey's translation (1902): "and of whom is Christ according to the flesh. Who is over all, God blessed forever: amen." Other renderings which have seemed unclear are found in Bartlett and Peters (1886), Wand (1944), and Tomanek (1958). Overbury (1925) and probably Wilson (1938) should be placed in the category of versions which deny the θεός to Christ. Overbury finds that Christ "is above all worthy of God's praise throughout the ages," and Wilson speaks of the Christ who "is above all, God [be] blessed forever." Living Letters (1962) understood Paul to say that Christ "now rules over all things and is blessed of God forever." The Sacred Name Version (1950) simply neglects to translate θεός: "and of whom as concerning the flesh the Messiah *came*, who is over all, blessed for ever." Probably four of these versions with unusual renderings should be counted with the RSV group. The total number of this group would thereby be increased to twenty-seven.

The distribution of these versions by decades is as follows:

Dates	Number of Versions
1881-1890	0
1891-1900	2
1901-1910	2
1911-1920	1
1921-1930	3
1931-1940	3
1941-1950	3
1951-1960	6
1961-1973	7

If any trend can be detected from these figures, it would seem to be that the number of versions which have chosen to separate the θεός from Christ has increased conspicuously since the RSV New Testament appeared in 1946. For the sixty-five years between 1881 and 1946 only eleven versions of this type are listed; but in the twenty-seven years since RSV, fifteen have been issued. From 1881 until the publication of RSV versions of this class which have been included in this study have appeared on the average of about once every six years; since that time such versions have been issued on the average of slightly more than one every two years.

The versions which agree substantially with KJV in their interpretation of Romans 9:5 (including a few which give marginal or optional renderings of the RSV type) are very numerous. They are ERV (1881), Numerical Bible (1891), Moule (1893), Sanday-Headlam (1895), Jacobs (1896), Rotherham[3] (1897), 20th Century (1898), Stevens (1898), Hayman (1900), Rutherford (1900), American Standard (1901), Smith (1901), Ballentine (1902, 1909), W. G. Williams (1902), Weymouth (1903), Worrell (1904), Lloyd (1905), 1911 Bible (1911), F. B. Westcott (1913), Clarke (1913), Concordant (1914), Cunnington (1914, 1919), Panin (1914), Anderson (1918), Pallis (1920), Student (1921), Westminster (1921), Montgomery (1924), LeFevre (1928), Martin (1929), Lenski (1936), C. B. Williams (1937; Commentary, 1953), Spencer (1937), Clementson (1938), Lamsa (1940), Basic English (1941), Confraternity (1941), Knox (1944), Verkuyl (1945), Swann (1947), Phillips (1947, 1958), Letchworth (1948), Makrakis (1950), Authentic (1951), Norlie (1951, 1961), Moore (1953), Kleist-Lilly (1954), Wuest (1955, 1958), Amplified (1958), New American Standard (1960), Badley (1961), Rhys (1961), Noli (1961), Green (1962), Beck (1963), Bruce (1965), RSV (Catholic ed., 1965), Living Scriptures (1966), Jerusalem Bible (1966), New Scofield (1967), Original Name (1968), Modern Language (New Berkeley) (1969-70), Blackwelder (1971), New International (1973). The total number of these versions is sixty-four. Probably the number should be increased by the addition of at least two from the group with unusual or ambiguous renderings. The remarkable fact is that the versions in the KJV tradition outnumber those of the RSV type by more than two to one.

The distribution by decades is as follows:

Dates	Number of Versions
1881-1890	1
1891-1900	10
1901-1910	8
1911-1920	8
1921-1930	5
1931-1940	5
1941-1950	8
1951-1960	7
1961-1973	14

It will be noticed that these versions have been appearing steadily since the second decade listed above. They are not concentrated in the earlier part of the period, as some might have expected; but the tradition which they represent continues to be robust and productive right down to the present. In the twenty-seven years since RSV was published, twenty-five of these versions have appeared, ten more than the number of those which agree with RSV in the same span of years. However, in the sixty-five years from 1881 until the year when RSV was published, forty-one versions of this type were issued, more than three times the number of versions that favored the RSV line of interpretation. The percentage gap between the two types, according to our sampling, has been closing in recent decades.

Marginal Notes

From the versions themselves, with the exception of those which are ancillary to commentaries, one will learn very little about the battle which has been fought by commentators and others over the interpretation of our verse. The battle has been of great significance, and much learning, vigor, and emotion have gone into the conflict. However, only a very limited number of the versions considered regard it as necessary to acquaint their readers with the existence of rival interpretations.

The English Revised Version of 1881 did supply a marginal note about rival readings favored by certain scholars. For doing this it was censured on substantial grounds by John William Burgon. He could see no justification for giving such prominence as the marginal comment does to what he calls "the Socinian gloss." "Is it . . . the function," he inquires, "of Divines appointed *to revise the Authorized Version,* to give information to the 90 millions of English-speaking Christians scattered throughout the world as to the unfaithfulness of *'some modern interpreters'?*"[5] He seeks to support his position by a learned appeal to patristic testimony and he looks also to the oldest codices, the minuscule manuscripts, and the ancient versions for assistance.

Just how influential Burgon's vigorous protest has been is difficult to say. It certainly had little effect on the American Revised Version

---

5. *The Revision Revised* (London: John Murray, 1883), p. 211.

of 1901. As early as 1881 members of the American committee which was consulted by the British committee on revision wrote rather fully on the subject of rival interpretations of Romans 9:5. Two articles on the theme by members of the American committee appeared in 1881 in the first volume of the *Journal of Biblical Literature and Exegesis.* Timothy Dwight, taking a quite moderate stance, supports the traditional interpretation, but allows for the propriety of a marginal reading introducing another construction. He reasons: "The presentation of the subject, which has been made, shows the groundlessness and inappropriateness of the extreme assertions which have been indulged in by advocates of both views of this passage. . . . The fair and unprejudiced consideration of the words draws us away from all such extravagant statements, and brings us to the calm inquiry into the arguments for both sides, and the decision as to probabilities within the sphere of language and grammatical construction. The presence of the two renderings in the Revised Version, as it comes into general use, will tend to make all theologians and readers recognize that there is a possibility of both renderings, while yet there is a probability that the one given in the text is correct."[6] A second member of the American committee, Ezra Abbot, contributed a long article on the subject to the same volume[7] and another on "Recent Discussions of Romans ix.5," to the volume for 1883.[8] He opposed the traditional interpretation of the verse. Not altogether surprisingly, the American Revised Version of 1901, which was put into its final form by the surviving members of the American committee, chose to call attention to alternative interpretations. The text reads: "whose are the fathers, and of whom is Christ concerning the flesh, who is over all, God blessed for ever. Amen." The margin adds: or, *flesh: he who is over all, God,* be *blessed for ever.*" The marginal reading has here attained a somewhat higher status than the marginal comment in ERV. ERV simply reported the views of "some modern

---

6. "On Romans ix.5." I (1881):54.
7. Mentioned above in footnote 3, pp. 87-154.
8. Pp. 90-112.

interpreters." ARV dignifies a rival interpretation by introducing it with the word "or."

When we move on to RSV in 1946, as we have noticed, the traditional interpretation is relegated to the margin as an option, whereas a doxological construction is enshrined in the text: "to them belong the patriarchs, and of their race, according to the flesh, is the Christ. God who is over all be blessed forever. Amen." There naturally has been dissatisfaction with the RSV choice. And the roots of that dissatisfaction went deeper than those of mere traditionalism. The distinguished and perceptive student of Bible versions, the late Professor Oswald T. Allis, for example, was one of those who expressed emphatic and scholarly disapproval.[9] But such displeasure with the handling of Romans 9:5 in RSV did not discourage the New English Bible (1961) from similarly setting itself against the prevailing judgment and wisdom of the past. It chooses as its text: "Theirs are the patriarchs, and from them, in natural descent, sprang the Messiah. May God, supreme above all, be blessed for ever! Amen." The footnote reads: "*Or* sprang the Messiah, supreme above all, God blessed for ever; *or* sprang the Messiah, who is supreme above all. Blessed be God for ever!"

Another version which informs the reader about rival interpretations is the New International Version of the New Testament, which has recently been published.. It represents a major evangelical effort. At Romans 9:5 it places the traditional interpretation in its text: "Theirs are the patriarchs, and from them is traced the human ancestry of Christ, who is God over all, forever praised! Amen." A footnote, however, offers some options: "Or *Christ, who is over all.. God be forever praised! Or Christ. God who is over all be forever praised!*" This setting forth of readings which do not ascribe deity to Christ as alternatives would not have elicited a very favorable review from John William Burgon.

The *Translator's New Testament,* published by the British and Foreign Bible Society (1973), casts its vote on the side of the type

---

9. *Revision or New Translation?* (Philadelphia: The Presbyterian and Reformed Publishing Company, 1948), pp. 116-17.

of rendering favored by RSV; but that is not all. It would inform us
that this type of rendering is adopted by most modern translators! It
chooses for its text: "theirs are the patriarchs and from them on the
human side comes the Messiah. May he who is God over all be
praised for ever! Amen." This translation in itself is ambiguous. As
it stands, "he who is God over all" could be taken to refer to the
Messiah, who has just been mentioned. But a note clearly indicates
that this version intended no such reference. The note says:

> This is the translation adopted by most modern translators,
> but possible alternatives should be noted.
>
> 1. The words here treated as a doxology may in fact be a
> continuation of the previous sentence, in which case they would
> refer to Christ, not God the Father, and the meaning would be,
> ". . . from them on the human side comes the Messiah who is
> God over all. May he be praised for ever!"
> 2. As above ". . . Messiah who is over all. May God be
> praised for ever!"

Only a small number of additional versions inform the reader
about rival interpretations, and not many of our translators attempt
any explanation or defense of their preferences. The reasons for
this silence will, of course, vary with different translators. Some
may be content to follow their basic texts with little if any emendation or comment. Some make a practice of providing no footnotes
or marginal readings at all. Goodspeed belongs to this group. In
his preface, however, he informs us that he has closely followed
the Greek text of Westcott and Hort, but he says that in a few
cases he has accepted the changes suggested by Hort in the "Notes
on Select Readings." Romans 9:5, although not specifically mentioned, would seem to afford an example. The Westcott and Hort
text is of the traditional sort, but the margin has a reading of the
opposing type. One learns from the "Notes" that Westcott favored
the reading given in the text, but Hort preferred the marginal
reading.[10] Goodspeed does not follow the marginal reading precisely
in his punctuation, but he adopts it in all essentials.

---

10. B. F. Westcott and F. J. A. Hort, *The New Testament in the Original
Greek,* 2 vols. (New York: Harper & Brothers, 1881–82), 2:109-110.

Moffatt will serve as an example of a translator who, unlike Goodspeed, does offer notes on textual matters. In the Preface to his *New Translation* he says that he has followed the Greek text of Von Soden, although not in every respect in arrangement and punctuation. He remarks that when he has considered it necessary to depart from Von Soden's readings he has provided a footnote. However, in the very important matter of the punctuation of Romans 9:5, he does disagree with Von Soden; but there is no footnote!

The Grounds for Choice

This paper is a study of versions, and our versions are on the whole conspicuously silent as to why they chose one interpretation rather than another at Romans 9:5. Perhaps the wisest course would be to emulate the greater number of them in their silence. But one cannot refrain from seeking further for an explanation of the important decisions which they have made.

The question naturally arises as to whether the choices have at times been theologically motivated. For some, such as the Jehovah's Witnesses, who are convinced that the Bible does not teach the deity of Christ, there may have been a basic assumption that it could not be right here to refer θεός to Christ. Charles Hodge, who has dealt with Romans 9:5 not only in his commentary on Romans, but also in his *Systematic Theology,* reports that it has been admitted by advocates of views that would divorce θεός from Χριστός here that "the reason for adopting them is to avoid making the Apostle assert that Christ is God over all. As they do not admit that doctrine, they are unwilling to admit that the Apostle teaches it."[11] Hodge continues: "It was universally referred to Christ in the ancient Church, by all the Reformers, by all the older theologians, and by almost all of the modern interpreters who believe in the divinity of Christ."[12] Professor Ned B. Stonehouse was prepared to assert that the influence of negative literary and historical criticism

---

11. *Systematic Theology,* 3 vols. (New York: Charles Scribner's Sons, 1898), 1:511.
12. *Ibid.*

and a misconception of the teaching of Paul played a role in the rejection by some of the traditional interpretation. ". . . we are prepared to state," he wrote in reviewing RSV, "that the really decisive argument which has brought many modern interpreters to the conclusion that Paul is not naming Jesus 'God' is the consideration that, as they suppose, the apostle would be at variance with his own evaluation of Jesus. While not prepared to deny that Paul thought of Jesus as divine in some sense or other, these interpreters appeal, for example, to 'the caution with which Paul treats the mystery of the divinity of Christ' (Lietzmann)." The fact that RSV in its translation of Romans 9:5 "wipes out one of the most explicit evidences" of the deity of Christ in the New Testament and yet is willing to translate Titus 2:13 in a way that seems favorable to that doctrine is attributable doubtlessly to critical conclusions regarding Paul's epistles. "There can be no serious doubt that the revisers, in common with the negative critics generally, reject the genuineness of the Epistles to Timothy and Titus, and assign them to a period long after the death of Paul, perhaps even to the second century." There would be no problem for them on their critical position to grant that at an advanced date, in a non-Pauline epistle, Jesus might be called God; but it would not accord with their assumptions to grant that in an admittedly genuine epistle written at an early date Paul explicitly affirmed that Jesus was God.[13]

Considerations such as Stonehouse opposes apparently were influential with the majority of the committee which worked on the text for the Bible Societies' Greek New Testament. They took the position that "on the basis of the general tenor" of Paul's theology "it was considered tantamount to impossible that Paul would have expressed Christ's greatness by calling him God blessed for ever."[14]

Unquestionably men holding unbiblical views of Christ and the Bible are represented in the company of those who have opposed the traditional interpretation of Romans 9:5. One would surely

---

13. "Is the *New* New Testament Modernistic?" *The Presbyterian Guardian* 15 (June 25, 1946):181.

14. Metzger, *Textual Commentary*, p. 522.

be naive and foolish to assume that their theological and philosophical assumptions have had no bearing on their decision. Indeed without taking account of their basic commitments one will never rightly understand why they interpret Romans 9:5 or any other verse of the Bible as they do.

However, one cannot justly assume that the choice of another than the traditional interpretation of Romans 9:5 is in every case an infallible indication of the rejection of the doctrine of the deity of Christ. It may, as Hodge has pointed out, indicate exactly that; but even he, by using the qualifying word "almost," grants that there may be some exceptions. And not every translator who in our times has failed to adopt the traditional interpretation can be regarded as non-evangelical. Professor F. F. Bruce in his commentary on Romans, although favoring the traditional position, nevertheless holds that an alternative view is legitimate and protests against casting doubt on the orthodoxy of those who prefer it.

Perhaps the argument against the traditional interpretation which merits most attention is what one might call biblico-theological rather than theological, or, more simply, the argument from Pauline usage. This approach would not necessarily deny that the Scriptures as a whole teach the deity of Christ and that Paul teaches that doctrine, but it would appeal to the terminology which Paul characteristically employs. It would insist that Paul elsewhere reserves θεός for the Father and that therefore it should not be assigned to the Son here. (It should not be overlooked that in determining Pauline usage, the witness of the Pastorals is ignored by some scholars. Thus a footnote in Metzger's *Textual Commentary on the Greek New Testament* remarks that Titus 2:13 is "generally regarded as deutero-Pauline.")[15] C. H. Dodd in his commentary on Romans takes the position that the direct designation of Christ as God would be unique in Paul's writings: "Even though he ascribes to Christ functions and dignities which are consistent with nothing less than deity, yet he pointedly avoids calling Him 'God' (e.g., I Cor. viii.6; Phil. ii.6-11; see also note on Rom. x.9)."[16]

---

15. *Ibid.*   16. Dodd, *ibid.*, p. 152.

This, the most weighty argument against the traditional view, has been found seriously wanting by advocates of that position. To begin with, some of them properly accept the witness of the Pastorals as Pauline.[17] Thus Professor John Murray in his commentary on Romans takes due account of Titus 2:13. Further, he strikes at the heart of the argument from usage by insisting that "it may not be dogmatically affirmed that Paul *never* uses the predicate θεός of Christ."[18] He finds possible support for his position in I Thessalonians 1:12 and stronger evidence in Titus 2:13, and he points out: "Paul uses several expressions which predicate of Jesus the fulness of deity. Perhaps most notable is Phil. 2:6— ἐν μορφῇ θεοῦ ὑπάρχων. μορφή means the specific character and in this instance is more eloquent than the simple θεός because it emphasizes the fulness and reality of deity. To refrain from applying the predicate θεός to Christ when he is said to have been originally and continued to be 'in the form of God' could not possibly have arisen from any hesitation in respect of propriety and, if Paul should, on occasion, speak of Christ as θεός, this is what we should expect. Of no less significance is Col. 2:9 where πᾶν τὸ πλήρωμα τῆς θεότητος is said to dwell in Christ. This means 'the fulness of Godhood' and no expression could express the fulness of Christ's deity more effectively. Again in Phil. 2:6 the terms τὸ εἶναι ἴσα θεῷ refer to the dignity of Christ's station as the terms preceding deal with the dignity of his essential being and attribute to Jesus that equality which could belong to no other than to one who is himself also God. Other expressions in Paul could be adduced. These, however, place beyond any doubt the propriety, in terms of Paul's own teaching, of the predicate θεός after the pattern of John 1:1 and 20:28."[19]

Professor Murray thinks it not strange that Paul did not usually employ θεός in speaking of Christ, because he characteristically

---

17. On recent support for the genuineness of the Pastorals, see Donald Guthrie, *New Testament Introduction* (Downer's Grove, Ill.: Inter-Varsity Press, 1970), p. 596.

18. John Murray, *The Epistle to the Romans*, 2 vols. (Grand Rapids: Wm. B. Eerdmans Publishing Co., 1959, 1965), 2:247.

19. *Ibid.*

uses ὁ θεός as the personal name of the Father and ὁ κύριος as that of Christ. However, that "he should on one occasion (as supposed at this point) have expressly used θεός of Christ should not be surprising in view of what Paul's conception of Christ not merely allowed but demanded. In II Cor. 3:17 Paul says ὁ δὲ κύριος τὸ πνεῦμά ἐστιν. This is unusual and without knowing Paul's theology we would be staggered and ready to question the propriety of the predication. It is his conception of the relation of Christ to the Holy Spirit that explains it, not his characteristic use of titles. So in Rom. 9:5."[20]

Murray finds also that it is in accordance with Paul's teaching elsewhere to speak of Christ as ὁ ὢν ἐπὶ πάντων. He refers to Romans 1:4; 14:9; Ephesians 1:20-23; Philippians 2:9-11; Colossians 1:18, 19 and to parallel statements elsewhere in the New Testament.

Similar attention is directed to the exalted view which Paul held of Christ in the commentary on Romans by F. F. Bruce. This testimony is of particular interest to us in this study, for Bruce himself, as will be remembered, prepared an expanded paraphrase of the Letters of Paul in which he interpreted Romans 9:5 in the traditional way. One of the important points that he makes has to do with the significance of the title "Lord" as applied to Christ: ". . . when Paul gives Christ the title 'Lord', he does so because God the Father Himself has given Him that title as the 'name which is above every name' (Phil. ii.9). This title 'Lord' is given to Jesus by Paul as the equivalent of the Hebrew *Yahweh* (Jehovah): the way in which he applies Isaiah xlv.23 (cf. Rom. xiv.11) to Jesus in Philippians ii. 10f., indicates that, to him, the confession 'Jesus is Lord' means 'Jesus Christ is Jehovah'."[21]

An extended note on Romans 9:5 is provided by the Jerusalem Bible, in which it sets forth not only positive reasons for accepting the traditional interpretation of the verse, but also deals in a scholarly way with the Pauline teaching about the deity of Christ and the apostle's use of titles in referring to the Father and the Son. It finds that the title "Son of God" became Christ's in a new

---

20. *Ibid.*, p. 248.
21. (Grand Rapids: Wm. B. Eerdmans Publishing Company, 1963), p. 187.

fashion with the resurrection, but that He did not receive it then, because of His preexistence, "not only as prefigured in the O.T., but ontologically." It asserts that into His own person is gathered the fulness of the Godhead and of the universe. Christ is mentioned, it would remind us, in the trinitarian formulæ.[22]

Likewise Sanday and Headlam, who are to be classed with translators as well as with commentators—for they furnish a translation of Romans in their commentary—mention the fact that Paul ascribes to Christ a dignity not below that which θεός would imply. They examine the question which they consider fundamental: "was θεός so definitely used of the 'Father' as a proper name that it could not be used of the Son, and that its use in this passage as definitely points to the Father as would the word πατήρ if it were substituted?"[23] This they find not to be the case. A consideration of I Corinthians 12:4-6; 1 Corinthians 3:5; and II Corinthians 3:6 indicates that Paul did not use absolutely fixed designations in referring to the three persons of the Godhead.

Testimonies of this sort could be multiplied, but one more should suffice. J. Gresham Machen in his classic work, *The Origin of Paul's Religion,* puts it plainly: "The Pauline doctrine of the divinity of Christ is not dependent upon individual passages; it does not depend upon the question whether in Rom. ix.5 Paul applies the term 'God' to Christ. Certainly he does so by any natural interpretation of his words. But what is far more important is that the term 'Lord' in the Pauline Epistles, the characteristic Pauline name of Christ, is every whit as much a designation of deity as is the term 'God.' Everywhere in the Epistles, moreover, the attitude of Paul toward Christ is not merely the attitude of man to man, or scholar to master; it is the attitude of man toward God."[24]

---

22. *The Jerusalem Bible* (Garden City, N. Y.: Doubleday & Co., 1966), *ad loc.*

23. William Sanday and Arthur C. Headlam, *A Critical and Exegetical Commentary on the Epistle to the Romans* (Edinburgh: T. & T. Clark, 1895), p. 237.

24. *The Origin of Paul's Religion* (New York: The Macmillan Company, 1928), p. 198; and see Machen's *What Is Christianity?* (Grand Rapids: Wm. B. Eerdmans Publishing Company, 1951), pp. 37-50.

In the light of all the considerations adduced by Machen and the other writers who have been cited above, the argument against the traditional interpretation of Romans 9:5 which appeals to the Pauline usage must be adjudged anything but compelling. It is not at all strange if it has failed to convince a majority of our translators of its validity.

On the other hand, very powerful and persuasive reasons have been advanced in support of the view that θεός in our verse is to be understood of Christ. A very convenient, concise summary of considerations in support of the traditional interpretation can be found in Metzger's *Textual Commentary*, to which reference has previously been made. A minority of the committee which worked on the Bible Societies' Greek New Testament favored understanding θεός of Christ, and Metzger sets forth five reasons for the minority's position.[25]

The first consideration is that the traditional type of construction is in accord with the sentence structure, but that it is awkward and unnatural to introduce, as the rival construction requires, an asyndetic doxology to God. B. F. Westcott is quoted pertinently as holding that the "juxtaposition of ὁ χριστὸς κατὰ σάρκα and ὁ ὢν κ.τ.λ. seems to make a change of subject improbable." The grammarian Nigel Turner is cited as pointing out that it is grammatically unnatural that a participle in agreement with χριστός "should first be divorced from it and then given the force of a wish, receiving a different person as its subject."[26] It might further be noticed that Turner has made a plausible use of the argument from the construction in II Corinthians 11:31. He says: "That the [traditional] interpretation [of Romans 9:5] is the natural one and ought not to be relegated to the margin, can be seen by comparing the same construction in II Corinthians 11[31] where again the participle of the verb 'to be' occurs in close conjunction with this adjective, 'blessed.' No one would submit that the participle in this context was a wish or exclamation, or that it introduced an entirely new person. No one would deny that it refers back to the

---

25. Pp. 521-22. 26. *Ibid.*, p. 521.

previous subject, and that surely is the correct way to view the same construction in Romans 9⁵. The Messiah is God."²⁷

It might also be stressed that the reference to Christ κατὰ σάρκα in the former part of the verse naturally suggests that a balancing or contrasting idea is to be expressed or understood. Earlier in Romans there has been a similar construction (1:3-4). There κατὰ σάρκα receives an appropriate balance or contrast. In I Peter 3:18 we meet with another completed contrast of the same type. Sanday and Headlam and also Philippi develop this point further. The former refer to the parallel with Romans 1:3-4. They hold that "here [Romans. 9:5] the course of the argument having led him [Paul] to lay stress on the human birth of Christ as a Jew, he would naturally correct a one-sided statement by limiting that descent to the earthly relationship and then describe the true nature of him who was the Messiah of the Jews. He would thus enhance the privileges of his fellow-countrymen, and put a culminating point to his argument. τὸ κατὰ σάρκα leads us to expect an antithesis, and we find just what we should have expected in ὁ ὢν ἐπὶ πάντων θεός."²⁸

The traditional interpretation is not only the most natural, Philippi argues; it is also the one which is absolutely necessary: "For as τὸ κατὰ σάρκα clearly postulates an antithesis, if such an antithesis, as is here actually the case, is found in the subjoined words (ὁ ὢν κτλ.), it is most natural to take these words as expressing the antithesis . . . . In the opposite case the antithesis to κατὰ σάρκα would be suppressed, and must therefore be supplied in thought. . . . But the suppression of the antithesis, and its supply in thought merely, cannot take place where, as here, the thesis only occurs for the sake of the antithesis. τὸ κατὰ σάρκα stands merely for the sake of the following ὁ ὢν ἐπὶ πάντων θεός. Without this contrast the words would imply a diminution of the prerogative of Israel. The apostle would then have written simply καὶ ἐξ ὧν ὁ Χριστός; for that the

---

27. Nigel Turner, *Grammatical Insights into the New Testament* (Edinburgh: T. & T. Clark, 1965), p. 15. See also Metzger, "Punctuation," pp. 105-106.
28. Sanday and Headlam, *Commentary*, p. 235. Cf. Metzger, "Punctuation," pp. 103-105.

Messiah springs from the Jews is a higher privilege than that He springs from them after the flesh merely. But that *He* springs from them after the flesh who is God over all, this is the highest conceivable prerogative."[29]

The sum of the whole matter is briefly and clearly expressed by the eminent grammarian A. T. Robertson. He finds that we have here "a clear statement of the deity of Christ following the remark about his humanity. This is the natural and the obvious way of punctuating the sentence. To make a full stop after *sarka* (or colon) is very abrupt and awkward."[30]

The second reason which seemed plausible to the minority of the Bible Societies' committee was this: "If the clause ὁ ὢν κ.τ.λ. is an asyndetic doxology to God the Father, the word ὢν is superfluous, for 'he who is God over all' is most simply represented by ὁ ἐπὶ πάντων θεός. The presence of the participle suggests that the clause functions as a relative clause (not 'he who is . . .' but 'who is . . .'), and thus describes ὁ Χριστός as being 'God over all.' "[31]

The other important considerations to the minority of the committee were that Paul's doxologies are never asyndetic, but are always joined to something before; that asyndetic doxologies in the Bible and in Semitic inscriptions are not constructed as the proposed doxology would be here; and that a doxology in this context would be out of place and not in harmony with the tone of the passage: "In the light of the context, in which Paul speaks of his sorrow over Israel's unbelief, there seems to be no psychological explanation to account for the introduction of a doxology at this point."[32]

It is not necessary here to elaborate on the considerations just mentioned. Further material on them is readily available in commentaries. Nor is it necessary to seek out other reasons which

---

29. Friedrich Adolph Philippi, tr. J. S. Banks, 2 vols. (Edinburgh: T. & T. Clark, 1878-79), 2:69-70.

30. *Word Pictures in the New Testament*, 6 vols. (New York: Harper & Brothers), 4(1931):381.

31. Metzger, *Textual Commentary*, p. 521.

32. *Ibid.*, p. 522. See also Metzger, "Punctuation," pp. 106-109.

may have contributed to the decisions made by the great company of witnesses from patristic times to the present who have found in Romans 9:5 a clear testimony to the deity of Christ. The case for the traditional view is clearly of the first order.

The force of the arguments in favor of the traditional interpretation has been felt to a degree even by some who have not accepted it. Timothy Dwight in the article previously mentioned remarks:

> It is a fact worthy of notice, that of the most prominent opponents of the reference of the passage to Christ—such writers, for example, as de Wette, Grimm, Rückert, Meyer, Jowett— each one admits a peculiar force as belonging to some particular argument among those which are urged in favor of that reference. . . . We cannot but regard the fact that these scholars find a strength in the various arguments, which it is hard to overcome— one looking upon one point as presenting very serious difficulty, and another upon another, until, as we read what is said by them all, we see that they are pressed by the weight of all the considerations—as showing that there is a real force in each one, taken by itself, and a cumulative force in the sum of them, when united together. If such advocates of the opposite view acknowledge that the argument, from stage to stage, causes even themselves to give it their most respectful consideration, the position of those who interpret the clause of Christ must be a strong one, and the reasons which support it must be such as ought to influence candid minds.[33]

It is true that not many translators in the period since 1881 have told us in their versions why they chose one construction or another at Romans 9:5; but it is also true that there are considerations of a most powerful and persuasive type in support of the interpretation which modern English versions have adopted by a margin of more than two to one, that Romans 9:5 testifies that Christ is "God over all, blessed forever. Amen." Quite possibly some translators have been so deeply convinced that the traditional interpretation of this verse is correct and that rival constructions are so obviously wrong that they have thought it unnecessary to attempt to justify their choice. Indeed, in view of the overwhelming strength of the

---

33. Dwight, *ibid.*, pp. 54-55.

reasons for adopting the traditional position, the present writer would conclude that a translator moved by them is under no obligation to acquaint his readers with rival interpretations which he rightly regards as implausible and unprofitable. It would also seem that to dignify these rival constructions as legitimate alternatives to the natural and traditional interpretation is without warrant.

LIST OF VERSIONS

1881–1973

American Revised Version. Standard Edition. New York: Thomas Nelson and Sons, 1901.

Amplified New Testament. Grand Rapids: Zondervan Publishing House, 1958.

Anderson, H. T. The New Testament, translated from the Sinaitic manuscript. . . . Cincinnati: The Standard Publishing Co., 1918.

Authentic: The New Testament . . . The Authentic Version. Plattsburg, Mo.: Brotherhood Authentic Bible Society, 1951.

Badley, J. H. A Bible for Modern Readers . . . The New Testament. . . . London: James Clarke & Co., 1961.

Ballantine, William G. The Riverside New Testament. Boston: New York: Houghton Mifflin Company, 1923.

Ballentine, Frank Schell. The American Bible. 5 vols. Scranton, Pa.: Good News Publishing Company, 1902.

————. The Bible in Modern English or The Modern English Bible (New Testament). Perkiomen, Pa.: The Perkiomen Press, 1909.

Barclay, William. The New Testament: A New Translation. London: Collins, 1968-69.

Barrett, C. K. A Commentary on the Epistle to the Romans. New York: Harper & Row, 1957.

Bartlett, Edward T., and Peters, John P. Scriptures Hebrew and Christian. 3 vols. London: New York: G. P. Putnam's Sons, 1886-93.

Basic English: The New Testament in Basic English. New York: E. P. Dutton & Co., 1941.

Beck, William F. The New Testament in the Language of Today. St. Louis: Concordia Publishing House, 1963.

Blackwelder, Boyce W. Letters from Paul. Anderson, Indiana: Warner Press, 1971.

Bruce, F. F.   The Letters of Paul: An Expanded Paraphrase.
Grand Rapids: Wm. B. Eerdmans Publishing Company, [1965].
Clarke, Edward. The New Testament: The Authorised Version,
Corrected. London: Smith, Elder & Co., 1913.
Clementson, Edgar Lewis. The New Testament. A Translation.
Pittsburgh: The Evangelization Society of the Pittsburgh Bible
Institute, 1938.
Concordant: Concordant Version. The Sacred Scriptures. "New
Testament." Los Angeles: Concordant Publishing Concern,
1914-26.
Confraternity: The New Testament. . . . Paterson, N. J.: St.
Anthony Guild Press, 1941.
Cunnington, E. E. The New Covenant. London: George Rout-
ledge & Sons, 1914.
————. The New Testament. A Revision of the Version of A.D.
1611. London: T. Fisher Unwin, 1919.
English Revised Version. The New Testament. Cambridge: Uni-
versity Press; Oxford: University Press, 1881.
Fenton, Ferrar. The New Testament translated from the Greek
into Current English. London: J. S. Dodington, [n.d.].
————. The New Testament in Modern English. 9th ed. Lon-
don: S. W. Partridge and Co., [n.d.].
————. The Holy Bible in Modern English. London: A. & C.
Black, 1903; reprinted 1931, 1933.
Godbey, W. B. Translation of the New Testament from the Origi-
nal Greek. Cincinnati: Office of God's Revivalist, [1902].
Good News for Modern Man: The New Testament in Today's Eng-
lish Version. New York: American Bible Society, 1966.
Goodspeed, Edgar J. The New Testament: An American Trans-
lation. Chicago: The University of Chicago Press, 1923.
Greber, Johannes. The New Testament. New York: J. Felsberg,
1937.
Green, Jay P. The Children's "King James" Bible: New Testa-
ment. Evansville, Indiana: Modern Bible Translations, [n.d.]
————. The Children's Version of the Holy Bible. New York:
McGraw-Hill Book Company, 1962.
————. King James II Version of the Bible. Grand Rapids:
Associated Publishers and Authors, 1971.
————. Modern King James Version of the Holy Bible. (Printed
by McGraw-Hill, 1962)
————. The Teen-Age Version of the Holy Bible. (Printed by
McGraw-Hill, 1962)

Griffith, Gwilym O. St. Paul's Gospel to the Romans. Oxford: Basil Blackwell, 1949.
Hayman, Henry. The Epistles of the New Testament. London: Adam and Charles Black, 1900.
Hudson, James T. The Pauline Epistles. London: James Clarke & Co., 1958.
Jacobs, Henry E. Annotations on the Epistles of Paul to the Romans and I Corinthians (The Lutheran Commentary). New York: The Christian Literature Co., 1896.
The Jerusalem Bible. Garden City, N. Y.: Doubleday & Company, 1966.
Jordan, Clarence. The Cotton Patch Version of Paul's Epistles. New York: Association Press, [1968].
Kleist, James A., and Lilly, Joseph L. The New Testament. Milwaukee: The Bruce Publishing Company, 1954.
Knox, R. A. The New Testament. New York: Sheed & Ward, 1944.
Lamsa, George M. The New Testament according to the Eastern Text. Philadelphia: A. J. Holman Company, 1940.
Laubach, Frank C. The Inspired Letters in Clearest English. New York: Thomas Nelson & Sons, 1956.
LeFevre, George N. The Christian's Bible—New Testament. Strasburg, Pa.: George N. LeFevre, 1928.
Lenski, R. C. H. The Interpretation of St. Paul's Epistle to the Romans. Columbus: Lutheran Book Concern, 1936.
Letchworth: The New Testament. . . . The Letchworth Version in Modern English. By T. F. Ford and R. E. Ford. Letchworth, Herts: Letchworth Printers, 1948.
Living Bible: The Living Bible Paraphrased. Wheaton, Illinois: Tyndale House, 1971.
Living Letters: The Paraphrased Epistles. By Kenneth N. Taylor. Wheaton, Illinois: Tyndale House, 1962.
Living Scriptures: A new translation in the King James tradition. Marshalltown, Delaware: The National Foundation for Christian Education, 1966.
Lloyd, Samuel. The Corrected English New Testament. London: The London Bible Warehouse, 1905.
Makrakis, Apostolos. Interpretation of the Entire New Testament, vol. 2. Tr. Albert George Alexander. Chicago: Orthodox Christian Educational Society, 1950.
Martin, William Wallace. Epistles. . . . 2 vols. Nashville: Press of Marshall and Bruce Co., 1929.

Modern Language New Testament. The New Berkeley Version. Grand Rapids: Zondervan Publishing House [1969, 1970].

Moffatt, James. The Historical New Testament. Edinburgh: T. & T. Clark, 1901.

————. The New Testament. A New Translation. London: Hodder & Stoughton, 1913.

Montgomery, Helen Barrett. Centenary Translation of the New Testament. Philadelphia: The American Baptist Publication Society, 1924.

Moore, George Albert. The New Testament. Chevy Chase, Maryland: Country Dollar Press, 1953-54.

Moule, Handley C. G. The Epistle of St Paul to the Romans. London: Hodder & Stoughton, 1893.

New American Bible. Paterson, N. J.: St. Anthony Guild Press, 1970.

New American Standard Bible. Carol Stream, Illinois: Creation House (1963).

New English Bible: New Testament. Oxford and Cambridge University Presses, 1961.

New International Version: The New Testament. Grand Rapids: Zondervan Bible Publishers, 1973.

New Scofield Reference Bible. New York: Oxford University Press, 1967.

New World Translation of the Holy Scriptures. Brooklyn: Watchtower Bible and Tract Society of New York, 1961. 1st ed., 1950.

1911 Bible. New York: Oxford University Press, 1911.

Noli, Fran S. The New Testament. Boston: Albanian Orthodox Church in America, 1961.

Norlie, Olaf M. The New Testament in Modern English. 2 vols. Privately issued, 1951.

————. Norlie's Simplified New Testament. . . . Grand Rapids: Zondervan Publishing House, 1961.

Numerical Bible. 7 vols. New York: Loizeaux Brothers, 1891-1931.

Original Name New Testament. The New Testament of Our Master and Saviour. . . . Junction City, Oregon: Missionary Dispensary Bible Research, 1968.

Overbury, Arthur E.: The People's New Covenant. Monrovia, California: Arthur E. Overbury, 1925.

Pallis, Alex. To the Romans. A Commentary. Liverpool: Liverpool Booksellers' Co., 1920.

Panin, Ivan. The New Testament from the Greek Text as Established by Bible Numerics. Toronto: The Book Society of Canada, 1945 [originally published in 1914].

Phillips, J. B. Letters to Young Churches. New York: The Macmillan Company, 1951 [originally published 1947].

————. The New Testament in Modern English. New York: The Macmillan Company, 1958.

Rhys, Howard. The Epistle to the Romans. New York: The Macmillan Company, 1961.

Rotherham, Joseph Bryant. The Emphasized New Testament. 3rd ed. New York: John Wiley & Sons, 1897.

Rutherford, W. G. St. Paul's Epistle to the Romans. London: Macmillan and Co., 1900.

Revised Standard Version. New Testament. New York: Thomas Nelson & Sons, 1946.

Revised Standard Version. Catholic Edition. New York: Thomas Nelson & Sons, 1965.

Sacred Name. The New Testament. . . . Irvington, N. J.: Scripture Research Association, 1950.

Sanday, William, and Headlam, Arthur C. A Critical and Exegetical Commentary on the Epistle to the Romans. Edinburgh: T. & T. Clark, 1895.

Schonfield, Hugh J. The Authentic New Testament. London: Dobson Books, 1955.

Smith, William Wye. The New Testament in Braid Scots. Paisley: Alexander Gardner, [1901].

Spencer, Francis Aloysius. The New Testament. New York: The Macmillan Company, 1937.

Stevens, George Barker. The Epistles of Paul in Modern English. A Paraphrase. New York: Charles Scribner's Sons, 1899.

Student. A Plain Translation of the New Testament. By a Student. Melbourne: McCarron, Bird & Co., 1921.

Swann, George. New Testament. Louisville: (3rd ed., New Testament Publishers), [1947].

Tomanek, James L. The New Testament. Pocatello, Idaho: Arrowhead Press, 1958.

Translator's New Testament. The Translator's New Testament. London: The British and Foreign Bible Society, [1973].

Twentieth Century. The Twentieth Century New Testament. London: Mowbray House, 1898-1901.

Verkuyl, Gerrit. Berkeley Version of the New Testament. Berkeley, California: James J. Gillick & Co., 1945.

Wade, G. W. The Documents of the New Testament. London: T. Murby & Co., 1934.

Wand, J. W. C. The New Testament Letters. Prepared and Paraphrased. Melbourne: Oxford University Press, 1944.

Way, Arthur S. The Letters of St. Paul. London: Macmillan and Co., 1901.

Weekes, Robert D. . . . The New Dispensation. New York: Funk & Wagnalls Co., 1897.

Westcott, Frederick Brooke. St. Paul and Justification. London: Macmillan and Co., 1913.

Westminster: The Westminster Version of the Sacred Scriptures. The New Testament was published in fascicles 1913-1935 and in four volumes. Volume 3, Paul's Letters to the Churches, appeared in 1921. London: Longmans, Green and Co.

Weymouth, Richard Francis. The Modern Speech New Testament. London: J. Clarke & Co., 1903.

Williams, Charles B. The New Testament. Boston: Bruce Humphries, 1937.

Williams, Charles Kingsley. A New Translation in Plain English. London: Longmans Green and Co., 1952.

Williams, Warren G. An Exposition of the Epistle of Paul to the Romans. Cincinnati: Jennings and Pye, 1902.

Wilson, R. Mercer. The Book of Books. London: The Lutterworth Press, 1938.

Worrell, A. S. The New Testament. Philadelphia: The American Baptist Publication Society, 1904.

Wuest, Kenneth S. Romans in the Greek New Testament. Grand Rapids: Wm. B. Eerdmans Publishing Company, 1955.

————. Wuest's Expanded Translation of the Greek New Testament. 3 vols. Grand Rapids: Wm. B. Eerdmans Publishing Company, 1956-59.

Chapter 6

ROBERT STRONG

Articles on the Second Coming of Christ

The Rev. Robert Strong, S.T.D., now professor of homiletics in the Reformed Theological Seminary, Jackson, Mississippi, published in the *Presbyterian Guardian* years ago a series of articles on eschatological matters entitled "Amillennialism in the New Testament." These articles were based on his doctoral dissertation on the same theme, but naturally, as more popular in design, they do not reproduce the footnotes and the documentation of that study. We are pleased to be able to present, with the permission of Dr. Strong and of the *Presbyterian Guardian,* the first five of these articles, and we hope to include others in coming volumes.

All our readers, whether or not they agree with the position which Dr. Strong takes, will appreciate the clarity and conciseness of his style and the temperateness and courtesy of his presentation. We shall welcome in the future other articles on eschatological subjects and will much appreciate constructive discussions of differences of interpretation.

The five articles included and the dates of their appearance in the *Presbyterian Guardian* are as follows:

I. Amillennialism in the New Testament   January 10, 1942

II. The Second Coming and the Second Century
January 25, 1942

III. The Millennial Discussion Continues   February 10, 1942

IV. The Structure and Terms of New Testament Eschatology
February 25, 1942

V.   The Day of the Lord Jesus Christ   March 10, 1942

I. *Amillennialism in the New Testament*

Among Bible-believing people there is almost no subject on which more disagreement is to be found than on the doctrine of the second coming of Christ. Every true Christian must of course believe in the personal return of the Lord Jesus Christ, for the Bible plainly teaches that the Saviour will one day appear from heaven. It is another matter entirely to gain consent to an outline of the doctrine of the second advent. And so we hear of some who believe in a postmillennial return of Christ, of others who subscribe to the view that Christ's coming will be premillennial, and of still others who hold to the view of the Lord's return that has come to be known as amillennialism.

I have been asked in this series of articles to condense a fairly long study I have written on the general subject: *Amillennialism in the New Testament*. Increasing notice is being taken of the amillennial view by both premillennialists and postmillennialists, and it may serve a useful purpose to present the main outlines of the amillennial understanding of the New Testament advent teaching.

To fulfill this purpose there will be the constant, inevitable necessity of contrasting the interpretations of Scripture advanced by representatives of the various views. The aim will be to be objective rather than controversial. It ought to be possible to discuss even prophetic subjects on the high plane of courtesy and mutual respect!

Reference has been made to three leading points of view about the second coming of Christ. It will be well to set them forth clearly at the outset of this study.

These three views may be distinguished by the attitude they take toward what is popularly known as "the millennium." The term derives from the twentieth chapter of the Book of Revelation, where is found repeated reference to a period of one thousand years. The relation one sees between the thousand years of Revelation 20 and the second coming of Christ determines his general prophetic point of view.

The first-mentioned of the three generally held views about the return of Christ was postmillennialism. This view has it that the thousand years of Revelation 20 precede the return of Christ, which is thus a postmillennial return. J. H. Snowden was not a consistent supernaturalist, but he presented a common form of postmillennialism when he wrote:

> The kingdom of God is now in existence and has been from the beginning of the world, but Christ came to reveal it more clearly and extend it over the world. This process is now going on as a slow growth, and the means by which it is being carried on are the preaching and ordinances of the gospel together with all the means of grace and agencies of good as they are energized by the Holy Spirit, who is immanent in the world. This process is to go forward until the world is practically Christianized, and this state and period of the world, which may or may not be referred to in the thousand years of Rev. 20:1-7, is commonly known as the millennium. Evil will not be wholly eradicated from the world at the height of the millennium, though Satan will be restrained, and at the end of this period there will be an outbreak of wickedness. Then will follow the final coming of Christ, which will be attended with the general resurrection and judgment, issuing in the eternal state.

Among liberal theologians a view prevails that the world will more and more come under the influence of Christianity until the kingdom of God will come on earth. When the world does come to an end, it will be in the manner predicted by naturalistic science: through a collision with a heavenly body, through the cooling of the sun, or some such cause. This evolutionary conception of eschatology we are not concerned to treat, lacking completely, as it does, biblical foundation.

Sharply opposed to Snowden's view stands premillennialism. Writing critically of postmillennialism, S. H. Kellogg says:

> Premillennialists insist that this view reverses the Scriptural order, and is inconsistent with revealed facts. Their belief is as follows. Agreeing that the Scriptures warrant the expectation of a future age of triumphant righteousness upon the earth, they maintain that the second Advent will not follow, but introduce,

that period, and that until that time, not "the wheat" merely, but "the tares" also, "the children of the wicked one," must continue to grow (see Matthew 13:30). They, therefore, expect no universal triumph of holiness till Christ returns.

As to its details, premillennialism usually follows this scheme of end-time events. A period of general apostasy from the true faith will immediately precede the return of Christ. The Lord Jesus will come in secret to catch away the living saints, at the same time raising from the grave the bodies of those who have died in the Christian faith. A seven-year period of tribulation will ensue, during which the personal Antichrist will rule the earth. At the end of this era of trouble, Christ will appear from heaven openly and will overthrow in the Battle of Armageddon the hosts of Antichrist. Then will be ushered in the Redeemer's glorious reign upon the earth, which will last a thousand years. Satan will be bound during this age of peace and righteousness, but at its end he will be released to stir up once more rebellion against the Lord. His crushing defeat is followed by the resurrection of the wicked, the last judgment, and the eternal state.

Historically speaking, this view with its two-stage coming of Christ has only recently appeared on the doctrinal scene.

There are many premillennialists, however, who do not accept this scheme. Those, for example, whom we might term old-fashioned premillennialists—because they agree with the millennial views held by certain fathers in the early church—place the rise and reign of Antichrist before the catching away of the saints. The coming of Christ is thus one unified coming and not in two stages.

Some of the writer's closest associates, both ministerial and lay, in his work in the Orthodox Presbyterian Church are premillennialists.* He would pay tribute to their zeal and faith and would point out, moreover, that lack of complete agreement with them on unfulfilled prophecy is definitely not a barrier to happy coöperation and fellowship.

---

*Editor's Note: Dr. Strong is at present a minister in the Presbyterian Church in the United States.

The third of the three views on the second advent of Christ is amillennialism. This view holds that the postmillennialist and the premillennialist have incorrectly interpreted Revelation 20 in seeing in it a millennium of *earthly* blessedness, an age whose joys will be shared by multitudes of Christ-rejecting men who survived the tribulation and the advent. The amillennialist contends that Christ returns not merely to set up a temporary kingdom but to achieve the final victory of His cause. and, in the new heavens and new earth which He will fashion out of the world purged by judgment fire, to establish His people in everlasting righteousness. The amillennialist sees no ground in Scripture for holding to a millennium of righteousness before the Lord's coming, and he sees the possibility of such a millennium after the second advent expressly excluded by the New Testament teaching. Amillennialism agrees with premillennialism that the Scriptures do not promise the conversion of the world through the preaching of the gospel. It agrees with postmillennialism that the coming of Christ ushers in the last judgment and the eternal state.

Briefly outlined, the amillennial view is that, preceding the coming of Christ, there will be a widespread apostasy from the true faith, climaxed by the manifestation of the personal Antichrist. This the final great rebellion against Christ will be overthrown at the personal appearing of the Son of God, who will come from heaven to take unto Himself His own people and to demolish the forces of Antichrist. The wicked dead will be raised unto judgment. The earth and its works will be overwhelmed in fire, and a new heaven and a new earth will appear in which only righteousness will dwell.

It is the amillennial view of which W. Masselink writes, when he says:

> We believe that when Christ comes again there will be a new heaven and a new earth. Creation will be restored and the curse shall be removed. This is not the millennium of which the Chiliast [millennialist] speaks, but this is the beginning of eternity on earth. Joyfully anticipating the renewing of all things, including the restoration of the whole creation of God, which shall accompany the complete consummation of the great purpose of redemption, the whole Christian church looks

forward to Christ's coming. The Bride shall then be united with the Bridegroom. Sin and death shall be abolished and the Prince of Peace shall establish His final kingdom.

Occasionally one will find amillennialism referred to in the prophetic literature of the day as a new and strange belief held by a very few obscure persons. This is a mistaken impression. As the next article will attempt to show, the amillennial view is a very old and a very honorable one.

It may at this point be appropriate to answer a question some will ask on reading the title of the series of articles: why simply "Amillennialism in the New Testament"? Now it is true that the doctrine of the return of Christ has its roots in the Old Testament. To limit the field of investigation to the New Testament, as lack of space requires that we do, is not, however, too greatly to circumscribe the study. For in matters of doctrinal definition it is obvious that the teaching of the New Testament is normative. It is axiomatic that the New Testament brings into their proper clearness and relation all those truths which in the Old Testament are to be found in germ. The often quoted saying of Augustine is very much in point, that what is latent in the Old Testament is patent in the New. By the plain teaching of the New Testament, therefore, a full outline of the events connected with the second advent may be achieved. It will then perhaps appear which of the three views of Christ's coming that have been described may properly lay claim to correctness.

The method that will be employed in the development of this series of articles is this: Two articles will be devoted to a résumé of the history of the millennial question. Although the solution to the problem is in no sense to be rested upon the opinions of church fathers or of church theologians, the history of the millennial discussion may not safely be slighted. The advocates of the premillennial view, for example, place a fairly heavy emphasis on the argument from tradition. And it may readily be admitted that the ability to adduce a body of confirming testimony to a belief, particularly if that testimony comes from the very early days of

Christian history, is of significant assistance in establishing the validity of one's belief.

An article will be given to a survey of what may be called the eschatological structure of the New Testament, and to a brief discussion of the terms used in the New Testament to denote the second coming of Christ.

Several articles will then be devoted to a fairly detailed study of the leading New Testament passages that deal at some length with the return of Christ or bear significantly upon it—passages like Matthew 13:24-30, 36-43; Matthew 24 and 25; Acts 15:13-21; I Corinthians 15:20-28; II Thessalonians 1:5-10; and II Peter 3:3-13.

The last two articles of the series will discuss the methods of interpretation applied to the Book of Revelation and the various interpretations of the much controverted section, Revelation 20:1-10.

A vast amount of material, more or less closely related to the principal subject of the study, cannot be touched upon. The following topics all bear upon the question to be treated: The Kingdom of God and the Church, The Nation of Israel and the Kingdom of God, The Unity of the Covenant of Grace, The Promise Made to Israel. These headings do not, however, lead to the heart of the millennial question as directly as the outline of procedure given above promises to do. And, again, these topics bear rather upon modern dispensationalism than upon millennialism in general. It is true that modern dispensationalism will inevitably find some place in the following discussions, but not a principal place. Modern dispensationalism is, of course, a type of teaching closely associated with premillennialism in the minds of many. (Books of particular value to those interested in the topics mentioned are Theodore Graebner's *War in the Light of Prophecy,* A. Reese's *Approaching Advent of Christ,* and Philip Mauro's *Hope of Israel—What Is It?)*

The course of the investigation to be undertaken in this series of articles has now been plotted and major terms have been defined. In the next article we shall ask the early Christian centuries what men were then saying about the return of the Lord Jesus Christ. May our study of these things to which for the next few months we are invited to give attention serve not merely to unfold to us the various advent viewpoints but to stimulate our hearts to greater love for Christ's appearing.

II. *The Second Coming and the Second Century*

In this article we are to consult the leaders of the Christian church who lived in the second century and ask them what they taught about the second coming of Christ. Let us first, however, take note of the dispute among the historians about this teaching.

A claim often made by advocates of the premillennial view of the return of the Lord is that their doctrine was all but universally held in the church during the early ages of Christian history. J. H. Brookes, in his widely read book *Maranatha,* devotes a whole chapter to the effort to prove this. He quotes from the historian Mosheim:

> Long before this period [the third century] an opinion had prevailed that Christ was to come and reign a thousand years among men, before the entire and final dissolution of the world. This opinion, which had hitherto met with no opposition, was variously interpreted by different persons.

Brookes quotes also from Philip Schaff:

> The most striking point in the eschatology of the ancient church is the widely current and very prominent chiliasm, or the doctrine of a visible reign of Christ in glory on earth with the risen saints for a thousand years.

Special stress is laid by Brookes on a statement of Gibbon paying tribute to the influence of the millennial doctrine during the period A.D. 150–325. Much is also made of the admission of Whitby, often called the father of postmillennialism, that chiliasm "passed among the best Christians for two hundred and fifty years for a tradition apostolical."

S. H. Kellogg, in his *Are the Premillennialists Right?,* even goes so far as to say that "it is commonly agreed by the best modern historians that from the death of the apostles till the time of Origen, premillennialism was the general faith of those who were regarded as strictly orthodox Christians."

A recent writer of the dispensational school, Charles Feinberg, goes to the extreme of saying in his *Premillennialism or Amillennialism?*: "Every book that we have read and studied on the question of the millennium, whether it was favorable to the doctrine, or whether it gave full force and value to the testimony or tried to dissipate its implications, admitted freely that the entire early church for the first three centuries was premillennial, almost to a man."

W. G. T. Shedd is an authority Dr. Feinberg must have overlooked, for in his review of the teachings of the fathers of the early second century Shedd observes:

> There are no traces of chiliasm in the writings of Clement of Rome, Ignatius, Polycarp, Tatian, Athanagoras, and Theophilus of Antioch. The inference from these facts, then, is, that this tenet was not the received faith of the church certainly down to the year 150. It was held only by individuals. These, in some instances, as in that of Cerinthus, were in hostile and positively heretical relations to the church. And in the instance of those whose general catholicity was acknowledged, (as Papias,) there was by no means such a weight of character and influence, as would entitle them to be regarded as the principal or sole representatives of orthodoxy. . . . A further incidental proof of the position that millenarianism was not the received authoritative faith of the church from the death of the apostles to the year 150, is found in the fact that it does not appear in the Apostles' Creed. In this symbol there is not the slightest allusion to two resurrections and a corporeal reign of Christ between them. The only specifications are that Christ shall come from heaven "to judge the quick and the dead;" and that there is a "resurrection of the body;" and a "life everlasting" (immediately succeeding is the implication).

To the same effect is the following sentence from Dr. N. B. Stonehouse, a careful student of the literature of the church fathers: "Inasmuch as Papias and Justin are the only writers of whom it can be said with any degree of certainty that they are chiliasts, and the eschatological expressions of many others exclude chiliasm, the assertion that this doctrine was an essential element in the faith of early Christianity needs revision."

Let us turn from the disagreements of the historians and see what the early fathers themselves had to say. Although the epistles of

Clement, Ignatius, and Polycarp (all to be dated in the first part of the second century) have nothing to say one way or another about a millennium, they do refer to the coming of the Lord.

Clement of Rome makes mention of a sudden coming of the Lord to execute judgment and give reward to His saints, and a time when those who possess a place among the godly "shall be made manifest at the revelation [visitation] of the kingdom of Christ." The kingdom is not, however, described as a thing of earth and time; it is merely said in the words of Paul that eye, nor ear, nor heart have perceived the things, prepared of God for them that wait for Him.

Ignatius pictures the life awaiting the believer as eternal. In speaking of the last times as "come upon us," he urges as a spur to holiness "fear of the wrath to come." There is nowhere a suggestion that he anticipates for the Christian a reigning with Christ in Jerusalem. He speaks of the coming of Christ as to occur "at the end of the world," when they that pierced Him will recognize Him and "mourn for themselves."

Polycarp writes in the same way of the coming of Jesus Christ, as a judgment for the living and the dead. Christ has authority to judge because God, having raised Him from the dead, has given Him a throne at His right hand, making subject to Christ all things in heaven and on earth, so that "Him every spirit serves." At the coming of Christ, "His blood God will require from them who disobey Him." But Christians will be raised as Christ was raised; they will receive the future world, and there they will reign with Christ.

In his *Ecclesiastical History*, Eusebius (fourth century) recounts a tradition handed down by Hegesippus, a tradition that is of interest because it purports to come from the sub-apostolic age. The grandsons of Jude are said to have been brought before the Emperor Domitian, accused of being descendants of David and related to Christ. When the emperor asked them about the nature, origin, and time of the appearance of the kingdom of Christ, they replied "that it was not a temporal nor an earthly kingdom, but celestial and angelic; that it would appear at the end of the world, when coming in glory He would judge the quick and the dead, and give to everyone according to his works."

It is from Eusebius also that we learn of the first chiliast who appears in the second century. Eusebius mentions that in Papias's *Exposition of the Dominical Oracles* is found the idea of a "certain millennium after the resurrection, and that there would be a corporeal reign of Christ on this very earth." Apparently this writer of the early second century was influenced to some extent by the Jewish apocalyptic literature, for Irenaeus quotes Papias as saying: "The days will come in which vines shall grow, having each ten thousand branches, and in each branch ten thousand twigs, and in each twig ten thousand shoots, and in every one of the shoots ten thousand clusters, and on every one of the clusters ten thousand grapes." Language of this extravagant kind probably was inspired by a Jewish work, the *Apocalypse of Baruch,* which also predicts a ten thousand-fold fruitfulness of the earth in a coming age.

Justin Martyr, who may be dated at about the middle of the second century, is thought by some scholars to owe his millennial theories to Papias. In Justin's *Apologies* there is nothing to suggest chilasm, and there are even elements which tend to contradict this view, as when he states: "And when you hear that we look for a kingdom, you suppose without making any inquiry that we speak of a human kingdom; whereas we speak of that which is with God." And Justin thus speaks of the coming of Christ: "According to prophecy, He shall come from heaven with glory, accompanied by His angelic host, when also He shall raise the bodies of all men who have lived, and shall clothe those of the worthy with immortality, and shall send those of the wicked, endued with eternal sensibility, into everlasting fire with the wicked devils." In the *Dialogue,* the second coming of Christ is explained to involve the destruction of the devil and his angels, the end of death, and a crisis such that "some are sent to be punished unceasingly into judgment and condemnation of fire; but others shall exist in freedom from grief and in immortality." He says further: "There shall be a future possession for all the saints in this same land [of Palestine]. And hence all men everywhere, who believe in Christ, know that they shall be with Him in that land, and inherit everlasting and incorruptible good." Justin makes no place for a final conversion of the Jews. He consistently maintains that Christians are the true Israel and the inheritors of the promises made to the fathers.

In view of this teaching, much of which is rather clearly out of harmony with chiliastic belief, it comes as an interesting inconsistency that Justin in one place endorses millennial ideas. Acknowledging that "many who belong to the pure and pious faith and are true Christians, think otherwise," he yet says that he and others, "who are right-minded Christians on all points," are assured that there will be a resurrection of the dead, followed by a thousand-year period in rebuilt Jerusalem. At the end of the thousand years, says Justin, come the final resurrection and the judgment of all men.

The name of Justin Martyr may thus be added to that of Papias as a witness to the presence of premillennialism in the second century.

Sometimes claimed as another witness to chiliasm is *The Epistle of Barnabas,* a pseudonymous writing from the first half of the second century. Although it has much to say about the last things, it is without any reference whatever to a millennial reign of the saints with Christ in Jerusalem. "Barnabas" makes it plain that his idea of the coming of Christ is that of final judgment when he says: "The day is at hand, in which everything shall be destroyed with the Evil One. The Lord is near, and His reward." Barnabas's scheme of history was patterned after the creative week of Genesis 1. He held that the expression, "He finished in six days," implies that "the Lord will finish all things in six thousand years." The rest on the seventh day is said to contain the prophetic meaning: "when His Son coming [again] shall destroy the time of the wicked man, and judge the ungodly, and change the sun and the moon and the stars, then shall He truly rest on the seventh day." This is decidedly not according to the program of premillennialism. Neither the seventh day, nor the eighth day, of which Barnabas also speaks, is said to be a thousand years. The seventh day of rest will come only when iniquity has been abolished and the Lord has made everything new. The eighth day is the "beginning of another world." Any real

distinction between the seventh and eighth days is denied when Barnabas says that the Lord, in the act of giving rest to all things, will
make the beginning of the eighth day.

Barnabas cannot be adduced as a witness of early premillennialism. The course of future events as he deals with them rules out
the idea of a millennium of earthly blessedness for unregenerate
men brought forcibly under the reign of Christ and the saints.

Also to be dated from the first half of the second century is *The
Didache* or *The Teaching of the Twelve Apostles*. In the last chapter of this work of unknown authorship some have seen a testimony
to premillennialism. The pertinent part is as follows:

> Then shall appear the world-deceiver as a Son of God, and shall
> do signs and wonders, and the earth shall be given into his hands,
> and he shall commit iniquities which have never yet been done
> since the beginning. Then all the race shall come into the fire
> of trial, and many shall be made to stumble and perish. But
> they that endure in their faith shall be saved from under this
> curse. And then shall appear the signs of the truth; first the
> sign of an opening in the heaven, then the sign of a trumpet's
> sound, and thirdly the resurrection of the dead, yet not of all,
> but as it hath been said—The Lord will come and all the saints
> with Him. Then shall the world see the Lord coming upon the
> clouds of heaven.

It may be observed in the first place that the order of events
given here is very different from the common premillennial teaching.
There is nothing said about a rapture of the saints before the end-
time tribulation and the rule of Antichrist. Up to this point the
Didache is quite in line with what was seen to be the view of amillennialism and the view we called old-fashioned premillennialism.
When it is urged that the *Didache* advocates the premillennial view
because it makes an apparent distinction between the resurrection
of the saints and that of sinners, the ancient writer's point seems to
have been missed. His point is that the resurrection of the saints
is the final sign which will precede the Lord's coming. To this form
of language amillennialism can consent as well as old-fashioned
premillennialism. As the *Didache* does not develop the subject of
the consummation any further, it cannot be determined whether its

author was a millennialist or not. It may possibly be said that he was not apparently interested in the subject.

The survey of the literature of the first half of the second century would appear to call for the conclusion that the sweeping claims of premillennialists for the all but universal acceptance of their doctrine in the early church are not valid. Only two orthodox witnesses for chiliasm may be identified, and Justin, as was seen, is at best a highly inconsistent witness. There would seem to be good grounds for saying that most of the writers of this half century expected the coming of Christ to usher in the judgment of all men and the eternal kingdom of God. In my first article I said of amillennialism that it is an ancient and honorable view. Surely this is simple fact, these early Christian writers being witness.

That some of the historians should have represented the Christians of the second century as predominantly premillennial is probably due to a failure to see that a reference to the second coming of Christ is not necessarily also a confession of chiliastic views. Such a reference may indeed imply a point of view quite opposed to premillennialism and in line instead with the view of Christ's coming now popularly called amillennialism.

Let us now go on to make at least a beginning of the study of the period called by church historians the era of the Old Catholic Church.

Shedd says that "the period between the year 150 and 250 is the blooming age of millenarianism." He holds, however, that even at this time "it does not become the catholic faith, as embodied in the catholic creed."

Irenaeus, who wrote in the last quarter of the second century, is the name most often cited by premillennialists from this time. He was the first fully to develop a system of chiliastic teaching. He differs from the premillennialists of our day in failing to mention any period of conflict after the millennium. This is no doubt because of his view that the earthly kingdom is but a stage in the process of preparing the saints to inhabit eternity. He says: "The resurrection of the just takes place after the coming of Antichrist, and the destruction of all nations under his rule; in [the times of] which [resurrection] the righteous shall reign in the earth, waxing stronger by the sight of the Lord; and through Him they shall become accustomed to partake in the glory of the Father, and shall enjoy in the kingdom communion with the holy angels, and union with spiritual beings; and [with respect to] those whom the Lord shall find in the flesh, awaiting Him from heaven, and who have suffered tribulation, as well as escaped the hands of the Wicked One." To Irenaeus the millennium has no reference to the wicked; its benefits are exclusively for the saved. An amillennialist would not be too greatly troubled by the views of Irenaeus, for he avoids the—to the amillennialist—fatal mistake of extending to the unregenerate a "second chance," following the coming of the Lord. It would simply be said about his scheme that the rapture and resurrection of the saints are fully sufficient preparation for the eternal kingdom, the millennial era of preparation for that kingdom hardly appearing to be necessary.

In the next article our pace will be more rapid. We shall survey the fortunes of millennialism in the third and fourth centuries, see why it disappeared, note its reemergence centuries later in new forms, and complete, though perhaps all too cursorily, our history of the millennial discussion.

III. *The Millennial Discussion Continues*

In the second half of the second century arose the movement known as Montanism. Chiliasm was prominent in the teaching of the Montanists. Tertullian was influenced by Montanism. It is chiefly in his Montanist writings that his eschatological views are to be found. Although at times Tertullian seems to think of eternity as immediately following the resurrection, chiliasm is an essential element in his teaching.

A strong reaction soon set in against the Montanists. The Montanist prophets claimed to be special organs of the Holy Spirit giving a last authoritative message to the church before the consummation. The Montanist extravagances were a telling factor in stirring up the opposition that was to arise to chiliasm in the third century.

About the year 200, Gaius, a presbyter of Rome, attacked the chiliastic ideas of the Montanist Proclus. Gaius declared that millennialism was the invention of the heretic Cerinthus. In his opposition to the materialistic interpretations placed upon the Book of Revelation by the Montanists, Gaius went to the extreme of asserting that its author was Cerinthus.

Besides Gaius there was still another Roman presbyter in the first quarter of the third century who was interested in eschatology. This was Hippolytus, who, according to Dr. Stonehouse, "as an exegete, apologist and polemicist . . . is the best representative of his time, and in many respects presages the conclusions to which the church as a whole was to come only after a longer development."

Hippolytus was active in opposing Montanism in the West, but he avoided the radical extremes of Gaius. Hippolytus did not share in the chiliastic expectations held by many in his day. In his treatise on the Antichrist, he says that his aim is to discuss Antichrist's character and the time of his coming, "and how he shall stir up tribulation and persecution against the saints; and what his end shall be; and how the sudden appearing of the Lord shall be revealed from heaven; and what the conflagration of the whole world shall be; and what the glorious and heavenly kingdom of the saints is to be, when they reign together with Christ; and what the eternal punishment of the wicked by fire." This is evidently the general outline of events to which Hippolytus holds. As he enlarges his theme in the course of his treatise, quoting extensively from the Old Testament prophets and from all parts of the New Testament, it is made clear that he expects the saints to undergo tribulation at the hands of Antichrist. Then the Lord will come—to use Hippolytus's own words, "What remains but the coming of our Lord and Saviour Jesus Christ from heaven, for whom we have looked in hope? who shall bring the conflagration and just judgment upon all who have refused to believe on him."

In a passage in his commentary, Hippolytus again speaks of the last events of history. When he tells how the Son of God will come from heaven, he insists that the earthly is done away and the heavenly begins, "that the eternal and indestructible kingdom of the saints may appear." And he says, "When the Judge of judges and King of kings comes from heaven He will destroy all His enemies, and punish all with an eternal fire, and will give the eternal kingdom to His servants."

Harnack lists Hippolytus among the chiliasts, but this is an evident mistake. It is perhaps to be explained by the fact that Hippolytus uses the familiar idea of the creative week as a pattern for human history. The seventh day, however, is, in his teaching, clearly a type of the believer's eternal rest, for he says of the kingdom to be established then: "Finally earthly things shall end, and heavenly things begin; that the indissoluble and everlasting kingdom of the saints may be brought to view, and the heavenly king manifested to all . . . Son of God and Son of man—coming from heaven as the world's Judge."

The testimony of Hippolytus is especially significant because of the fact that he gave so much attention to the prophecies of Scripture. His views are entirely out of accord with both the chiliasm of his day and dispensational premillennialism. To use a modern term, the distinguished leader Hippolytus was an amillennialist.

It was from the Alexandrian school of theologians that chiliasm was to receive its deathblow in the early church. Clement of Alexandria was not primarily concerned about the last things, but he often refers to the second coming and to the great final judgment. He makes no mention of a millennium, but this has been explained as due more to philosophical than exegetical considerations. Clement's Platonism inclined him to take a spiritual view of the future age.

Origen was the successor of Clement as the head of the school at Alexandria. He also was influenced by Platonism, and in his exegesis of Scripture he was often guilty of extreme allegorizing. His spiritual viewpoint excluded chiliasm. He was outspoken against those who looked for the setting up of a material kingdom on earth. Yet Origen's method of interpretation did not lead him to the length of ignoring the great facts of Bible teaching. He regarded as sure the coming of Antichrist and the personal return of the Lord Jesus.

Hagenbach, in his *History of Doctrines,* says that the contest in which Origen had engaged with the chiliasts ended, soon after his death, in practically complete victory for his opinions. Origen's disciple Dionysius became bishop of Alexandria and succeeded in persuading the followers of a certain bishop Nepos, headed by the presbyter Coracion, to give up their millennial views. Hagenbach observes that "millenarianism was from that time supported by but a few of the eastern theologians."

Cyprian of Carthage is another prominent name from this period. Although he was a disciple of Tertullian and has often been listed among the chiliasts, it does not appear that he looked for an earthly kingdom. He held with Tertullian that the end was imminent, and he shared the notion, so often found in the teaching of chiliasts that the world was to last six thousand years. He is very clear, however, that when Christ comes it will be as a judge. He conceives Christ's rule as king to be a reign in eternity, in a kingdom which is not to be thought, in any sense, as of this world, and a kingdom that is unending.

Methodius, bishop of Olympus in Lycia, who was martyred in 311, held to a spiritualized form of chiliasm. The historian Eusebius, who lived at this same general period, had a very low opinion of chiliasm and chiliasts. Western leaders who were millennialists were Commodian, Lactantius, and Victorinus. Lactantius, says Shedd, was "the only man of any note in the fourth century who defended the system."

Athanasius, bishop of Alexandria from 329 to 373, had a simply stated eschatology. Nowhere does he speak of the future kingdom of Christ as earthly and temporary. When Jesus comes He will judge the world; the good will receive the heavenly kingdom and the evil will be cast into the eternal fire and outer darkness spoken of by the Lord. The Athanasian Creed expresses his view succinctly: "at whose [Christ's] coming all men shall rise again with their bodies, and shall give account of their own works."

Reference must be made to Augustine, the greatest theologian of his age. In the *City of God*, he says that he was once himself a millennialist, but has come to reject the chiliastic view as "carnal." He understands the binding of Satan referred to in Revelation 20 as the fulfilment of Jesus' cryptic words: "No man can enter into a strong man's house, and spoil his goods, except he first bind the strong man." Augustine says that Satan is the strong man, and he is bridled and restrained in power so that he cannot seduce and gain possession of those who are to be freed. The reigning of the saints with Christ is to be regarded as a present actuality. The first resurrection is unto spiritual life; the second resurrection is unto physical life and occurs at the coming of Christ. The living saints will be caught up to meet Him in the air. The unrighteous will be raised for their everlasting judgment. Then will appear new heavens and a new earth in which the glorified people of God shall dwell.

The views of Augustine were so generally accepted that S. J. Case was led to remark that Augustine laid "the ghost of millenarianism so effectively that for centuries the subject is practically ignored."

The survey of eschatological teaching from the year 150 to the age of Augustine indicates that chiliasm, though for a season flourishing in both the East and the West, was still by no means at any time universally held. In every generation there were those who rejected it in favor of the view that when Christ comes it will be to judge the wicked and to set up, not an earthly and temporary kingdom, but a heavenly and eternal one. The weight of early Christian opinion would seem to be much more on the side of what is now called amillennialism than on that of premillennialism.

Millennialism Since Augustine

Millennialism appeared occasionally in the Middle Ages, though Hagenbach says it was the heretical sects that from time to time revived it. The approach of the year 1000 stirred an almost universal apprehension that the end of the world was at hand. This was due, however, not to premillennial beliefs but to a widely held notion that the thousand years spoken of in Revelation 20 commenced with the first advent of Christ. The establishment of the church was regarded as the first resurrection and as the first epoch of the kingdom of a thousand years. This explains the great excitement that prevailed as the year 1000 drew close.

At the time of the Reformation, millennialism reappeared: it was an item in the teaching of the heretical sect, the Anabaptists. The last article of the Lutheran Augsburg Confession reflects the prevailing Protestant opinion and condemns chiliasm. The Confession states that its framers "reject all those who spread the Jewish opinion, that prior to the resurrection of the dead the pious shall receive the administration of the world and then shall bring the ungodly under subjection."

Calvin reveals what amounts to contempt for millennial ideas when, in Book III, Chapter 25, of the *Institutes,* he says that Satan has tried to corrupt the doctrine of the resurrection by various fictions: "not to mention that he began to oppose it in the days of Paul, not long after arose the millenarians, who limited the reign of Christ to a thousand years. Their fiction is too puerile to require or deserve refutation." Calvin's treatment of the resurrection makes it plain that he regards the coming of Christ as having reference both to the eternal blessedness of the saints and the eternal condemnation of the wicked.

The English Confession of Edward VI, which was later condensed into the Thirty-nine Articles, condemns millennialism in nearly the same terms as those used in the Augsburg Confession. Shedd points out that the Belgic Confession "guards the statement respecting the second advent of Christ, by teaching that the time of its occurrence is unknown to all created beings, and that it will not take place until the number of the elect is complete." The Confession thus rules out the possibility of a millennial salvation for those who had not received Christ prior to His return. The Second Helvetic Confession is very strongly worded; the article on judgment contains this sentence: "Moreover, we reject the Jewish dreams that there will be before the day of judgment a golden age upon the earth and that the pious will take possession of the kingdoms of the world, after their enemies, the ungodly, have been subdued. For the truth of the Evangelists (Matthew XXIV and XXV; Luke XVIII in like manner) and the Apostolic teaching (II Thessalonians II and in II Timothy III and IV) are found to present something very different" (Chapter XI, Article 14).

As a final example of the position taken in the creeds of Protestantism, I cite the teaching of the Westminster Confession of Faith and Catechisms as given in the answers to Questions 87 and 88 of the Larger Catechism:

> We are to believe, that, at the last day, there shall be a general resurrection of the dead, both of the just and unjust: when they that are then found alive shall in a moment be changed; and the self-same bodies of the dead which are laid in the grave, being then again united to their souls for ever, shall be raised up by the power of Christ. ·The bodies of the just, by the Spirit of Christ, and by virtue of his resurrection as their head, shall be raised in power, spiritual, and incorruptible, and made like to his glorious body: and the bodies of the wicked shall be raised up in dishonor by him as an offended judge.

> Immediately after the resurrection shall follow the general and final judgment of angels and men: the day and hour whereof no man knoweth, that all may watch and pray; and be ever ready for the coming of the Lord.

Although there were several premillennialists in the membership of the Westminster Assembly, it is abundantly clear that the premillennial view received little comfort in the doctrinal statements handed down to us by that justly revered body of learned theologians.

The foregoing review of the creeds of the leading Protestant bodies shows a consensus of formal opinion that is definitely opposed to millennialism. It is the historic position of Protestantism that the coming of Christ is the signal for the general and final judgment. The amillennial view of the Lord's return has at least the advantage of being squarely in line with the great Reformation creeds.

It was early in the seventeenth century that postmillennialism began to be seriously advanced among Protestants. Whitby's treatise on the millennium is often credited with being the first statement of the point of view that Revelation 20 refers, as Brookes phrases it, "to a spiritual millennium, consisting in a universal triumph of the Gospel, and the conversion of all nations, for a thousand years before the coming of Christ." The origins of postmillennialism, however, go much further back. As was seen, there is an approach to postmillennialism in some medieval expositors. The Scottish divine, James Durham (1622-1658), expressed the opinion that the millennium began about the year 1560. John Bunyan slightly antedates Whitby; in his tract, *The New Jerusalem*, he expounds Revelation 20 in terms of the postmillennial conception.

The foremost defender of postmillennialism in the last century was David Brown, whose *Second Advent* is an able presentation of the view. The leading postmillennialists since Brown were Charles Hodge and B. B. Warfield. Postmillennialism never found expression in any of the great creeds. Its influence in our own day seems to be very slight in conservative circles.

Premillennialism is today, as has been the case for fifty years, the most vocal of the three leading views of the Lord's coming. In the eighteenth and nineteenth centuries a great interest in chiliasm arose that continues strong to the present moment. The expositor Bengel is recognized as the one who gave the real impetus to the revival of premillennialism. Other great names associated with its rising tide of acceptance were Alford, Lange, Delitzsch, Bonar, Tregelles, and Zahn.

Notice ought to be taken of the origin of the prevailing form of premillennialism—that which was, in my first article, called dispensational premillennialism. Old-fashioned premillennialism, which is not without numerous adherents in our time, holds that the second coming of Christ will be open, glorious, visible to all the world. Dispensational premillennialism holds to a coming of Christ in two stages: the first is marked by the secret rapture of the saints, who are caught away to meet the Lord in the air; the second reveals the Lord to all the world, which for seven years has lain in the grip of the Antichrist and is at Jesus' return to the earth released to enjoy His millennial reign.

This new form of premillennialism was introduced about 1830 in the writings of J. N. Darby, a leader of the group that came to be known as the Plymouth Brethren. W. E. Blackstone's *Jesus Is Coming* spread the view far and wide in America. In recent years *The Scofield Reference Bible* has been the great textbook of dispensational premillennialism.

Any contest that is being carried on with premillennialism today is being waged mainly by amillennialism. Some critics of the latter view have been disposed to regard it as a form of postmillennialism, or as a retreat of a rather recent origin from that prophetic position. The preceding review of the history of the millennial discussion has, however, made it plain that what is now called amillennialism for lack of a better term, is an exceedingly ancient and respectable point of view. The conclusion has already been stated that the great weight of traditional opinion. is to be characterized as amillennial. And the claim of some premillennialists to have the support of the overwhelming testimony of church history has been shown to be groundless. The judgment of Shedd has been seen to be entirely correct that "millenarianism was never the ecumenical faith of the church, and never entered as an article into any of the creeds; that millenarianism has been the opinion of individuals and parties only —some of whom have stood in agreement with the catholic faith, and some in opposition to it."

The question of the relative merit of the three views of the coming of Christ is not, of course, to be settled by a weighing of historical testimony or the adding together of names of authorities. We can only be satisfied of the correctness of a doctrine if it is found to be clearly taught in the Holy Scriptures. In the next article we shall begin to consider the teaching of the New Testament on the doctrine of the return of the Lord Jesus Christ.

IV. *The Structure and Terms of New Testament Eschatology*

A large assignment is to be undertaken in this article. Here we must quickly examine the broad patterns of the New Testament teaching about the things to come, and we must begin the survey of the terms the New Testament uses to denote the second advent of the Lord Jesus Christ. This done we shall be in a position to look closely, in the several following articles, at the passages dealing in detail with the return of Christ.

Three main patterns are to be found in New Testament eschatology. The first is what we may call the "last days" concept. The New Testament point of view is that the "last days" began with the first advent of Jesus Christ (cf. Heb. 1:1, 2; Acts 2:17; I John

2:18; James 5:3; I Pet. 1:20; Heb. 9:26). The impression one gains from such passages as these is that with the incarnation of Christ was introduced the final period of the world's history.

A second pattern found in New Testament eschatology is called by the noted scholar Geerhardus Vos the "semi-eschatology" of the New Testament. By this term he refers to the way in which Paul, for example, regards the heavenly world and the earthly sphere as parallel states, to both of which believers in Christ belong. The advent, death, and resurrection of Christ have thus not only brought in the last days or period of world history, but have actually introduced the Christian into the eternal order. This has come about through the ascension of Christ to the right hand of God. Believers in Christ are mystically united to Him, and they therefore in a spiritual sense inhabit with Him the eternal world (heaven) while they are physically in this world. This is the thought to be taken from Ephesians 2:6: "God hath raised us up together and made us sit together in heavenly places in Christ Jesus" (cf. Phil. 3:20; Eph. 1:3; Col. 3:1-3).

It is to be pointed out that Paul's emphasis on the Christian's relation to the upper world by virtue of his union with Christ does not in the least tone down the hope of the Lord's personal return. Paul's purpose was to drive home the truth that a believer in Jesus is primarily an other-worldly person. It is as he sees this that a Christian will really cherish the hope of Christ's second coming, that glorious coming which will make an actuality the experience of spiritual exaltation now possessed only incipiently by the believer. The personal return of Christ is presented as all that awaits to complete the transition through which God's people are passing from the earthly to the heavenly state. For then will occur the resurrection of their bodies, so that body as well as soul may inhabit the eternal order, redemption thus becoming complete.

Two lines of eschatological development in the teaching of the New Testament have now been very quickly traced. The third has to do with the frequent antithesis that is made between the age in which we live and the age which is to come. This antithesis appears clearly in Paul's writings in such a passage as Ephesians 1:21, where he speaks of Christ as having been exalted "far above all principality, and power, and might, and dominion, and every name that is named, not only in this world [age], but also in that which is to come." Here the evident intention is to assert the absolute supremacy of Christ. By his comprehensive language, the apostle brings all history, present and future, under the sway of Christ.

There are several other passages in Paul where the antithesis is found, though in these by implication. Romans 12:2, for example, bids believers not to be conformed "to this world [age]," but to be transformed; and the thought is evidently that they are to pattern themselves after the life that will be theirs in the age to come. I Corinthians 1:20 asks the rhetorical question: "Where is the disputer of this world [age]? hath not God made foolish the wisdom of this world?" Here the wisdom of this world is set plainly in contrast with that of the world to come, or more specifically, with that of the world above, which is, as we have seen, also to be the world that is to come. (Cf. also II Cor. 4:4; Gal. 1:4; Eph. 2:2.)

The antithetical structure often to be found in Paul's eschatology is not first encountered there. It is introduced to us in the teaching of our Lord. There also the distinction between the two ages appears both explicitly and by implication. A passage where the contrast between the ages is made is Mark 10:30. Jesus has said that no man shall leave family or possessions for His sake and the gospel's "but he shall receive an hundred-fold now in this time, houses, and brethren, and sisters, and mothers, and children, and lands, with persecutions; and in the world to come eternal life." Here the two members of the antithesis are "this time" and "the world to come." Evidently the world to come is the final order, for in it the follower of Christ is to have eternal life.

Even more significant is Jesus' word in Matthew 12:31, 32: "Wherefore I say unto you, All manner of sin and blasphemy shall be forgiven unto men: but the blasphemy against the Holy Ghost shall not be forgiven unto men. And whosoever speaketh a word against the Son of man, it shall be forgiven him: but whosoever speaketh against the Holy Ghost, it shall not be forgiven him, neither in this world [age], neither in the world to come [neither in the coming one]." The thought is plain that by the expressions "this world" and "the world to come" Jesus comprehends universal history. This is made still more clear by the parallel passage, Mark 3:29: "He that shall blaspheme against the Holy Ghost hath never forgiveness, but is in danger of eternal damnation [is guilty of an eternal sin]."

One more reference remains to be examined, Luke 20:34-36: "And Jesus answering said unto them, The children of this world marry, and are given in marriage: but they which shall be accounted worthy to obtain that world, and the resurrection from the dead, neither marry, nor are given in marriage: neither can they die any more: for they are equal unto the angels; and are the children of God, being the children of the resurrection." Again there is the distinction between "this age" and "that age" which is to come; again the whole panorama of the future is presented. But there is an important added detail. It has to do with the great event which introduces the age to come. The great eschatological crisis which is to usher in the coming age is said to be the resurrection of the dead; it is this momentous event which bisects universal history. We thus gain the following outline of events: 1. This age (of the gospel of Christ); 2. The resurrection; 3. That age, or the age to come.

The step may now be taken of identifying with the second advent of Christ the dividing-point between this age and the age to come. Among prophetic students of all shades of opinion it is agreed that the bodies of believers will be raised at the second coming of the Lord (cf. I Thess. 4:16). The outline thus becomes: 1. This age; 2. The second advent of Christ; 3. That age, or the age to come.

The question may now be asked: Do these preliminary considerations in the analysis of New Testament eschatology tend to favor any one of the three views about the coming of Christ more than the others?

Let it be at once admitted that a case has not yet been made for any view. And yet premillennialism must be felt to have received something of a reverse from the fact that the New Testament sums up universal history in terms of "this age" and "the age to come."

The premillennial scheme looks upon universal history as consisting of "this age," the millennial age, and the eternal age.

A point appears against modern postmillennialism also. The New Testament characterizes the age that is to run until the second advent as "this present evil world [age]." Such a characterization tends to negate the common postmillennial notion that the world will be converted before the return of Christ and enjoy an age of righteousness.

The amillennial view has it that Christ will come back to a world still torn by strife and wickedness, that He will deliver His saints and raise the dead (the righteous to be with Him, the wicked to their final judgment), that Christ at His return will introduce the eternal order. The conclusion may be ventured that the broad outlines of New Testament eschatology do not seem to embarrass the amillennial view. It must remain for the detailed exegesis of the advent passages to settle the issue.

New Testament Expressions for the Second Coming

Every New Testament writer makes mention of the return of Jesus Christ. A variety of terms is used to denote this great consummating event. It is important to survey these terms. One reason is that many premillennialists seek to represent the coming of Christ as in two stages, stages which in certain instances are to be distinguished from each other on the basis of the term used. The two stages or aspects are called respectively "the rapture" and "the revelation." By the rapture is meant the sudden and possibly secret coming of Christ in the air to catch away from the earth the resurrected bodies of those who have died in the faith and with them the living saints. Then is supposed to ensue a seven-year tribulation (some do not limit it to seven years), which is concluded by the glorious and visible appearing of Christ upon the earth. This is "the revelation" and marks the beginning of the millennium. By many premillennial interpreters a sharp distinction is thus made between the coming of Christ for His saints and the coming of Christ with His saints.

Admitting that not all of the terms used to denote the second coming of Christ make exact reference to one or the other aspect of the second advent, premillennialists of this persuasion hold that some of these terms apply exclusively to one stage of the Saviour's coming. Dr. Feinberg, for example, distinguishes between "the day of Christ" and "the day of the Lord." The following quotation will indicate his reasoning:

> In the Rapture the Church is seen removed from the earth; in the Revelation she is seen returning with Christ. At the first event Israel is unaffected; in the second she has all her covenants fulfilled. Evil does not come into view when Christ takes His own to Himself; when He comes with them, evil is ended, Satan is judged, and the man of sin and the false prophet are destroyed. In the first event there are no signs to mark its approach and it is a timeless event; in the second event there are signs to precede its approach and it has a specific time and place in the prophetic scheme of the Scriptures. One is spoken of as the "Day of Christ" and the other is referred to as the "Day of the Lord." . . . Surely, then, premillennialists are warranted in distinguishing between the Rapture, which is solely Church truth, and the Revelation, which concerns all on the earth also.

The New Testament never speaks of the return of Christ as His "second coming." The leading New Testament terms for the return of Christ are, in transliterated form, as follows: *parousia, apokalupsis epiphaneia, to telos, he sunteleia tou aionos, hemera* (which appears in a variety of combinations, as "day of judgment," "the last day," "the day of the Lord," "that day," "that great day," "day of God," "day of redemption," etc.).

The term *parousia* means presence; it is often translated "coming." It is recognized to be a technical term for the return of Christ. Sixteen instances of such use are to be found: Matthew 24:3, 27, 37, 39; I Corinthians 15:23; I Thessalonians 2:19; 3:13; 4:15; 5:23; II Thessalonians 2:1, 8; James 5:7, 8; II Peter 3:4, 12; I John 2:28. An examination of these passages discloses that associated with the coming of Christ are the resurrection of the sainted dead, the rapture of them and of living believers, the destruction of Antichrist, and tremendous cosmical changes. The *parousia* will be open and visible, like lightning, and will occur with great and startling suddenness.

The use of the word *parousia* gives no trace of the idea of a duplication or series of comings. It denotes a point of eventuation; it strikes a note of momentous finality. Its use in II Peter 3 would seem to indicate that the *parousia* introduces the eternal age to come. The exegesis of that chapter—to be later attempted—will disclose whether this is a legitimate inference.

The term *apokalupsis* means revelation. In most instances it denotes the disclosure of divine truth previously unknown. Dr. Feinberg connects four of the obviously eschatological uses of the term with the coming of Christ *for* His saints, "the rapture"; three passages using this word he refers to the coming of Christ *with* His saints, "the revelation." A reading of the passages (Rom. 8:19; I Cor. 1:7; I Thess. 1:7-10; I Pet. 1:7, 13; 4:13) indicates that the distinction drawn is purely arbitrary. The term *apokalupsis* denotes the second coming of Christ in glory. In its eschatological use it is synonymous with *parousia*. It shows that there will be associated with Christ's coming the blessing and comforting of the living saints and the pouring out of wrath upon the wicked and unbelieving. The emphasis is not on the retributive aspect of the *apokalupsis* of Christ but rather on the deliverance that will then be brought to believers. There is the same element of momentous finality, however, in this term as was seen to be associated with *parousia*.

The word *epiphaneia* is used six times in the New Testament, five times being translated "appearing" and once "brightness." The latter translation is found in II Thessalonians 2:8, where it is said that when the Lord comes He will destroy the man of sin "with the *epiphaneia* of His coming." In I Timothy 6:14 *epiphaneia* stands alone as the term used for Jesus' coming; the apostle has enjoined Timothy to keep his charge unrebukable "until the appearing of our Lord Jesus Christ." II Timothy 1:10 uses the word for the first advent of Christ. II Timothy 4:1, however, uses *epiphaneia* in the clear eschatological sense: "The Lord Jesus Christ shall judge the quick and the dead at his *appearing* and his kingdom." In the eighth verse of the same chapter Paul speaks of the reward that will be given to all those who love Christ's appearing (*epiphaneia*). The term by its use in this one chapter is seen to have reference to the advent of Christ, the judgment of living and dead, the bringing in of Christ's kingdom, and the rewarding of His faithful people. Titus 2:13 completes the list of verses using *epiphaneia*.

Even though used only infrequently, *epiphaneia* is clearly a term that may safely be classed with *parousia* and *apokalupsis* as a technical designation of the second coming of Christ. It too suggests the thought of the manifesting of Christ's glory openly and visibly, and the thought of reward for Christ's servants and judgment for the wicked.

Dr. Feinberg makes a significant admission when he says after his own examination of these words: "We conclude, then, that from a study of the Greek words [*parousia, apokalupsis, epiphaneia*] themselves, the distinction between the coming of Christ for His saints and with His saints is not to be gleaned." As our study of these terms has indicated, the conclusion may also be stated that their use in the New Testament all but forbids the making of any such artificial distinction as that made by some premillennialists between "the rapture" and "the revelation." The use of these terms for the second coming of the Lord shows that the second advent of Christ is one coming, having reference both to the righteous and to the wicked.

To telos—"the end"—is the standing New Testament designation for the end of the world. This is the meaning the expression has in the teaching of our Lord (cf. Matt. 24:6-14). Paul uses the expression in I Corinthians 1:8. He speaks of the Corinthians as waiting for the coming of Christ, "who shall confirm [them] unto the end, that they may be blameless in the day of our Lord Jesus Christ." Thus *to telos* comes into connection with the second coming of Christ. This it does also in I Corinthians 15:24. The detailed exegesis of the passage must wait for later treatment, but it may be pointed out that here it is apparently taught that the coming of Christ brings in "the end": "But every man in his own order: Christ the first fruits, afterward they that are Christ's at his coming. Then cometh the end [literally: then the end], when he shall have delivered up the kingdom to God." II Corinthians 1:13, 14 also connects "the end" with the day of Christ's coming. (Cf. also I Peter 4:7.)

There is reason to conclude that *to telos* used eschatologically designates the return of Christ in glory. It is a term well fitted to convey the same idea of momentous finality that was seen to be conveyed in the other expressions we have studied.

In a continuation of this article we shall conclude the survey of the New Testament terms for the second coming.

V. *The Day of the Lord Jesus Christ*

Our study of the terms used in the New Testament to refer to the second coming of Christ has introduced to us these expressions: *parousia* or coming, *apokalupsis* or revelation, *epiphaneia* or appearing, *to telos* or the end. Now let us consider the phrase *sunteleia tou aionos* or consummation of the age, and the word *hemera* (day) in the various combinations in which it bears an eschatological significance.

Jesus uses the expression *sunteleia tou aionos* twice in the parable of the wheat and the tares (Matt. 13:36-43) and once in the related parable of the drag-net (Matt. 13:49). Each time it is translated "the end of the world [the age]." The term clearly denotes the final harvesting of the world, when the wicked are to be separated from the good and destroyed. The phrase comes again from the lips of Jesus in Matthew 28:20, where the Saviour gives that great promise to His disciples: "Lo, I am with you alway, even unto the end of the world." Here the suggestion is plain that the Lord will maintain fellowship with His followers so long as time runs on, that is, until the very end of time—"the end of the world." All agree that the end of the period to which Jesus was referring in the promise that accompanied the Great Commission is marked by the personal return of the Son of God. The conclusion that is therefore reached for the significance of the expression *sunteleia tou aionos* is the same as that for the terms already studied. The consummation of the age has associated with it the return of Christ, the blessing of the righteous, and the judgment of the wicked.

The word *hemera* appears in a variety of combinations. Sometimes standing alone as "the day" or "that day," it more often is joined with modifying phrases, as "day of judgment," "the last day," "the day of Christ," "the day of the Lord," "the day of God."

Matthew 10:15; 11:22, 24; 12:36; and Luke 10:12 speak of "the day of judgment," when it will be "more tolerable" for Sodom and Gomorrah than for the cities that have rejected the ministry of Christ, and when men shall give an account even for the idle words that they have spoken. II Peter 2:9 says that the ungodly will be reserved for punishment until "the day of judgment." In the next chapter Peter indicates (3:7) that "the day of judgment and perdition of ungodly men" will be a day of fiery destruction for the earth and the heavens. This day he also calls the "day of the Lord," which, he goes on to say, will come as unexpectedly as a thief in the night. This is the same way in which, in other places in Scripture, it is said that the coming of Christ will occur. And indeed the subject under discussion in the third chapter of II Peter is the *parousia*. The inference seems an entirely legitimate and even inescapable one that the day of judgment is at the coming of the Lord.

Romans 2:5, Jude 6, and I John 4:17 are general references to the day of judgment.

It is in the Gospel of John that the expression "the last day" appears. John 6:39-54 has four instances of its occurrence. In each case Jesus is teaching that He will at the last day raise up those who believe on Him. Martha shows that she has grasped this truth when, in John 11:24, she says that she knows her dead brother Lazarus will rise at the resurrection in the last day. Very significant is John 12:48, for it shows that not only will the righteous be raised at the last day, but the wicked will then be judged: "He that rejecteth me, and receiveth not my words, hath one that judgeth him: the word that I have spoken, the same shall judge him in the last day."

Related to these passages dealing with the last day is the section, John 5:22-29, in which Jesus expounds His authority as judge and life-giver. The Saviour thus concludes: "Marvel not at this: for the hour is coming, in the which all that are in the graves shall hear his voice [the voice of the Son of God], and shall come forth: they that have done good, unto the resurrection of life; and they that have done evil, unto the resurrection of damnation." Here "the hour" is evidently used as the equivalent of "the last day." According to the premillennial scheme, "the hour" and "the last day" of which Jesus speaks refer to a period of at least a thousand years' duration, for that length of time is supposed to intervene between the resurrection of the righteous and the resurrection of the wicked. It is difficult to accept this interpretation in view of the way our Lord places the two resurrections in closest connection with no slightest hint of any separation in time between them. It would rather seem that the terms "the hour" and "the last day" carry with them the same absolute finality found to be associated with the more usual designations of the coming of the Lord.

In the synoptic teaching of Jesus the expression "that day" is often used: Matthew 7:22, "that day" when Jesus judges and casts out the workers of iniquity who falsely claim to have served Him; 24:36, "that day" of His coming, of which no man knows, but only the Father; 26:29, "that day" of His kingdom when the Lord will again drink of the fruit of the vine with His disciples; Luke 21:34, 35, "that day" for which Jesus' disciples are to watch lest it come on them unawares, "for as a snare shall it come on all them that dwell on the face of the whole earth"; Luke 17:24-37, "that day" when the Lord's people are taken to be with Him and judgment fire falls on the rest of the world.

In Paul's teaching also "that day" has an aspect of reference to the wicked. Some attention has already been given to the eschatological section in II Thessalonians 1, so that now it is necessary but to mention that it is there taught that when the Lord comes to comfort and deliver His afflicted people, it will also be His purpose to judge and punish the wicked "in that day." In II Timothy 4:8 Paul again uses "that day" in connection with the second coming of Christ.

We come finally to the consideration of the use of the word *hemera* in such phrases as "the day of the Lord," "the day of Christ," "the day of God." It is at this point that premillennialists who hold to the idea of a secret rapture assert that the distinction they make between "the rapture" and "the revelation" is marked out. In the Scofield Reference Bible, for example, is a footnote on page 1212* which says that the "day of Christ" relates wholly to the reward and blessing of saints at His coming, as "day of the Lord" is connected with judgment. In the course of the examination of the passages using these terms, it will be seen whether the distinction claimed by C. I. Scofield, Dr. Feinberg, and others is a valid one.

The Scofield Reference Bible lists only six occurrences of the phrase "the day of Christ." Properly to be included in such a list, however, are the verses in Luke 17 that speak of "the day of the Son of man," a phrase that is exactly equivalent to "the day of Christ." Luke 17:24, for example, in comparing the second advent to the flash of lightning across the sky, says, "So shall also the Son of man be in his day." Verses 29 and 30 add: "But the same day that Lot went out of Sodom it rained fire and brimstone from heaven, and destroyed them all. Even thus shall it be in the day when the Son of man is revealed." These texts would seem to make it very clear that the "day of Christ [or the day of the Son of man]" has by no means reference exclusively to the righteous. The passage referred to makes it unmistakable that in the day when Jesus comes again for His people, destruction is meted out to the wicked.

The remaining passages where the term "the day of Christ [day of Jesus Christ, day of the Lord Jesus]" appears are I Corinthians 1:8; 5:5; II Corinthians 1:14; Philippians 1:6, 10; 2:16. In these the reference is exclusively to Christians; Paul's purpose is to impress on them the need of holiness and to comfort them with the promise of Christ's return.

The expression "the day of the Lord" appears in three passages: I Thessalonians 5:2-5; II Thessalonians 2:2 (where the translation in the King James Version is "day of Christ" but should be, according to the best manuscripts, "day of the Lord"); II Peter 3:10. In Acts 2:20 Peter quotes from Joel concerning the coming of the "great and notable day of the Lord." With this we are not so much concerned, for in Old Testament prophecy the day of the Lord does

---

*Editor's Note: The pagination is that of the older *Scofield Reference Bible*. The *New Scofield Reference Bible* (New York: Oxford University Press, 1967) did not appear until long after this article was written. In it, see p. 1233.

not have a fixed reference. (Cf. Isa. 10:3; 13:6; Amos 5:18; Hos. 1:11; Joel 2:31; 3:14; Mal. 4:5.) It is, however, true that the most characteristic features of the Old Testament "day of Jehovah" have their consummate fulfilment in the New Testament "day of the Lord."

The expression "the day of the Lord" first appears in the New Testament (elsewhere than in a quotation) in I Thessalonians 5. Paul has dealt in the preceding chapter with the comforting hope of the coming of Christ to gather His people unto Himself. Paul goes on then to say:

> But of the times and the seasons, brethren, ye have no need that I write unto you. For yourselves know perfectly that the day of the Lord so cometh as a thief in the night. For when they shall say, Peace and safety; then sudden destruction cometh upon them, as travail upon a woman with child; and they shall not escape. But ye, brethren, are not in darkness, that that day should overtake you as a thief.

It is difficult to see how in the face of this passage any distinction between the "day of Christ" and the "day of the Lord" can be maintained. It seems to be clearly taught here that the day of the Lord is to be looked for by Christians. It is the time when the righteous dead shall be raised and living believers transformed and translated with them. It is also the time when the wicked shall be overwhelmed; the day of the Lord will come unexpectedly upon them and they shall not escape from its vengeance.

Almost as great an obstacle in the way of the distinction some would make between the rapture and the revelation is imposed by II Thessalonians 2. Here Paul says in part:

> Now we beseech you, brethren, by the coming of our Lord Jesus Christ, and by our gathering together unto him, that ye be not soon shaken in mind, or be troubled, neither by spirit, nor by word, nor by letter as from us, as that the day of the Lord is at hand. Let no man deceive you by any means: for that day shall not come, except there come a falling away first, and that man of sin be revealed, the son of perdition.

This passage seems to say plainly that Paul views the day of the Lord as the time when Christ shall come for His people. Here he seeks to enlarge on the thought given in I Thessalonians 5 that the day of the Lord will not overtake Christians "as a thief." They are to understand that certain events must occur before Christ appears. There will be a falling away, or an apostasy; and the man of sin, or Antichrist, will come forth to oppose God and His truth.

The force of this is evaded by C. I. Scofield, who advances the interpretation that verse 7 of II Thessalonians 2 indicates that the rapture of the church occurs before the appearance of Antichrist. The verse is as follows: "For the mystery of iniquity doth already work; only he who now letteth will let, until he be taken out of the way [more accurately: only until he who now hindereth be removed]. And then shall that wicked be revealed." Scofield says about this that the restrainer is a person—"he," and since a "mystery" always implies a supernatural element, this Person can be no other than the Holy Spirit in the church, to be "taken out of the way." In my judgment this is curious reasoning and may even be called a forced interpretation. The related passage, I Thessalonians 5, and the obvious connection of the day of the Lord as spoken of in II Thessalonians 2:2 with the earthly life of believers make it impossible to understand the phrase "the day of the Lord" as in any way different in meaning from the day of Christ's return for His people.

There remains to be considered the use of "day" in II Peter 3. The word appears here in two combinations: "the day of the Lord" and "the day of God." Peter says:

> But the day of the Lord will come as a thief in the night; in the which the heavens shall pass away with a great noise, and the elements shall melt with fervent heat, the earth also and the works that are therein shall be burned up. . . . [Ye ought to be] looking for and hasting unto the coming of the day of God, wherein the heavens being on fire shall be dissolved, and the elements shall melt with fervent heat.

"The day of the Lord" is at once seen to be the same in meaning as "the day of God." But it is also the same in meaning as *parousia*. As was earlier pointed out, Peter's purpose in this chapter of his epistle is to assure believers that in spite of the skepticism of the scoffers the Lord will surely come again. For the scoffers His coming (*parousia*) will mean overwhelming destruction, like that of the earth. It is a dread day indeed for the unbeliever. But for the Christian it is a day for which he is to prepare by a holy manner of life, by true godliness; it is a day for which he is to look and toward which he is to hasten with eagerness, because for him it will mean the ushering in of eternal glory in a new heaven and a new earth.

I have often wondered why the Scofield Bible offers no explanation of this passage. Dr. Feinberg, who in so many ways follows the Scofield system and thus is also a representative of dispensational premillennialism, speaks passingly of II Peter 3, as follows:

> It is objected further [to premillennialism] that a great conflagration takes place at the coming of Christ, according to the prophecy of Peter. The apostle speaks in his Second Epistle of the burning of the heavens and the earth and their displacement by the new heavens and new earth wherein dwelleth righteousness. It is impossible, so goes the objection, for all this to happen before the alleged millennium. Premillennialsits do not place this before the millennium, but after it.

Now it is all very well for premillennialists to say that they place II Peter 3 after the millennium; there is of course nothing else to do and maintain any semblance of the chiliastic scheme. It is another matter entirely for them to show that they have the right so to treat II Peter 3. Careful Bible study does not permit the arbitrary assignment of passages of Scripture to a place that will accommodate them to a particular system of interpretation. The only sound method is that of accurate exegesis; our system of belief must be drawn out of the Scripture, not imposed upon it. I do feel that the almost offhand manner in which II Peter 3 has been dealt with by some premillennialists has had an unfortunate effect upon the credit of the premillennial position. A more detailed examination of this passage will be undertaken later on in these studies. Enough has been said, however, to show that there is strong reason to hold that the events Peter describes are to occur at the coming of the Lord. Another argument is therefore forged against the distinction some would make between the "day of Christ" and the "day of the Lord."

The study of the terms used to denote the second coming of Christ has served to disclose that they may be fairly held to be interchange-able. *Parousia, apokalupsis, epiphaneia, to telos, sunteleia tou aionos,* and *hemera* in its various combinations, all have reference to the coming of Christ in glory, to the resurrection and blessedness of the saints at His coming, to the judgment that will befall the wicked, to cosmical changes that will occur at Christ's return. No distinction may be made on the basis of the use of these terms be-tween "the rapture" and "the revelation." The return of Christ, insofar as these New Testament designations permit us to describe it, is one unified event having final reference to all men and to creation itself.

It is evident, I think, that the study of the New Testament ex-pressions for the second coming of Christ has raised serious objec-tions to the validity of the premillennial system. It may be asked whether any implications may be taken concerning the relative merits of postmillennialism and amillennialism. The answer would seem to be that amillennialism has received support. The world to which Christ comes is not, in the Scripture passages considered, a world that has been converted. It is a world which has been hostile to the gospel of Christ and which has heaped tribulation upon His people. The postmillennialism with which we are most familiar has not been in the habit of so picturing the course of world history as it approaches the second advent. The picture is after the amillennial view of things rather than the postmillennial. Although a verdict can by no means yet be entered, those preliminary steps have now been taken which were necessary to prepare for the exegesis of the conclusive passages of Scripture which are to be studied in detail in the articles which shall follow. . . .

Chapter 7

RONALD SCHARFE*

Significant Periodical Articles (1973-74) for New Testament Specialists

Barrett, C. K. "John and the Synoptic Gospels." *Expository Times,* 85:8 (May, 1974), 228-33.

An excellent survey of the debate as to whether John's gospel was or was not written independently of the Synoptic tradition. The summaries of scholarly views are lucid and Barrett's own conclusion is "it is natural rather than difficult to believe that he [i.e., John] had read at least Mark, and had pondered—and understood—its meaning."

Drane, John W. "Gnosticism and the New Testament (2 parts)." *Theological Students' Fellowship Bulletin,* 68 (Spring, 1974), 6-13; 69 (Summer, 1974), 1-7.

This two part article deals with a description of the central motifs of Gnosticism, the origins of classical (second-century) Gnosticism, a survey of positions taken during the last seventy years on the issue of Gnosticism and the N.T., and finally with the problem of definition.

Dunn, J. D. G. "The Messianic Secret in Mark." *Theological Students' Fellowship Bulletin,* 69 (Summer, 1974), 1-14.

A detailed examination of Wilhelm Wrede's thesis that the messianic secret in Mark is theological rather than historical in origin. Contains three penetrating criticisms by the author, who holds that "to speak of a messianic *secret* is misleading and

---

*Mr. Scharfe is assistant professor of Bible and head librarian at the Fort Wayne Bible College, Fort Wayne, Indiana.

unjustified. So far as Jesus' Messiahship was concerned there was no secret as such, only a cautious disavowal of false views."

Epp, Eldon Jay. "The Twentieth Century Interlude in New Testament Textual Criticism." *Journal of Biblical Literature*, 93:3 (Sept., 1974), 386-414.

20th century textual criticism is characterized in terms of an "interlude" on the basis of (a) lack of progress in popular critical editions, (b) lack of progress toward a theory and history of the earliest NT text, (c) lack of progress in major critical editions/ apparatuses, (d) lack of progress in the evaluation of readings, and (e) the return of the textus receptus. A carefully reasoned article though not without its biases.

Fuller, R. H. "Aspects of Pauline Christology." *Review and Expositor*, 71:1 (Winter, 1974), 5-17.

Currently Professor of NT at the Protestant Episcopal Theological Seminary in Alexandria, Virginia, Fuller holds that the study of Christological titles in Paul's writings leads to a failure to distinguish between tradition and redaction. A better methodology he thinks is the thematic approach and his conclusion—Paul's achievement is his rescuing the earthly Jesus from being relegated to the archives in the Hellenistic church.

Gasque, W. W. "Did Luke Have Access to Traditions about the Apostles and the Early Churches?" *Journal of the Evangelical Theological Society*, 17:1 (Winter, 1974), 45-8.

In contrast to the views of Dibelius and Haenchen, who hold that no sources were available to Luke for his writing of Acts, Gasque examines with approval the thesis of Jacob Jervell that in fact conditions were not unfavorable for the formation of traditions about the apostles and the apostolic churches.

Grayston, Kenneth. "Foreign Theological Literary Survey: 1973-74 (New Testament)." *Expository Times*, 85:10 (July, 1974), 309-13.

Grayston provides for English-speaking students a helpful survey and analysis of contemporary trends in European NT scholarly circles as evident in their theological journals. Succinct summaries and critical annotations are included.

Groh, Dennis E. "Hans von Campenhausen on Canon." *Interpretation*, 28:3 (July, 1974), 331-43.

Groh, who teaches at Garrett Evangelical Theological Seminary,

Evanston, Illinois), carefully reviews von Campenhausen's views on the canon of the NT as set forth in his work *The Formation of the Christian Bible* (1972). From Groh's presuppositions the strengths as well as the weaknesses of von Campenhausen's position are delineated.

Guthrie, Donald. "History and the Gospels." *Themelios,* 10:1 (1974), 11-19.

In this articulated survey, Guthrie focuses the reader's attention on the pertinent problem of history versus the gospel narratives. Source criticism and historical skepticism are clearly portrayed, followed by the tracing of those movements away from historical skepticism. The article concludes with a section devoted to a positive approach to the history of the Gospels.

Hoehner, Harold W. "Chronological Aspects of the Life of Christ (4 parts, to be continued)." *Bibliotheca Sacra,* Part 1: The Date of Christ's Birth, 130:520 (Oct.–Dec., 1973), 338-51; Part 2: The Commencement of Christ's Ministry, 131:521 (Jan.–Mar., 1974), 41-54; Part 3: The Duration of Christ's Ministry, 131:522 (Apr.–June, 1974), 147-62; Part 4: The Day of Christ's Crucifixion, 131:523 (July–Sept., 1974), 241-64.

A closely knit series of articles, historical and critical in the best sense of the word, based on the highest form of conservative biblical scholarship, which validate and sustain against the views of negative critics the trustworthiness of gospel tradition as it pertains to the events in Christ's life. Rewarding.

Hoekema, Anthony A. "The Perfection of Christ in Hebrews." *Calvin Theological Journal,* 9:1 (April, 1974), 31-7.

An investigation of the usage of the concept *teleiōsis* as Hebrews employs the term in regard to Christ. The prominence of the term in Hebrews demands diligent consideration, and Hoekema's study, though not as painstaking as it might be, indicates some of the factors involved in a proper understanding of what it means when Christ is said to have been made "perfect."

Hughes, Philip Edgcumbe. "The Blood of Jesus and His Heavenly Priesthood in Hebrews" (4 parts). *Bibliotheca Sacra,* Part 1: The Significance of the Blood of Jesus, 130:518 (Apr.–June, 1973), 99-109; Part 2: The High-Priestly Sacrifice of Christ, 130:519 (July–Sept., 1973), 195-212; Part 3: The Meaning of 'The True Tent' and 'The Greater and More Perfect Tent,' 130:520 (Oct.–Dec., 1973), 305-14; Part 4: The Present Work of Christ in Heaven, 131:521 (Jan.–Mar., 1974), 26-33.

This series of articles was originally delivered as lectures at Dallas Theological Seminary. Taken together they form a compact theology on the soteriology of Hebrews. The main emphasis throughout is to highlight the meaning and implications of the blood of Christ and his priesthood ministry. The articles are both exegetical and theological in nature, and the author's insights help to illuminate the message of this extremely important NT epistle.

Karris, R. J. "The Background and Significance of the Polemic of the Pastoral Epistles." *Journal of Biblical Literature,* 92 (Dec., 1973), 549-64.
This well-documented analysis of the Pastorals is a study in the use of form and redaction criticism as applied specially to the polemic of these epistles. The result, according to the author, tends to prove that the heretics involved are not of Greek origin but Jewish Christians who teach the law, Jewish myths, genealogies, forbid marriage, and enjoin abstinence from food.

Marshall, I. Howard. "The Problem of New Testament Exegesis." *Journal of the Evangelical Theological Society,* 17:2 (Spring, 1974), 67-73.
A discussion by a British evangelical scholar on the faculty of the University of Aberdeen which concentrates on the hermeneutical problems unique to NT exegesis. Some of the problems briefly encountered are textual criticism, translation, background, function, symbolism, etc. Marshall uses as a test case John chapter 4.

Morris, Leon. "Luke and Early Catholicism." *Westminster Theological Journal,* 35:2 (Winter, 1973), 121-36.
Morris scrutinizes the case which is often made nowadays that Luke perverted the original gospel and replaced it with an institutional "early Catholicism." Luke according to the author is "not wrestling with the problem of the delayed parousia—he is putting on record an accurate account so that Theophilus (and others with him) may know the certainty of the tradition in which he has been instructed (*katēchēthēs*)."

Reicke, Bo. "The Historical Setting of Colossians." *Review and Expositor,* 70:4 (Fall, 1973), 429-38.
Reicke describes for the reader such background material as place and date, the church of Colossae, the recipients and the setting. The study is based not on stylistic and theological matters, but rather on an objective analysis of names involved and events

alluded to. This particular issue of *Review and Expositor*, devoted completely to Colossians, also includes the following articles: John Polhill, "The Relationship between Ephesians and Colossians," 439-50; Eduard Schweizer, "Christ in the Letter to the Colossians," 451-67; George Beasley-Murray, "The Second Chapter of Colossians," 469-79; C. F. D. Moule, " 'The New Life' in Colossians 3:1-17," 481-93; E. Glen Hinson, "The Christian Household in Colossians 3:18-4:1," 495-506; George E. Ladd, "Paul's Friends in Colossians 4:7-16," 507-14.

Saucy, Robert L. "The Husband of One Wife." *Bibliotheca Sacra,* 131:523 (July-Sept., 1974), 229-40.

Saucy's article treats the requirement for eldership set forth in I Timothy 3:2 in the light of present-day problems, particularly that of divorce. The author is prepared to hold (1) that adultery is probably not a continual state of sin, but can be forgiven even as murder, and (2) that divorce does dissolve marriage so that one married again is not considered to be the husband of two wives.

Thiselton, Anthony C. "New Testament Commentary Survey." *Themelios,* 10:2 (1974), 7-23.

This is a useful survey of commentaries on the individual books of the NT. Evaluations are provided in terms of strengths and weaknesses, and then works recommended for possible purchase are suggested. The author's introductory remarks are addressed to the need for several types of commentary, individual commentaries or sets, older commentaries, and one-man sets.

PART II
THE STUDENT AT WORK

Chapter 8

LEON MORRIS*

On Writing a Commentary

The editor has asked me to write an article on how to prepare a commentary. This I fear is too big a task for me. I cannot pretend to say how a commentary ought to be written. I can say only how I go about it and leave the reader to judge whether there is any merit in the procedure.

For me, the first step in writing a commentary is to let the book on which I am to write speak to me. Sometimes I find myself caught up with deadlines, and then I must proceed with haste in a way I do not like. But left to myself I would not write a line for months. If I can, I take the book on which I am to write as a book for special study in my own quiet times day by day. I work slowly through it in the original language with no aids whatever and simply listen to what God is saying to me through it. I take very seriously the idea that the Bible is the word of God and I do not see how I can write anything useful on it unless I have first heard that word of God to me. So, as I say, I listen. I make some notes. And I try to put into practice in my own life what I learn in these quiet times.

When the time comes to write, the first question to be resolved is which comes first, the commentary or the introduction. My preference is to do the commentary first, for only after one has immersed oneself in the thought of the writer is one in a position to handle satisfactorily the questions that arise in the introduction.

*Dr. Morris is principal of Ridley College, University of Melbourne.

If I am not working to a rigid space limit I would always do it this way. But if a publisher sets a firm limit it may be better to do it the other way round. The important part of the work is the commentary, and I like to get through the introduction secure in the knowledge that questions of date, authorship, and the like have been dealt with in the space I have tentatively allotted them. And, of course, there is always the possibility of a bonus. One may find that the introduction can be shortened a bit and then there is some extra space for the commentary proper.

It is good when working to a space limit to plan out the whole work beforehand. One should, of course, respect a limit and not try to crib some extra words. The publisher has planned out the series and it is not the place of any individual author to upset the perspective by enlarging his contribution (which always seems to him the most important part of the series) and making it longer in comparison with the others. Of course, it may turn out that way. For example, my commentary on Ruth in the Tyndale series is on a much larger scale than the commentary on Judges in the same series and with which it is bound up. I do not know why the publishers wanted Ruth on the larger scale. But they did, and I was glad to do the work under those conditions. But a commentator who is writing for a series does not have the decision as to scale. If he is not satisfied with the wordage allotted to him, he should refuse the invitation to write. If he accepts it, he should respect the limits to which he has agreed. It is not fair to the publishers or the other contributors to do otherwise.

I find it helpful to work out a rough plan before I start writing. Unless one is in the fortunate position of having no limits of space, there is always the temptation to write at too great length on the earlier part of the book. There is always more to say about Scripture than one can include in a commentary and the commentator must be selective in his comments. One must not be in bondage to a plan, but it is useful to know whether at a given stage one is within the proper limits or not. Otherwise there is the risk that when the work is finished it will be found to be too long and must be abbreviated. Or, even worse, one may find that there is space allotted that has not been used! In drawing up a plan it is helpful to look at a few other commentaries. If other commentators seem all to take more space on say, chapter three, than other chapters, it is well to allow a little more space there.

The commentator should read the whole book carefully and draw up an anaysis of its contents. In some commentaries such an analysis is regularly published. But even if it be not published it is a help to the commentator to have it before him. He can then see how the section on which he is commentating at any time fits in to the plan of the whole, and he can relate it to the argument of the whole book. This is important for he is writing about a book, not a series of isolated texts.

When it comes to the actual writing of the commentary, I find it best to work through either the whole book or a section of it writing furiously but without making any reference to other commentaries or for that matter articles or general works. This gets onto paper what the book means for me and it means that the final shape of the book is my own, not a pale adaptation of some other writer who has impressed me. It may be that some other writers are more strong-minded than I, but I find that if in this first stage I refer to other writers I tend insensibly to be influenced by what they say. So at this stage I write out of my own head, with the comforting assurance that this draft is invariably headed for the waste paper basket anyway.

I make one exception to my rule of using no other writers at this stage. I do not hesitate to use concordances, lexicons, and tables of statistics. It simplifies the work to be able to compare the passage under discussion with other passages and to have statistics handy. An occasional resort to the grammar books may also be useful at this stage. But not much. This is the stage when my own views in all their horror are set forward. There will be many errors which will be eliminated later (and others, alas, that will not). But putting the comments down with all the errors and infelicities is the only way I know of making sure that any insights I may have gained will be included.

The weeding out of the errors and the gaining of fresh insights is the next stage. I go systematically through as many commentaries on the book as I can, noting carefully what earlier commentators have had to say. This is a humbling, but salutary experience. Over and over I find myself saying, "How could I have been so blind as to put that in? Or to leave that out?" I find that I can learn something from every commentator, whether his standpoint is roughly my own or diametrically opposed. So I read as many commentators as I have time for and profit from them all. In this process, of course, I pick up a lot of footnotes. I reason that, if some comment has meant a good deal to me, presumably it will be useful to anyone who reads what I write. Limitations of space will, of course, keep the number down. But I like to put them in where I can.

I add other books to the commentaries. Here the grammars come into their own. Many grammars have useful indexes to passages of scripture as well as to subjects. It is a good plan to work systematically through the references to the book on which one is commenting. Often the grammar will say little enough, but every now and then there will be a very useful comment on the meaning of a particular construction. The process can be continued indefinitely with books other than grammars. Many works on the Bible carry indexes to Bible passages and these can often be followed through with profit. The individual writer will have to decide where to stop, for this opens up such a wide field that there is virtually no limit.

Another source of help is, of course, one's own reading. I suppose we all have our favorite authors and we know instinctively that they will have a useful remark on such and such a passage. In addition one's general reading will be carried on while the commentary is being thought of and written. From the time I accept an invitation to write a commentary I make it a practice to jot down the reference any time I come across anything significant on the book in question in any of my reading. Then when I am doing the writing I look up all these references and see what bearing they have on what is before me.

Yet another source is one's friends. It is helpful to submit what one has written to the judgment of those who are well disposed but critical, before it has to run the gauntlet of the pitiless criticisms of others. A fresh mind will often pick up errors and infelicities which elude their perpetrator. And a friend will often suggest a line of thought which may profitably be followed up.

Throughout the process it is important to bear in mind the readership at which the series is aimed. If the publisher is producing a series aimed at the general Christian public, it is not profitable to produce a magnificent work replete with footnotes aimed exclusively at the specialist. On the other hand if the work is meant to be on a scholarly level, there is no point in producing a simple primer. Occasionally one can write for more than one group as in the New International series. There one is asked to make the text straightforward, so that the ordinary Christian layman can profit from it. No language other than English is to be used, and so on. But there are no such restrictions on the footnotes, and in them the commentator can use any language and discuss intricate scholarly points to his heart's content. But this kind of approach is rare and even here it is important not to confuse the text with the footnotes.

At whatever level one is writing there is no substitute for a determined wrestling with the text in the original language. Much of what one learns in this process cannot be produced if the commentary is to be pitched at a "popular" level. But it will be misleading unless the author has done his best to get to grips with the meaning of the original.

Special attention has to be given to difficult passages. The temptation is always to gloss over these in favor of the purple passages, where the commentator feels that he has something he very much wants to say. But he must always bear in mind that many of those who will use his commentary will do so because they want enlightenment on a point that is a problem to them. Of course the commentator may not be able to solve all the problems (certainly this one cannot). But he must face them honestly and set out the issues as he sees them. This will enable the reader at least to see what is known and what is not and will enable him to get a grip on the issues involved.

I guess what I am saying is that for me writing a commentary up to this point divides broadly into three phases. In the first I write nothing, but simply let the Scripture speak to me. Unless it has spoken to my soul I do not feel myself in a position to write on it at all. In the second I write what I see and take little or no notice of what anyone else has written. I know of no other way of ensuring that in the end it will be *my* commentary and not a pale imitation of the authors I admire. Then in the third phase I submit my ideas to the scrutiny of as many others as I can—grammarians, commentators, general writers, friends.

But there remains another stage and this final process is perhaps the most arduous of all. It consists in working over the whole with a view to improving the English style. I write very badly, and I must spend a lot of time working over and over what I have written, trying to eliminate ambiguities and make sure that readers will be able to understand what I have said, even if they cannot accept it. I am sure that for people with real writing ability this process is not difficult. But for me it is. It means going over and over what I have written and working through draft after draft. The waste paper basket really comes into its own at this stage.

I suppose I ought to continue the process until the work is just right. But I find I am never satisfied. Every time I read through what I have written I find something more that ought to be altered. I keep this up as long as I can stand it. But when I have been through it so often that I am sick of the sight of it, when I am convinced that any further improvement is going to be marginal, I parcel it up and send it off to the publisher. Then it's up to him to decide whether the work is as bad as I fear, or whether he is ready to take his courage into his hands and launch it on to an unsuspecting public.

Chapter 9

JOHN H. SKILTON

Working Lists of Commentaries on the New Testament: An Invitation to Our Readers

I. EXTENT OF THE LISTS

These lists of commentaries are not intended to be final or exhaustive. Numerous works which have been indexed by the compiler have not yet been included. The omission of a work is not to be interpreted as representing an adverse judgment about its merit. For supplementation of these working lists the student is referred to scholarly commentaries, works on special introduction to the New Testament, and Bible dictionaries and encyclopedias.

II. COMPILATION OF THE LISTS

In the compilation of "VII. A Brief List of Useful Commentaries," account has been taken of the judgment of a number of scholars, including Dr. George W. Knight, III, and Dr. Edwin H. Palmer ("A Suggested Book List for Ministers"). Commentaries in the Brief List are included in italic type in section IX, "Commentaries on Individual Books." Comments about the merit of any works on the Brief List or the larger lists and suggestions about commentaries which might be included in the future will be welcomed. It is hoped that with the help of our readers annotated and more useful bibliographies can be published.[1]

---

1. Suggestions and comments might be addressed to the editor at Westminster Theological Seminary, Chestnut Hill, Philadelphia, Pa. 19118.

III. TYPES OF COMMENTARIES

The Commentaries included represent various theological viewpoints, different types of exegesis and interpretation, different periods of church history, and different parts of the world. In addition to scientific exegetical commentaries, works of a more general explanatory type and of a more popular and practical nature have been included.

IV. DESIGNATIONS OF COMMENTARIES

Very brief designations are generally used for the commentaries listed (usually the last name of the author is given); but these designations should not occasion much difficulty to the student who has access to a good theological library.

V. USE OF THE LISTS

For those doing special exegetical work in connection with graduate programs, it will be wise to consult all of the scientific exegetical commentaries mentioned and such other works on the lists as may help to establish the history of the interpretation of given texts. Undergraduate exegetical assignments will, of course, be less demanding, but at least two or three scientific exegetical commentaries should be studied in preparation for recitations and class discussions.

Before consulting commentaries, the student might find it profitable to follow some such procedure as the following:

(1) Make his own translation of the given text or passage and compare his translation with those in such versions as AV and ARV.

(2) Attempt to settle problems of textual criticism which may be involved.

(3) Attempt to exegete the text or passage on his own. After careful reflection, he might list tentative conclusions and also questions requiring research.

(4) As needed, consult lexicons, Kittel's *Theological Dictionary,* and concordances (including at times concordances on the Hebrew and Greek texts of the Old Testament). In this, as in all of the subsequent preliminary steps, tentative conclusions and also questions might be listed.

(5) As needed, consult works on grammar and syntax.

(6) Consult works intermediate between lexicons and commentaries such as A. T. Robertson's *Word Pictures.*

(7) Consult atlases, works on archaeology, Bible dictionaries and encyclopedias, introductions to commentaries, and works on general and special introduction for background information.

When the student does at length turn to the exegetical treatments in the commentaries, he should look specifically for answers to the questions which he has raised in his preliminary investigations and should seek to test his tentative conclusions. (Of course, commentaries may raise questions which had not previously occurred to the student and may perform various additional services.) The first commentaries to be consulted will normally be of the scientific exegetical type; after that, as the student's purposes may require, commentaries of a more practical and devotional sort may be used with profit.

After consulting a sufficient number of commentaries, the student might list his conclusions and any questions which still remain unanswered. He might then consult special studies related to his text or passage and works on biblical and systematic theology which will help him to test his conclusions, obtain additional insights, and answer problems in the light of broader contexts and relationships.

VI. PURCHASE OF COMMENTARIES

The following suggestions are concerned only with commentaries in the English language. Students who can read various other languages will find suitable works mentioned in the main lists (VIII and IX).

A good set with which to begin one's collection of commentaries on the New Testament is an English translation of the H. A. W. Meyer series, containing a number of commentaries by the distinguished exegete Meyer himself. Also meriting consideration for early purchase are Alford's Greek Testament, Calvin's commentaries, and a set of Matthew Henry. The student will also wish to acquire outstanding commentaries on particular books. Very useful volumes in the *International Critical Commentary* are Plummer on Luke, Sanday-Headlam on Romans, Robertson-Plummer on I Corinthians, Plummer on II Corinthians, Burton on Galatians, Abbott on Ephesians and Colossians, Vincent on Philippians and Philemon, Frame on I and II Thessalonians, Lock on the Pastorals, Ropes on James, and Bigg on I and II Peter and Jude. Other volumes in this series are also profitable. Among gifted commentators who have written on more than one book of the New Testament (but not on the whole New Testament) are Alexander, F. F. Bruce, Brown, Eadie, Ellicott, Godet, Hendriksen, Hengstenberg, Hodge, Hort, Johnstone, Knowling, Lange, Lightfoot, Plummer, Morris, Swete, and Westcott. The student might examine the collection of commentaries in an ample theological library with a view to determining which volumes would best meet the requirements for his own library.

VII.   A BRIEF LIST OF USEFUL COMMENTARIES
(For Abbreviations, see VIII)
A. *Commentaries on the Entire New Testament or on Much of It*
Alford, Calvin, Meyer (English), Matthew Henry
Gospels: Ryle (*Expository Thoughts*)
B. *Commentaries on Individual Books*
Matthew: Alexander, Broadus, Hendriksen, McNeile, Plummer
Mark: Alexander, Lane (NIC), Plummer (CGT), Swete, Taylor
Luke: Arndt, Geldenhuys (NIC), Godet, Morris (T), Plummer (ICC), Oosterzee (L)
John: Barrett, Godet, Hendriksen, Hengstenberg, Morris (ICC), Westcott (both on the Greek and on the English texts)
Acts: Alexander, Bruce (NIC and Commentary on the Greek text), Hackett, Gloag, Knowling (EGT), Page, Rackham (W)
Romans: Barrett (B-H), Bruce (T), Denney, Godet, Haldane, Hodge, Luther, Moule, H. C. G. (CBSC; Ex B), Murray (NIC), Sanday-Headlam (ICC)
I Corinthians: Barrett (B-H), Godet, Grosheide (NIC), Hodge, Morris (T), Robertson-Plummer (ICC)
II Corinthians: Barrett (B-H), Denney, Hodge, Hughes (NIC), Plummer (ICC)

Galatians: Brown, Burton (ICC), Eadie, Hendriksen, Lightfoot, Machen (*Machen's Notes on Galatians*), Ramsay, Ridderbos (NIC), Stoeckhardt

Ephesians: Abbott (ICC), Eadie, Hendriksen, Hodge, Simpson (NIC), Westcott

Philippians: Eadie, Hendriksen, Johnstone, Lightfoot, Moule, H. C. G. (*Philippian Studies*), Müller (NIC), Vincent (ICC)

Colossians: Abbott (ICC), Bruce (NIC), Eadie, Hendriksen, Lightfoot, Moule, C. F. D.

I, II Thessalonians: Best (B-H), Eadie, Frame (ICC), Hendriksen, Milligan, Morris (NIC; T), Plummer

I, II Timothy, Titus: Fairbairn, Guthrie (T), Hendriksen, Kelly, J. N. D. (B-H), Lock (ICC), Simpson

Philemon: Hendriksen, Lightfoot, Moule, C.F.D. (CGTC), Müller (NIC), Vincent (ICC)

Hebrews: Brown, Bruce (NIC), Delitzsch, Moffatt (ICC), Montefiore (B-H), Owen, Vos (*The Teaching of the Epistle to the Hebrews*), Westcott

James: Hort, Johnstone, Manton, Mayor, Plummer (ExB), Ropes (ICC), Ross (NIC), Tasker (T)

I, II Peter: Bigg (ICC), Brown, Green II (T), Hort I, Johnstone I, Kelly (B-H), Leighton I, Mayor II, Selwyn I, Stibbs I (T)

I, II, III John: Brooke (ICC), Candlish I, Cotton, Plummer (CGT), Ross (NIC), Stott, Westcott

Jude: Bigg (ICC), Green (T), Manton, Mayor, Plummer

Revelation: Charles (ICC), Elliott, Hendriksen (*More Than Conquerors*), Hengstenberg, Hoeksema, Hort, Kuyper, Ladd, Morris (T), Swete

VIII. CHIEF WORKING LIST OF COMMENTARIES ON THE ENTIRE NEW TESTAMENT OR ON A LARGE PORTION OF IT

	Abbott
ABC	*Abingdon Bible Commentary*
AGT	Alford's *Greek Testament*
	Alford's *New Testament for English Readers*

AB	*Anchor Bible*
	Annotated Bible
	Annotated New Testament (in Japanese)
	Auslegung Neutestamentlicher Schriften
	Barclay (*Daily Study Bible*)
	Barnes's *Notes*
	Baumgarten-Crusius
	Beacon Bible Commentary
	Bengel's *Gnomon*
	Benson
	Beza
	Bibelstunden
	Bible for Home and School
	Biblia Comentada
B-H	*Black's (Harper's) New Testament Commentaries*
	Bloomfield
	Broadman Bible Commentary
	Burkitt
	Calmet
	Calvin
CBSC	*Cambridge Bible for Schools and Colleges*
CGT	*Cambridge Greek Testament*
CGTC	*Cambridge Greek Testament Commentary*
	A Catholic Commentary on Holy Scripture
	Century Bible
	New Century Bible
CB	*Clarendon Bible*
NCB	*New Clarendon Bible*
	Clarke
ComNT	*Comentario al Nuevo Testamento*
C	*Commentaire du Nouveau Testament*
	Concise Bible Commentary
	Cornelius a Lapide
	Cramer (*Catenae*)
	De Wette
	Doddridge (*Family Expositor*)
	Dummelow
EBC	Ellicott's *Bible Commentary*
EP	Ellicott's *Critical and Grammatical Commentary on the Epistles of Saint Paul*
ENT	Ellicott's *New Testament Commentary*
	Erdman

EB	*Études bibliques* (Commentaries in this series)
	Euthymius Zigabenus
EvBC	*Evangelical Bible Commentary*
EC	*Evangelical Commentary*
	Everyman's Bible Commentary
ExB	*Expositor's Bible*
EGT	*Expositor's Greek Testament*
	Gaebelein
	Gill
	Gore, Goudge, and Guillaume
	Graebner
	Grinfield
	Grotius
	Hammond
	Handbooks for Bible Classes and Private Students
HNT	*Handbuch zum Neuen Testament*
H-C	*Hand-Commentar zum Neuen Testament*
	Hermeneia
	Die heilige Schrift des Neuen Testaments
	Die heilige Schrift für das Leben erklärt
H	Hendriksen
	Matthew Henry
HTK	*Herders theologischer Kommentar zum Neuen Testament*
SB	*The Holy Bible . . . . (Speaker's Bible,* ed. Cook)
	Honert
	Hugh of St. Cher
IC	*Indian Church Commentaries*
ICC	*International Critical Commentary*
	International Revision Commentary
IB	*Interpreter's Bible*
	Jamieson, Fausset, and Brown
	Jerome Bible Commentary
	Kang (in Korean)
	Knox, Ronald A.
KNT	*Kommentaar op het Nieuwe Testament* (Revisions and new editions under the title:
CNT	*Commentaar op het Nieuwe Testament*)
	Koolozaki (in Japanese)
	Koppe
	Kuinoel
KV	*Korte Verklaring der Heilige Schrift*

L   Lange
         Layman's Bible Commentary
         Le Clerk, J.
         Lee (in Korean)
         Lenski
         Les Livres de la Bible
         Lutheran Commentary
         Maclaren
         Makrakis
M   Meyer, H. A. W. (Editions in English and German)
Mo   Moffatt
         Moody Press: Paperback Commentaries
         Morgan
NTD   *Das Neue Testament Deutsch*
         New Bible Commentary
NIC   *New International Commentary*
         New Testament for Spiritual Reading
         The New Testament in the Apostolic Fathers (Although
             this is not a commentary, it has some hermeneutical
             value)
         Nichol's Series of Commentaries
         Olshausen
         Park, Y. S. (in Korean)
         Patrick, Lowth, Arnald, and Whitby
         Peake's Commentary on the Bible
PC   Pelican Gospel Commentaries
         Piscator
         Poole
         Popular Commentary of the Bible
PCNT   *Popular Commentary on the New Testament,* ed. Schaff
PNT   *De Prediking van het Nieuwe Testament*
P   *Prophezei:* Schweizerisches *Bibelwerk für die Gemeinde*
             (later called *Zürcher Bibelkommentare*)
         Pulpit Commentary (for expository material)
         Raphel (Raphelius)
RNT   *Regensburger Neues Testament*
         Rosenmüller (*Scholia*)
         La Saccra Bibbia
         La sainte Bible ("Bible de Jérusalem")
         La sainte Bible (Pirot, Clamer, eds.)
         Die Schriften des Neuen Testaments
         Schlatter (*Erläuterungen zum Neuen Testament*)

Thomas Scott
Shield Bible Study Series
Standard Bible Commentary
Strack and Billerbeck (*Kommentar zum Neuen Testament aus Talmud und Midrasch*)
Strack und Zöckler
Tekst en Uitleg
THNT *Theologischer Handkommentar zum Neuen Testament*
Theophylact
TB *Torch Bible Commentaries*
Trapp
Trollope
T *Tyndale New Testament Commentaries*
VS *Verbum Salutis*
Von Gerlach
Weiss, B.
Wesleyan
W *Westminster*
Westminster Assembly (*Annotations*)
Wettstein (*Novum Testamentum Graecum*)
Wolf (Wolfius)
Wordsworth
Wycliffe Bible Commentary
Z Zahn (*Kommentar zum Neuen Testament*)

IX. COMMENTARIES ON INDIVIDUAL BOOKS

Note: Often works included in the commentaries listed under VIII are not mentioned here.

Matthew

Allen (ICC), *Alexander,* Aquinas (*Catena*), Augustine (on V-VII), Bonnard (C), *Broadus,* Campbell, Chrysostom, Civit (ComNT), Cowles, Dausch, Dickson, Filson (B-H), Gaechter, Gander, Glover, Grosheide (KNT), *Hendriksen,* Hilary of Poitiers, Hill, Jacobus, Jerome, Keil, Klostermann (HNT), Kuinoel, Lagrange (EB), Lange (L), Lohmeyer-Schmauch (M), Loisy, McNeile, Maldonatus, Major-Manson-Wright (*The Mission and Message of Jesus*), Montefiore, Origen, *Plummer,* Ridderbos (KV), *Ryle,* Schlatter, Schmid (RNT), Schniewind (NTD), Simcox, Smith, B. T. D. (C.G.T.), Smith, H. (*Ante-Nicene Exegesis of the Gospels*), Spurgeon, Stier, Tasker (T), Watson, Wellhausen, Zahn (Z).

Mark

Alexander, Aquinas (*Catena*), Bacon, Beasley-Murray (on XIII), Bede, Berkelbach van der Sprenkel, Branscomb (Mo), Campbell, Carrington, Chadwick (ExB), Cole (T), Cowles, Cranfield (CGTC), Dausch, Earle (EC), Glover, Gould (ICC), Grob, Groenewald (KB), Haenchen, Jacobus, Johnson (B-H), Klostermann (HNT), Kuinoel, Lagrange (EB), *Lane* (NIC), Lange (L), Linn, Lohmeyer (M), Loisy, Maldonatus, Major-Manson-Wright (*The Mission and Message of Jesus*), Menzies, Montefiore, Morison, Nineham (PC), *Plummer* (CGT; CBSC), Rawlinson (W), *Ryle,* Schlatter, Schmid (RNT), Schniewind (NTD), Schweizer, Smith, H. (*Ante-Nicene Exegesis of the Gospels*), Stier, *Swete,* Taylor, Turner, Weidner, Wellhausen.

Luke

Ambrose, Aquinas (*Catena*), *Arndt,* Balmforth (CB), Bede, Campbell, Caird (PC), Cowles, Creed, Dausch, Easton, *Geldenhuys* (NIC), *Godet,* Gollwitzer (*Die Freude Gottes*), Greijdanus (KNT; KV), Harrington, Jacobus, Jerome-Origen, Klostermann (HNT), Kuinoel, Lagrange (EB), Leaney (B-H), Loisy, Luce (CBSC; CGT), Major-Manson-Wright (*The Mission and Message of Jesus*), Maldonatus, Manson (Mo), Martin, Montefiore, *Morris* (T), Plummer (ICC), Rengstorf (NDT), *Ryle,* Schlatter, Schmid (RNT), Smith, H. (*Ante-Nicene Exegesis of the Gospels*), Stier, Van Andel, *Van Oosterzee* (L), Walker (IC), Wellhausen, Zahn (Z).

John

Aquinas (*Catena*), Augustine, Barrett, Bauer (HNT), Bernard (ICC), Bouma (KV), Brown (AB), Büchsel (NTD), Bultmann (M), Campbell, Chrysostom, Dodd, Dods (ExB), *Godet,* Grosheide (KNT), *Hendriksen, Hengstenberg,* Hobbs, Holtzmann (H-C), Hoskyns, Hutcheson, Jacobus, Kuinoel, Lagrange (EB), Lampe, Lange (L), Lightfoot, R. H., Linn, Loisy, Lücke, Lüthi, Macgregor (Mo), Major-Manson-Wright (*The Mission and Message of Jesus*), Maldonatus, Marsh (PC), Morris (ICC), Origen, Owen, J. J., Pink, Plummer (CGT), Richardson (TB), *Ryle,* Sanders-Mastin (B-H), Schlatter, Schnackenburg (HTK), Semler, Smith, H. (*Ante-Nicene Exegesis of the Gospels*), Stier,

Strachan, Strathmann (NTD), Tasker (T), Temple, Tenney, Tholuck, Titus, Turner-Mantey (EC), Van Andel, Von Loewenich (*Das Johannes-Verständnis im zweiten Jahrhundert*), Wellhausen, *Westcott* (on both the Greek and the English texts), Whitelaw, Wright, Zahn (Z).

The Acts

Alexander, Allen, Barde, Baumgarten, Bede, Beyer (NTD), Blaiklock (T), Blass, Blunt (CB), Browne (IC), *Bruce, F. F.* (NIC; *Commentary on the Greek Text*), Carter-Earle (EC), Chrysostom, Conzelmann (HNT), Cowles, Du Veil, Foakes-Jackson (Mo), Furneaux, *Gloag,* Grosheide (KNT; KV), *Hackett,* Haenchen (M), Hoennicke, Humphrey, Jacobus, Kelly, *Knowling* (EGT), Kuinoel, Lake-Cadbury (in *Beginnings of Christianity*), Lechler (L), Loisy, Macgregor (IB), *Page, Rackham* (W), Ricciotti, Schlatter, Smith, J., *The Voyage and Shipwreck of St. Paul*), Smith, R., Stählin, Stokes (ExB), Streso, Thomas, Walker (IC), Wielenga (*Van Jeruzalem naar Rome*), Williams (B-H), Zahn (Z).

Romans

Althaus (NTD), Ambrosiaster, Asmussen, Augustine, Bardenhewer, Barnhouse, *Barrett* (B-H), Barth, Baulès, Beck, Beet, Brown, J., *Bruce* (T), Brunner, Chalmers, Chrysostom, Deluz, Denny (EGT), Dickson, Dodd (Mo), Ferme, Forbes, Fritzsche, Gaugler, Gifford, *Godet,* Gore, Greijdanus (KNT), *Haldane,* Hamilton, *Hodge,* Hunter, Kelly, Köllner, Koppe, Kraemer, Kühl, Kuss, Lagrange (EB), Lange-Fay (L), Lekkerkerker (PNT), Leenhardt (C), Liddon, Lietzmann (HNT), Lightfoot (*Notes*), *Luther* (*Lectures*), Melville, Michel (M), Moule, H. C. G. (CBSC; ExB), *Murray* (NIC), Newell, Nygren, Parr, Pelagius, Philippi, Plumer, Reiche, Ridderbos (CNT), Rückert, *Sanday-Headlam* (ICC), Schlatter, Scott, Shedd, Staab (*Pauluskommentare aus der griechischen Kirche*), Steele-Thomas (*Interpretive Outlines*), Stifler, Stöckhardt, Stuart, Theodoret, Tholuck, Thomas, Van Andel, Van Hengel, Vaughan, Wilson, Zahn (Z).

I and II Corinthians (No number indicates one work on both; I & II indicates two separate works.)

Allo I & II (EB), Ambrosiaster, Atto Vercellensis, Bachmann I & II (Z), *Barrett* I & II (B-H), Beet I & II, Bernard II (EGT), Billroth, Chrysostom, Conzelmann I (M), Cürlis I, Deluz I,

Denney II (ExB), Dickson, Edwards I, Ellicott I (EP), Emmerling II, Estius, Evans, Findlay I (EGT), *Godet* I, Godet, G. II, Goudge I (W), *Grosheide* (CNT I & II; NIC I), Hanson (TB), Heinrici I & II (M), Héring I and II (C), Herveius Burgidolensis, *Hodge* I & II, *Hughes* II (NIC), Kennedy, Klöpper II, Krause, Leun II, Lietzmann I & II (HNT), Lightfoot part of I (*Notes*), McFadyen, Meyer, J. P., II (*Ministers of Christ*), Menzies II, Moffatt I (Mo), *Morris* I (T), Moule, H. C. G. II, Oecumenius, Parry I (CGT), Pelagius, *Plummer* II (ICC), Pop I & II (PNT), Pott I, *Robertson-Plummer* I (ICC), Rückert, Schlatter, Schmiedel, Staab (*Pauluskommentare aus der griechischen Kirche*), Stanley, Strachan II (Mo), Tasker II (T), Theodoret, Van Andel I, Van Veldhuizen, Weiss, J. I (M), Wendland (NTD), Wilson I & II, Windisch II (M).

Galatians

Allan (TB), Ambrosiaster, Asmussen, Augustine, Bayley, Beet, Bligh, Bonnard (C), Bosveld, *Brown, Burton* (ICC), Cole (T), Dehn, Dickson, Duncan (Mo), *Eadie*, Ellicott (EP), Emmet, Fergusson, Findlay (ExB), Gonzalez-Ruiz (ComNT), Greijdanus (KNT), Guthrie, *Hendriksen*, Hogg-Vine, Jager, Jerome, Koppe, Lagrange (EB), *Lightfoot*, Loisy, Lütgert, Luther, *Machen* (*Machen's Notes on Galatians*), Marius Victorinus, Maurer, Oepke (THNT), Pelagius, *Ramsay, Ridderbos* (NIC), Rückert, Ruiz, Schlatter, Schlier (M), Schott, Staab (*Pauluskommentare aus der griechischen Kirche*), *Stoeckhardt*, Tenney, Theodore of Mopsuestia, Theodoret, Venn, Wieseler, Williams, A. L. (CBSC), Wilson, Winer, Zahn (Z).

Ephesians

Abbott (ICC), Ambrosiaster, Bayne, Beare (IB), Beet, Berkelbach van der Sprenkel (PNT), Bruce, Candlish, Chrysostom, Dibelius (HNT), Dickson, *Eadie*, Ellicott (EP), Fergusson, Findlay (ExB), Foulkes (T), Frost, Gaugler, Gnilka (HTK), Goodspeed (*The Meaning of Ephesians*), Goodwin, Graham, Grosheide (CNT), Gurnall (on VI:10-17), Harless, *Hendriksen, Hodge*, Jerome, Koppe, Lightfoot (*Notes*), McGhee, Macpherson, Marius Victorinus, Masson (C), Moody (*Christ and the Church*), Moule, H. C. G. (*Ephesian Studies*), Neill, Pelagius, Pridham, Robinson, Rückert, Salmond (EGT), Schlier, Scott (Mo), Simpson (NIC), Staab (*Pauluskommentare aus der griechischen Kirche*), Stoeckhardt, Theodore of Mopsuestia, Theodoret, Westcott, Zanchius.

Philippians

Ambrosiaster, Barth, Beare (B-H), Beet, Boice, Chrysostom, Daillé, Dibelius (HNT), Dickson, Donner, *Eadie,* Ellicott (EP), Fergusson, Gnilka (HTK), Haering, *Hendriksen,* Huene, *Johnstone, Lightfoot,* Lohmeyer (M), Marius Victorinus, Martin (T), Meyer, F.B., Michael (Mo), Motyer, Moule, H. C. G. (*Philippian Studies*), *Müller* (NIC), Pelagius, Staab (*Pauluskommentare aus der griechischen Kirche*), Simcox, Tenney, Theodore of Mopsuestia, Theodoret, Thurneysen, Vaughan, *Vincent* (ICC), Von Huene, Walker (IC).

Colossians

Abbott (ICC), Ambrosiaster, Baynes, Beet, Biesterveld, *Bruce, F. F.* (NIC), Byfield, Carson (T), Chrysostom, Daillé, Davenant, Dibelius (HNT), Dickson, *Eadie,* Ellicott (EP), Elton, Fergusson, Firminger, Frost, *Hendriksen,* Hoeksema, *Lightfoot,* Lohmeyer (M), Lohse (M), Maclaren (ExB), Martin, *Moule, C. F. D.* (CGTC), Moule, H. C. G. (CBSC; *Colossian Studies*), Müller, Pelagius, Radford (W), Ridderbos (CNT), Scott (Mo), Staab (*Pauluskommentare aus der griechischen Kirche*), Steiger, Theodore of Mopsuestia, Theodoret, Uitman, Van Andel.

I and II Thessalonians (No number indicates one work on both; I & II indicates two separate works.)

Ambrosiaster, Bailey-Clarke (IB), *Best* (B-H), Bicknell (W), Brouwer, Chrysostom, Denney (ExB), Dibelius (HNT), Dickson, *Eadie,* Ellicott (EP), Fergusson, Findlay (CBSC; CGT), *Frame* (ICC), *Hendriksen,* Hogg-Vine, Holtzmann, Kelly, Koppe, Lightfoot (*Notes*), Lillie, Masson (C), *Milligan,* Moffatt (EGT), *Morris* (NIC; T), Neil (Mo; TB), Pelagius, *Plummer* I & II, Rigaux (EB), Schott, Staab (*Pauluskommentare aus der griechischen Kirche*), Theodore of Mopsuestia, Theodoret, Von Dobschütz (M), Walvoord, Wohlenberg (Z).

I and II Timothy and Titus (Indication is given if all are not included.)

Ambrosiaster, Barlow II, Barrett (NCB), Bernard (CGT), Bouma (KNT; KV), Borrmann I (*Siloah*), Brown (W), Chrysostom, Dibelius (HNT), Dibelius-Conzelmann (HNT), Dickson, Easton, Ellicott (EP), *Fairbairn,* Falconer, *Guthrie* (T), Haering, Hall, *Hendriksen,* Holtzmann, Huther (M), Jeremias (NTD), Jerome Tit., *Kelly, J. N. D.* (B-H), Kelly, W. I, II, Kent, *Lock*

(ICC), Moule, H. C. G. II (*Devotional Commentary*), Parry, Pelagius, Plummer (ExB), Schlatter (*Die Kirche der Griechen im Urteil des Paulus*), Scott (Mo), Simpson, Spicq (EB), Staab (*Pauluskommentare aus der griechischen Kirche*), Taylor Tit., Theodore of Mopsuestia, Theodoret, Van Andel I, II, White (EGT), Wohlenberg (Z).

Philemon

Ambrosiaster, Bieder (P), Carson (T), Chrysostom, Dibelius (HNT), Dickson, Dodd (ABC), Ellicott (EG), Firminger, *Hendriksen*, Jerome, *Lightfoot*, Lohmeyer (M), Lohse (M), Maclaren (ExB), Müller (NIC), *Moule*, C. F. D. (CGTC), Moule, H. C. G. (CBSC; *Colossian Studies*), Pelagius, Radford (W), Scott (Mo), Scroggie, Staab (*Pauluskommentare aus der griechischen Kirche*), Theodore of Mopsuestia, Theodoret, *Vincent* (ICC).

Hebrews

Baumgarten, Braun, Brochmand, *Brown*, Bruce, A. B., *Bruce, F. F.* (NIC), Chrysostom, Davidson, Delitzsch, Dickson, Edwards (ExB), Fudge (*Our Man in Heaven*), Gouge, Grosheide (CNT; KV), Héring (C), Hewitt (T), Javet (*Dieu Nous Parla*), Kendrick, Kent, Kuinoel, Kuss, Lindsay, Loew, Lowrie, McCaul, Maclean, Manson, Meyer, F. B., Michel (M), *Moffatt* (ICC), Montefiore (B-H), Moule, H. C. G., Murray (*The Holiest of All*), Nairne (CBSC), Neil (TB), *Owen*, Pink, Plumer, Rendall, Ridout, Riggenbach (Z), Sampson, Saphir, Schneider, Schulz, Spicq (EB), Staab (*Pauluskommentare aus der griechischen Kirche*), Strathmann (NTD), Stuart, Theodoret, Tholuck, Thomas (*"Let Us Go On"*), Turner, Van Andel, Vaughan, *Vos* (*The Teaching of the Epistle to the Hebrews*), Weiss, B. (M), *Westcott*, Wickham (W), Windisch (HNT).

James

Bardenhewer, Belser, Blackman (TB), Carr (CGT), Deems (*Gospel of Common Sense*), Dibelius (M), Dickson, Grosheide (CNT), Hauck (NTD), Horn, *Hort, Johnstone,* Knowling (W), *Manton*, Marty, *Mayor*, Moffatt (Mo), Mitton (EvBC), *Plummer* (ExB), Plumptre (CBSC), Pott, *Ropes* (ICC), *Ross* (NIC), Schlatter, Sikkel, Smelik (PNT), Spitta, Stier, *Tasker* (T), Thurneysen, Wardlaw.

I and II Peter and Jude (Indication is given if all are not included)

Adams II, Ames, Beare I, *Bigg* (ICC), Blenkin I (CGT), *Brown* I & II, Chaine (EB), Clark I & II, Cranfield I (TB), Demarest I, Dickson, *Green* II (T), Hauck (NTD), Holzmeister, *Hort* part of I, Huther (M), Jenkyn Ju., *Johnstone* I, Jowett I & II, Keil, Kelly (B-H), Knopf (M), Lawlor Ju., *Leighton* I, Lillie I & II (ExB), *Manton,* Ju., Masterman I, *Mayor* II & Ju., Meyer, F. B., I (*Tried by Fire*), Moffatt (Mo), Plummer Ju. (ExB), Plumptre (CBSC), Pott, Reicke (AB; *The Disobedient Spirits and Christian Baptism,* part of I), Schnackenburg (HTK), Schott II, Ju., *Selwyn* I, Spicq I, II, Steiger, *Stibbs* I (T), Stöckhardt I, Wand (W), Wohlenberg (Z), Wolff Ju.

I, II, and *III John* (Indication is given if all are not included)

Alexander, W. (ExB), Augustine, *Brooke* (ICC), Büchsel (THNT), Bultmann (M), *Candlish* I, Chaine (EB), Cocke, Cotton I, Dickson, Dodd (Mo), Ebrard, Findlay, Gaugler, Ghysels, Gore, Hardy I, Hauck (NTD), Haupt I, Horn, Huther (M), Lücke, Morgan I, *Plummer* (CBSC; *CGT*), *Ross* (NIC), Schnackenburg (HTK), Semler I, Smith (EGT), *Stott, Westcott,* White I.

Revelation

Alford (AGT), Allo (EB), Barclay, Bavinck, J. H. (*En voort wentelde de eeuwen*), Beckwith, Behn (NTD), Bonsirven (C; VS), Bousset (M), Brown, Buis, Bullinger, Bultema, Caird (B-H), Case, Cerfaux-Cambier, *Charles* (ICC), Clark (*The Message from Patmos*), Cowles, Cumming, De Burgh, De Haas, Douglas, Durham, *Elliott,* Ewald, Farrer, Frey (*Das Ziel aller Dinge*), Garratt, Glasgow, Govett, Gowan, Greijdanus (KNT; KV), Hadorn (THNT), Hartenstein, *Hendriksen* (*More Than Conquerors*), *Hengstenberg,* Hoeksema, Holden, Hort, Kelly, Kepler, Kiddle (Mo), *Kuyper,* Ladd, Lange (L), Latham, Lee, Laymon, Kohmeyer (HNT), Lilje, Little, Loisy, Lücke, Milligan (ExB), *Morris* (T), Newell (PCNT), Preston (TB), Ramsey, Scott, W., Seiss, Stuart, *Swete, Tenney,* Torrey, Trench (on II, III), Victorinus of Pettau, Visser (PNT), Vitringa, Waller (IC), Walvoord, Zahn (Z).

Chapter 10

LESLIE W. SLOAT*

On the Teaching of New Testament Greek

For some twelve years now I have been involved in giving instruction in New Testament Greek to seminary students. I myself learned the language when I was in seminary. During the years after graduation I had "kept up" with Greek after a fashion by regular reading from the Greek New Testament. But I admit it was somewhat of a traumatic experience to find myself, as the result of the untimely death Dr. Ned B. Stonehouse, invited to share in the responsibility of conducting Greek classes. I looked on the task as in all probability temporary, but temporary things have a tendency to take on a more permanent character.

At first I was assigned the task of helping the more advanced students with their reading. But before long I was also conducting an elementary course for beginners. This I have been doing now for some years.

From the inception of Westminster Seminary in 1929 instruction in elementary Greek has been based on the grammar *New Testament Greek for Beginners* by Dr. J. Gresham Machen. This is the book I use. It begins with the alphabet, goes through the declensions and conjugations in fairly systematic fashion, and includes a simplified explanation of essential points of grammar and syntax. In thirty-three lessons the student is taken through the basic material of the language, and given a minimal vocabulary. Each lesson includes

*Professor Sloat is lecturer in Greek at Westminster Theological Seminary.

sentences for translation, both from Greek to English and from English to Greek. Only near the end of the book are the sentences actually from the New Testament text, though the vocabulary throughout is biblical.

I know that others go about teaching the language in other ways. I have seen a programmed course in which a multitude of details are brought out step by step in numbered sequence. There are inductive grammars, in which a passage of the New Testament is taken and analyzed and explained, as a method of teaching. I am sure those who use these methods believe them to be better than the one we use, and I do not doubt that such methods have certain advantages. But I am satisfied that the method employed by Machen's grammar will, if carefully applied, bring the student to the position where he can handle the Greek of the New Testament with reasonable facility.

As a result of my own experience, I may be permitted to make a few comments. First, as everyone else well knows, the only way to learn a subject is to be compelled to teach it. I have learned more Greek through my teaching than I ever learned as a student. And I encourage my students to find someone to teach—their wives, or friends, or fellow students. Through the give and take of teaching, one learns.

There is nothing impossible about learning the language. The chief problem students have is that they do not know English grammar. It would appear that English grammar, as distinct from literature and composition, has largely disappeared from our lower schools. Students hardly know what adjectives and adverbs, phrases and clauses, are. That nouns have case, and that verbs have active and passive forms and tenses, is a feature of grammar that seems largely foreign to them. Students confess again and again that they have learned English grammar through the study of Greek. I have heard of Greek teachers who spend the first week of the course teaching English. It may not be a bad idea.

At the seminary we try to teach the proper accenting of words from the beginning. In some schools accents are not taught, or taught only in a most minimal fashion. It is true that there were no accents used in the early uncial manuscripts. But there is no doubt that as Greek was read by those who knew it as a native language the words were accented, either by tone or stress, and there was thus a correct pronunciation. The later insertion of accents was not an arbitrary thing, but represented the accepted pronunciation. The Greek texts which the student today uses carry accents, in accordance with established rules, and why should not the student of Greek learn the whole language as it is written, rather than only a part of it?

Learning the accents should not be difficult for students who have been able to graduate from college. And the accents not only contribute to a regular pattern of pronunciation, but often distinguish different forms of words which otherwise are spelled the same. I see no reason for denying the student this degree of familiarity with the language.

In Greek more than in English a good memory is required. A Greek verb may have more than one hundred distinct spellings—forms—to indicate the differences in tense, voice, mood, personal subject, etc. A large part of learning Greek is learning to recognize, at a glance, the different forms of verbs and nouns, so that the proper grammatical relationships and structure of a sentence may be determined. Students who have graduated from college often feel that they have gotten beyond the stage where they have to memorize a multitude of details. They have arrived in the great arena where people think and argue, but no longer memorize data. Dr. Machen more than once made the point that one cannot reason and think except on the basis of known facts. And one certainly does not know and cannot use Greek until he has well memorized the standard paradigms. Is there any miraculous mnemonic device for this? I know of none. I tell the students to sit down and copy out the paradigms a few times, until they can reproduce them accurately. This is no real hardship, and even provides a little extra practice in writing Greek.

Machen's book has exercises which call on the student to translate sentences from English to Greek, as well as from Greek to English. Occasionally students who have had some Greek elsewhere, where translating from English to Greek was not required, come to us confident that they are well prepared, but when asked to put English sentences into Greek they admit that "this is a whole new ball game." In my opinion unless a student has some facility in this type of exercise, he has not yet grasped the language.

It is of course true that in most instances a given English sentence may be translated into Greek in more than one construction. The student may have a harder job deciding on the construction to use than actually using it. Often several constructions are equally correct. As the student comes to see this, his understanding of the richness and variety of both languages is considerably enlarged.

Machen has given us an elementary course for beginning students. He makes no attempt to deal with all the variables of the language, and when the students advance to the New Testament it is inevitable that they will find things with which Machen has not dealt, or which seem to be exceptions to rules and forms he has presented. I seem to recall someone's saying that it was Machen's view that the study of Greek in seminary was not per se intended to produce Greek scholars. That task belongs rather to graduate schools specializing in language study. The seminary program is rather designed to provide students with a sufficient proficiency in the language so that they will be able to read commentaries intelligently and, with the help of grammars and lexicons, carry out responsible exegesis.

It is certainly true that the New Testament style is not elementary. Some of it is highly literary. It is also true that we are being confronted today with a plethora of translations, some very good, and some at points very misleading. The man whose business is the Word of God should be able to handle it aright, translate it accurately and interpret it properly. For this he needs more than a smattering of the original language. It may well be that the elementary course is not sufficient to equip the minister of the Word adequately. So at the seminary there is reading in the New Testament, not only in the Greek course itself, but also in other New Testament courses. I do believe that one who has completed and to a fair degree mastered the elementary course based on Machen's lessons, together with certain additional vocabulary and syntax material, is prepared to deal with most matters found in the New Testament, and he is prepared to look into the many more advanced and sophisticated grammars for additional light. I rejoice to hear seminary graduates reporting that they keep up their Greek, and regularly use it in sermon preparation.

My high regard for Machen's book has not kept me from making adjustments which seem to me desirable. For example I have tried bringing in the contract verbs and the rules of contraction while I am dealing with the present system of the verb. Machen delays this material until he has covered the four major tenses. But this means that some of the verbs introduced early cannot be used, for example, in the future or aorist because they are liquid at those points. I have found the students quite able to assimilate the principles and rules of contraction at the earlier stage, and this makes it possible to carry all the verbs through all the tenses, and I find this arrangement satisfactory.

I have made it the practice to provide students with supplementary material in mimeographed form. Students seem to like handouts from the teacher, even though these in the main repeat what appears in the textbook. Some of the material I have reduced to chart form, so the student can see at a glance where he is going. The danger here is, of course, that the student will confine himself to learning the mere data, and will bypass the explanatory material in the book. But I take this chance.

For several years now the seminary has arranged for a special course in Greek for incoming students, given during August. This concentrates a semester of work in one month—two hours a day five days a week for four weeks. I have taught this course and have been well satisfied with it. The student is taking no other course work, and can devote himself to the language, and in general the students have done this. In the one month we are usually able to cover twenty or more chapters of the grammar. And I have given the students the option of taking a final exam, or of writing an essay, in Greek, of at least two hundred and fifty words, using a fair sampling of the forms and constructions already covered. A goodly number of students have taken this option, and have done well.

This summer program makes it possible for the student in September to begin his second language, Hebrew, and also to start his other New Testament courses, for which some knowledge of Greek is required. Students who do not take the summer course, but who begin Greek in September, must normally take four years to complete the degree, while the others can finish in three.

Frankly I enjoy teaching Greek. It gets a little boring at times as students struggle with the paradigms or pronunciation and translation. But to have a group of students come to you knowing nothing of the language in which, in the providence of God, a large portion of His special revelation was communicated to His church, and to see those same students after a few months reading the New Testament in the original, discussing its meaning on the basis of grammatical and historical considerations, and suddenly discovering new depths of meaning with significance for their own lives and for their work—this is very rewarding.

It is highly proper that the Bible should be translated into the language of the people. And we believe that the most unlearned person, reading the Bible in his own language, may well come to understand its blessed message of salvation, and may come to know what he is to believe concerning God and what duty God requires of him. But we may never treat as unimportant that scholarship by which men are enabled to read and search more deeply the sacred treasure store of God's truth. It is just such scholarship and such ability that we hope to develop in the students, that they may "rightly divide the word of truth." And to God shall be all the glory.

Chapter 11

LESLIE W. SLOAT*

New Testament Verb Forms

As a student in Westminster Theological Seminary I learned that a traditional question in New Testament course exams was one requiring us to translate a passage from Greek to English, and to parse all the verb forms.

When years later I found myself teaching Greek in the same seminary, I naturally tried to prepare my pupils for the same sort of question. And it was not long before I came to the conclusion that, for my own benefit if for no other reason, I should myself actually parse all the verbs in the New Testament.

As I thought of this project, certain considerations immediately came to mind. First was the obvious one of the procedure for recording the information so as to make it readily available. I would need some sort of form sheet which would show and classify the information plainly, would reveal any interesting patterns which might exist, and would permit of easy summary and tabulation.

Then it seemed to me that (at least for the Gospels and Acts) I ought to use a variety of markings, so as to distinguish the verbs used, say, by Jesus, from those used by other speakers or by the author. Modern criticism is hardly prepared to admit that such distinctions can be made, since it is widely held that the speeches and discourses have been largely edited, or even originated, by the authors and are not truly genuine. I recognize that different authors

---

*Professor Sloat is lecturer in Greek at Westminster Theological Seminary.

may well report events and even speeches in somewhat different language, but I do believe that the sayings and discourses attributed to Jesus and to others constitute genuine historical reporting, and should be so treated.

Here, however, I faced another problem. It is not always easy to decide where a speech ends and the author's material is resumed. This problem is particularly acute at some points in the fourth Gospel. Here I simply had to use my own judgment. I am sure others would have made different decisions in at least some instances.

Other problems arose. There are a number of verb forms which may be classified in more than one way. The first person singulars of the future active indicative and the aorist active subjunctive are frequently identical. Some contract verbs have the same forms for indicative and subjunctive. The second person plural of the present imperative is the same as the indicative. So here again I have exercised my own judgment. Usually the context will determine, but not always.

At the beginning there was the question of what Greek text to use. I chose to follow the text of the United Bible Societies edition, first published in 1966, under the editorship of Kurt Aland and others. I am not convinced that this edition has the best text at all points. In a number of places it differs from, for example, the Nestle and the Souter texts. However, it is very readable so far as the type face is concerned, and I doubt that, over all, the variations are statistically significant.

As for the form sheet, I prepared one with space for the verb form to be copied in, and then thirty-four columns, representing the different forms. This allowed for five tenses—present, imperfect, future, aorist, and perfect—and five "moods"—indicative, subjunctive, imperative, infinitive, and participle, these however appearing only in the present and aorist, with the participle also in the perfect. In the future and aorist it was necessary to allow for three voice differences, but in the present, imperfect, and perfect tenses the middle and passive forms are identical, so only two columns were required.

I was not very far into the project, however, before I came upon forms that did not fit into the pattern sheet. These I lumped together to the right of the last column, and analyzed separately at a later stage. There are some sixteen of these other forms (optatives, future participles, pluperfects, etc.), which means that in all in the New Testament there are fifty different verb forms.

Each of the sheets took fifty-five verbs, and at the end I had identified a grand total of 28,006 verbs. I also totalled the individual columns for each New Testament book separately, and worked out the percentage of each type of form to the total, constructing charts to show these percentages also.

One may wonder whether, on the basis of this sort of analysis, any judgment could be made as to authorship, for example, of the various letters attributed to Paul, or of the material attributed to John. My own opinion at this point is a decidedly negative one, since I feel that there is not sufficient material, there is variation in the type of material which justifies different language styles, and there is too much possibility of the use of secretaries to do the actual writing, so that an author's own language style does not necessarily appear.

This does not mean, however, that there are not differences of style in verb usage on the part of different authors. An example is the use of the so-called historical present in the narrative portions of the Gospels. Thus in Mark 143 verbs out of 1,443 attributed to the author, are presents. This is just about ten percent. In Matthew about six percent are presents, while in Luke only fifteen out of 1,811 verbs attributed to the author, or less than one percent, are present tense. By contrast, in material attributed to Jesus in the synoptics, the percentage of present actives is twenty-one percent in Matthew, twenty-two percent in Mark, and eighteen in Luke. Incidentally, in Acts in the material attributed to the author, less than one percent of the verbs are present active. Luke did not use the historical present to any substantial degree.

In the narrative portions of the Gospels there would be little occasion to use the future tense. Neither Matthew nor Luke has a single instance, and Mark has only three. One of these is Mark 3:2, where the author reports that the people (subject indefinite) were watching Jesus to see whether he would heal (future) the man with the withered hand on the sabbath day. In the parallel in Luke the author reports that the scribes and Pharisees were watching to see whether Jesus heals (present) on the sabbath. Is Luke concerned more with the general policy followed by Jesus, while Mark's interest is in the immediate situation? Perhaps so.

Paul on more than one occasion attracts the reader's attention—and this would be even truer of a person hearing the material read—by doublets or repeats, the same verb in the same form repeated in successive clauses, or by the rapid alternation of two verbs (e.g., "it is sown . . . it is raised . . . it is sown . . . it is raised . . ." I Cor. 15:42ff.). It is easy to pass lightly over these features in normal reading, but they stand out clearly on a chart.

When the project was completed, I listed the different forms in the order of their frequency. The most frequently used forms were present active indicative 4,573, aorist active indicative 4,400, present active participle 2,654, aorist active participle 1,575, followed in order by the imperfect active indicative, future active indicative, and present middle/passive participle, etc. I found one future passive participle, two perfect active-imperatives, and five future infinitives.

Copies of some of the charts follow, showing how the work was carried out, and some of the results.

I. Verb Form Sheet

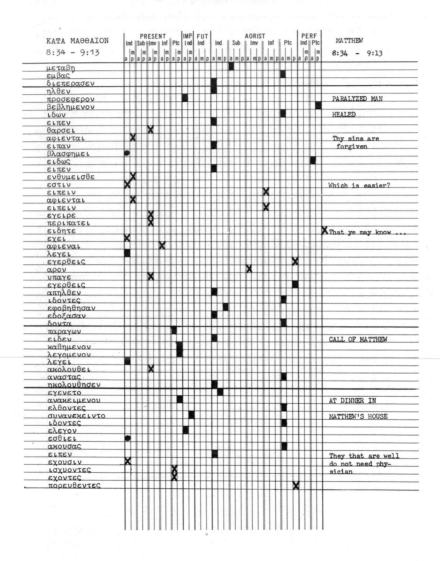

ΚΑΤΑ ΜΑΘΘΑΙΟΝ 8:34 - 9:13	PRESENT					IMP	FUT	AORIST					PERF		MATTHEW 8:34 - 9:13
	Ind	Sub	Imv	Inf	Ptc	Ind	Ind	Ind	Sub	Imv	Inf	Ptc	Ind	Ptc	
μεταβη															
εμβας															
διεπερασεν															
ηλθεν															
προσεφερον															PARALYZED MAN
βεβλημενον															
ιδων															HEALED
ειπεν															
θαρσει															
αφιενται															Thy sins are
ειπαν															forgiven
βλασφημει															
ειδως															
ειπεν															
ενθυμεισθε															
εστιν															Which is easier?
ειπειν															
αφιενται															
ειπειν															
εγειρε															
περιπατει															
ειδητε															That ye may know ...
εχει															
αφιεναι															
λεγει															
εγερθεις															
αρον															
υπαγε															
εγερθεις															
απηλθεν															
ιδοντες															
εφοβηθησαν															
εδοξασαν															
δοντα															
παραγων															
ειδεν															CALL OF MATTHEW
καθημενον															
λεγομενον															
λεγει															
ακολουθει															
αναστας															
ηκολουθησεν															
εγενετο															
ανακειμενου															AT DINNER IN
ελθοντες															
συνανεκειντο															MATTHEW'S HOUSE
ιδοντες															
ελεγον															
εσθιει															
ακουσας															
ειπεν															They that are well
εχουσιν															do not need phy-
ισχυοντες															sician
εχοντες															
πορευθεντες															

II. Chart Showing Number of Each Verb Form, by Section and Source
This Chart Shows Use by Jesus in Matthew

Section	PRESENT IND a	IND mp	PRES SUB a mp	PRES IMV a	IMV mp	PRES INF a	INF mp	PRES PTC a	PTC mp	IMP IND a mp	FUT IND a	IND m	IND p	AOR IND a	IND m	IND p	AOR SUB a	SUB m	SUB p	AOR IMV a	IMV m	IMV p	AOR INF a	INF m	INF p	AOR PTC a	PTC m	PTC p	PERF IND a	IND mp	PERF PTC a	PTC mp
13:7 – 19	12	1		1			1	6		1	2	1	3	9		1	6			1			3			1	1	4		2	1	
13:19 – 30	14	3				1		7			1	1		9		2	2		1	3			1	1		3	1	1			1	
13:30 – 44	12	3		1		1		3		1	6			2		1	1			1	1		1			4		2			1	
13:44 – 14:4	9		1					1		1	4			5		1	1			1		1	2			5						1
14:4 – 19	1			1																1	1											
14:19 – 31	1			1				3	2		1			4		1	1	1		1			3			1						
14:31 – 15:13	6	1	1	4				3	2		1			1		1	1	1	1	4			1			1		1			2	
15:13 – 28	8	3															6	5	4	5			1		2	1					1	
15:28 – 16:3	8	1		3	3			1		3	4			5		1	5			4	1		1			1		1		1	1	
16:3 – 19	11	2	1	2	2			3	1	3	5			10	1	2	3			1			1	1		1	3			1	3	
16:19 – 17:3	6		1	1	1			1	2	1	2	1		2		1	2		1	2	1		3			3	2	1				
17:4 – 16	2	1		1	1			3		3	3			5		2	1	5		2	1		2	1		7			1			
17:16 – 18:2	5		1	2		2		1		1	2			10	1	1	6		1	3			4		1	1	2	1		1	1	
18:2 – 16	14	2	1	1	1			2			3	1		2			5						6							2		
18:16 – 29	7			3	1	1		3		3	4			5			3			1										1		
18:29 – 19:7	2		1	3	1	1		3		3	3			10	1	1	2			2	1		1			3		1	1	1		
19:8 – 20	9	1		2	2			1	2	1	4	1		2		2	1			3			1			7						
19:20 – 20:4	7		1		1			2	1	3	3	1		5	1	1						2	2			1		1				
20:4 – 19	11		2			1		1		1	3			10					1	1			4						1			1
20:19 – 31	5	2	1	3				2		1	3	1		1		1	2	1	1	1			3			3		1	1			1
20:31 – 21:12	2			3		1		1			3	2	1	1		2	2	1	1	2	2		2	1		7	2		2			2
21:12 – 23	2		1	2	1									1	1		2	1	1	3			4	1	1	1				1	1	
21:23 – 33	7		1	1	1			2		3	2			13	1	1	1	1	1	1		2	1	1		3	3	3	1		1	

III. Chart Showing Percentage of Use of Each Verb Out of Total Verbs Used by Source

This Chart Shows Use by Jesus in Matthew

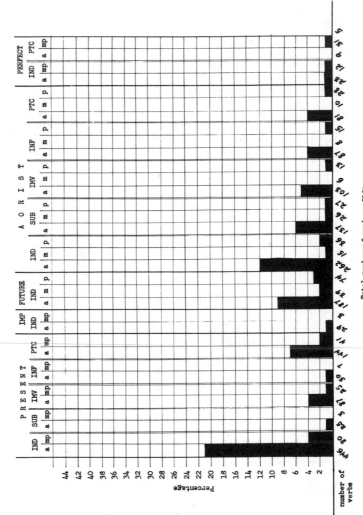

Total number of verbs – 2154

IV
Total Verbs in Greek New Testament

Tense	Active	Middle	Passive	M/P
Present Indicative	4573			
Aorist Indicative	4400			
Present Participle	2654			
Aorist Participle	1575			
Imperfect Indicative	1328			
Future Indicative	1013			
Present Participle				998
Aorist Subjunctive	964			
Aorist Infinitive	956			
Present Indicative				954
Aorist Indicative			852	
Present Infinitive	756			
Aorist Indicative		636		
Aorist Imperative	629			
Present Imperative	613			
Perfect Indicative	601			
Perfect Participle				447
Present Subjunctive	395			
Aorist Participle			388	
Future Indicative		311		
Aorist Participle		304		
Imperfect Indicative				298
Future Indicative			286	
Present Imperative				261
Aorist Subjunctive			253	
Present Infinitive				235
Perfect Indicative				231
Perfect Participle	223			
Aorist Infinitive			174	
Aorist Subjunctive		159		
Aorist Infinitive		115		
Pluperfect Indicative	78			
Aorist Imperative			77	
Present Subjunctive				60
Aorist Imperative		59		
Perfect Infinitive	37			
Aorist Optative	20			
Present Optative	19			
Aorist Optative		19		

Future Participle	9			
Perfect Subjunctive	9			
Perfect Infinitive				9
Pluperfect Indicative				7
Future Infinitive	(5)			
Aorist Optative			5	
Present Optative				4
Future Participle		2		
Perfect Imperative	2			
Perfect Imperative				2
Future Participle			1	
TOTALS	20,859	1,605	2,036	3,506

Total verbs in N.T.—28,006

Chapter 12

JOHN H. SKILTON

The Study of Modern English Versions of the New Testament

In his book, *The English Bible*,[1] Professor F. F. Bruce tells the story of a pastoral call which a young minister in Scotland made on an elderly woman. The minister read to her a chapter from Moffatt's translation of the Bible. She listened to him and said, "Well, that was very nice; but won't you just read a bittie of the Word of God before you go?"[2] For her Moffatt's version was one thing; the Word of God was something else.

The elderly parishioner's evaluation of Moffatt's version is probably representative of the spontaneous appraisal which many have made in our times of the versions which have been appearing for decades with bewildering frequency. They may have sincerely felt that the version with which they were most familiar was more reliable than its newer rivals. Not many may have gone so far as the gentleman who is reported to have said that if the King James Version was good enough for the Apostle Paul it was good enough for him, but it cannot be questioned that for a goodly number the Authorized Version has become virtually the *St.* James version! The present writer has much sympathy for their high esteem for that truly great version. He would still commend it for popular

---

1. New York: Oxford University Press, 1961.
2. *Ibid.*, p. 168.

and general use, for public reading, and for memorization of texts,[3] but he would suggest that sound reasons should be set forth in support of it or of any other version that one may recommend. Advocates of the use of certain modern versions as well as those who have favored continued use of the King James Version have often, in the writer's judgment, been hampered by a lack of information and have failed to make accurate and just appraisals. The zealous advocates of the King James Version just mentioned should not serve as our only bad examples. Too many in our times who are not really qualified to judge of the accuracy of modern versions seem to take the position: "If this sounds good to me, it must have been good enough for the Apostle Paul!"

How should one go about appraising modern English versions and evaluating the translation effort in general in the period since 1881? (1881 is a significant date for the student of English versions, for it was then that the New Testament in the English Revised Version appeared and then also that the highly influential Greek New Testament of Westcott and Hort was published. For our purposes here the modern period may be said to begin with that year.)

The first thing that the student should do in his effort to make an informed assessment of the translation activity since 1881 is to obtain or develop an adequate working bibliography of the English versions of the period. Despite the proliferation of translations of the New Testament in recent years, few persons have any proper conception or appreciation of the actual extent and diversity of the translation activity which has been going on since 1881. In his researches, the writer has been able to list on the average more than one new English translation or revision of an earlier translation of the entire New Testament or of much of it per year from 1881 to the present. Translations or revisions of portions of the New Testament for this period are to be numbered in the hundreds. Table I, which follows, will give an impression of the vastness of the translation activity in the years from 1881 to the early part of 1961. Table II

---

3. See John H. Skilton, "The King James Version Today," in *The Law and the Prophets*, ed. John H. Skilton (Nutley, N. J.: Presbyterian and Reformed Publishing Company, 1974), pp. 94-114.

lists some of the translations or revisions of earlier translations of the entire New Testament or of much of it for the years since 1881. Brief designations of the translations are given. The numbers which introduce each listing refer to the place in the writer's "Working Bibliography of English Translations of the New Testament, 1881-1961,"[4] where the full title may be found. Thus 1881:1 indicates that the work is listed in the bibliography under the year 1881 and is the first item mentioned for that year.

Table I

LIST OF NEW ENGLISH TRANSLATIONS,
PARAPHRASES, AND REVISIONS
1881–1961

Year	Bible and N.T.			Parts of N.T.			Totals for Year		
	New	Revised	Total	New	Revised	Total	New	Revised	Total
1881	0	5	5	6	1	7	6	6	12
1882	0	0	0	4	0	4	4	0	4
1883	1	3	4	5	0	5	6	3	9
1884	0	0	0	1	0	1	1	0	1
1885	1	0	1	5	0	5	6	0	6
1886	2	0	2	1	0	1	3	0	3
1887	0	0	0	2	0	2	2	0	2
1888	0	0	0	6	0	6	6	0	6
1889	0	0	0	3	0	3	3	0	3
1890	0	0	0	1	1	2	1	1	2
1891	2	0	2	3	1	4	5	1	6
1892	0	0	0	3	0	3	3	0	3
1893	0	0	0	3	0	3	3	0	3
1894	0	0	0	3	0	3	3	0	3
1895	1	0	1	6	0	6	7	0	7
1896	0	0	0	2	0	2	2	0	2
1897	3	1	4	5	0	5	8	1	9
1898	2	0	2	6	0	6	8	0	8
1899	2	1	3	4	0	4	6	1	7
1900	0	0	0	7	0	7	7	0	7
1901	3	1	4	7	0	7	10	1	11

4. John H. Skilton, "The Translation of the New Testament into English, 1881-1950: Studies in Language and Style" (doctoral dissertation, 1961, available through University Microfilms, Ann Arbor, Mich.), pp. 1-180.

Table I (Continued)

Year	Bible and N.T.			Parts of N.T.			Totals for Year		
	New	Revised	Total	New	Revised	Total	New	Revised	Total
1902	1	0	1	4	0	4	5	0	5
1903	1	0	1	4	0	4	5	0	5
1904	1	0	1	7	0	7	8	0	8
1905	0	2	2	5	0	5	5	2	7
1906	0	0	0	1	0	1	1	0	1
1907	0	0	0	5	0	5	5	0	5
1908	0	0	0	5	0	5	5	0	5
1909	2	0	2	6	0	6	8	0	8
1910	0	0	0	3	1	4	3	1	4
1911	1	1	2	6	0	6	7	1	8
1912	0	1	1	5	1	6	5	2	7
1913	2	2	4	5	0	5	7	2	9
1914	2	1	3	4	0	4	6	1	7
1915	0	0	0	4	0	4	4	0	4
1916	0	0	0	0	0	0	0	0	0
1917	0	0	0	2	0	2	2	0	2
1918	1	0	1	8	0	8	9	0	9
1919	0	1	1	5	0	5	5	1	6
1920	0	0	0	12	0	12	12	0	12
1921	1	0	1	2	0	2	3	0	3
1922	0	0	0	5	0	5	5	0	5
1923	3	0	3	4	0	4	7	0	7
1924	1	0	1	9	0	9	10	0	10
1925	1	0	1	2	0	2	3	0	3
1926	0	0	0	2	0	2	2	0	2
1927	0	0	0	2	0	2	2	0	2
1928	1	0	1	3	0	3	4	0	4
1929	2	0	2	5	0	5	7	0	7
1930	0	0	0	8	0	8	8	0	8
1931	0	0	0	4	0	4	4	0	4
1932	0	0	0	6	2	8	6	2	8
1933	0	0	0	8	0	8	8	0	8
1934	1	0	1	10	0	10	11	0	11
1935	0	1	1	8	0	8	8	1	9
1936	1	0	1	4	0	4	5	0	5
1937	3	0	3	10	0	10	13	0	13
1938	2	0	2	7	0	7	9	0	9
1939	0	0	0	4	0	4	4	0	4
1940	1	0	1	6	0	6	7	0	7
1941	2	0	2	5	0	5	7	0	7

Table I (Continued)

Year	Bible and N.T.			Parts of N.T.			Totals for Year		
	New	Revised	Total	New	Revised	Total	New	Revised	Total
1942	0	0	0	7	0	7	7	0	7
1943	1	0	1	2	0	2	3	0	3
1944	1	0	1	4	0	4	5	0	5
1945	1	0	1	1	0	1	2	0	2
1946	0	1	1	3	0	3	3	1	4
1947	1	0	1	7	0	7	8	0	8
1948	1	0	1	3	0	3	4	0	4
1949	0	0	0	7	0	7	7	0	7
1950	3	0	3	6	0	6	9	0	9
1951	2	0	2	6	0	6	8	0	8
1952	1	0	1	6	0	6	7	0	7
1953	1	0	1	8	0	8	9	0	9
1954	1	0	1	8	0	8	9	0	9
1955	1	0	1	15	0	15	16	0	16
1956	1	0	1	7	0	7	8	0	8
1957	0	0	0	13	0	13	13	0	13
1958	3	1	4	13	0	13	16	1	17
1959	0	0	0	7	0	7	7	0	7
1960	1	0	1	4	1	5	5	1	6
1961	1	0	1	1	0	1	2	0	2
Totals	67	22	89	416	8	424	483	30	513

Table II

THE BIBLE OR THE NEW TESTAMENT ALONE

(Complete or almost complete)

A working list of English versions and revisions

1881–1973

1881: 1 Speaker's Commentary
1881: 4 Revised Version. See 1885: 2.
1881: 5 American Version
1881: 6 Williams, S.
1881: 7 American Revised Edition
1883: 1 Darby
1883: 2 Bible Union. See 1913: 1.
1883: 3 Hanson
1883: 4 Tischendorf
1885: 3 Dillard
1886: 1, 2 Bartlett and Peters

Table II (Continued)

1890:	2	Rotherham. See 1897: 1, 4.
1891:	1	Numerical Bible
1891:	2	Sawyer
1895:	2	Fenton. See 1903: 1.
1897:	2	Berry
1897:	3	Morrow
1897:	1, 4	Rotherham. See 1890: 2.
1897:	5	Weekes
1898:	2	Twentieth Century
1898:	3	Horner. Bohairic.
1899:	1	Sanders and Kent
1899:	2	Murphy Bible
1899:	3	Ballentine. See also 1909: 3 and 1922: 1.
1901:	1	American Revised
1901:	3	Mackail
1901:	4	Moffatt. See 1926: 1.
1901:	5	Smith, W. W.
1902:	1	Godbey
1903:	4	Weymouth
1904:	3	Worrell
1905:	1	Genders
1905:	2	Lloyd
1909:	2	Kent
1909:	3	Ballentine
1911:	1	The 1911 Bible
1911:	4	Horner. Sahidic.
1912:	1	Wildermann-Brepols
1913:	1	Improved Edition. See 1883: 2.
1913:	2	Westminster
1913:	3	Clarke
1913:	5	Moffatt. See 1926: 1.
1914:	1	Concordant
1914:	3	Cunnington
1914:	4	Panin
1918:	1	Anderson
1919:	1	Hayes-Rheims
1921:	1	Student
1923:	1	Ballentine
1923:	2	Goodspeed. See 1935: 1 and 1939: 1.
1923:	3	Sommer
1924:	1	Centenary
1925:	1	Overbury

Table II (Continued)

1928:	2	LeFevre
1929:	1	MacLean, C.
1929:	3	Wolff
1934:	1	Wade
1935:	2	Carey
1936:	2	West China
1937:	1	Greber
1937:	2	Williams, C. B.
1937:	3	Spencer
1938:	1	Pittsburgh, Clementson
1938:	2	Wilson, R. M.
1940:	1	Lamsa. See 1957: 1.
1941:	1	Basic English. See 1949: 1.
1941:	2	Confraternity
1943:	1	Stringfellow
1944:	1	Knox. See 1955: 1.
1945:	1	Berkeley. See 1959:1.
1946:	1	RSV. See 1952: 1.
1947:	2	Swann
1948:	1	Letchworth
1950:	1	New World
1950:	2	Sacred Name
1950:	3	Mackail
1951:	1	Brotherhood Authentic
1951:	2	Norlie
1952:	2	Williams, C. K.
1953:	1	Moore
1954:	2	Kleist and Lilly
1955:	2	Schonfield
1956:	1	Wuest. See 1958: 7 and 1959: 2.
1958:	2	Amplified
1958:	4	Marshall
1958:	5	Phillips
1958:	6	Tomanek
1960:	1	Green
1961:	1	New English

The following versions, which have appeared between 1961 and 1973, have not yet been assigned a number in the working list. The dates given are either of first publication or of copyright. For more detailed bibliographical information, see the List of Versions appended to the article on "Romans 9:5 in Modern English Versions" elsewhere in this volume.

Table II (Continued)

1961	Badley
1961	Noli
1961	Norlie. See 1951: 2.
1962	Children's Version (Green)
1962	Modern King James Version (Green)
1962	Teen-age Version (Green)
1963	Beck
1963	Holy Name Bible. See 1950: 2.
1963	New American Standard
1965	Revised Standard Version, Catholic Edition
1965	Amplified Bible. See 1958: 2.
1966	Jerusalem Bible
1966	Todays English Version (Good News for Modern Man)
1966	Living Scriptures
1967	New Scofield
1967	Living New Testament (a paraphrase)
1968–1969	Barclay
1968	Original Name Version
1969	Modern Language (New Berkeley). See 1945: 1.
1970	New American
1971	King James II Version (Green)
1973	New International Version
1973	Translator's New Testament
1973	Better Version

The Working list given in Table II could be enlarged by including revised editions of certain versions. And unquestionably despite efforts to be comprehensive, some titles have been overlooked. It is indeed doubtful that a completely exhaustive list of English Versions of the New Testament and parts of it in the period since 1881 will ever be developed; but efforts to do so should be encouraged. Any supplementation of the working list which readers can provide will be most welcome.

The task of forming an adequate working bibliography of English Versions which have been made since 1881 is fascinating and arduous. One must, of course, consult such standard works as the *General Catalogue of Printed Books* of the British Museum, the *Library of Congress Catalogue,* the *National Union Catalog,* the *United States Catalogue,* and the *Cumulative Book Index.* But it is necessary to go far beyond these standard bibliographical tools and seek out various special sources of information such as other published (and unpublished) catalogues. Libraries public and private must be visited. In the case of many works, it is impossible to ascertain from their titles alone as they are given in catalogues whether they contain fresh translations, revisions or reprints of translations, or no translated material at all. There can be no substitute for actually seeing such works.[5]

Even a cursory acquaintance with the large company of new versions and revisions which have appeared since 1881 will indicate that there is a fascinating and challenging diversity among them in every respect. In the matter of basic text, for example, translators will be found using a Greek text or a secondary text such as Latin, Syriac, Coptic, Armenian, or German. In the case of the Greek texts used, the influence of Westcott and Hort will be observed to be very prominent, but the Greek base will be found to range all the way from a form of the textus receptus to the Greek text which underlies the English Revised Version, the Resultant Greek Text of Weymouth, the texts of individual manuscripts, and the texts of Tischendorf, Tregelles, Von Soden, Bover, the Bible Societies, and a number of eclectic texts.

The student who is concerned about obtaining an adequate impression of the nature of the basic text followed by a translator will naturally take account of any information about the matter that the translator himself provides. However, regardless of what the translators say, it is essential to check versions at numerous places of significant textual variation. A convenient list of important textual variants in the Gospels and Acts is found in Appendix I in Kenyon's *Our Bible and the Ancient Manuscripts.*[6] This list may be readily supplemented for the rest of the New Testament by consulting an edition with an adequate critical apparatus. Checking of this sort should give a good preliminary indication of the general nature of the basic text. One should be able to tell whether its leaning is toward the textus receptus or toward a modern critical text. And

---

5. Skilton dissertation, pp. 3-7.
6. Frederic G. Kenyon, *Our Bible and the Ancient Manuscripts.* Rev. by A. W. Adams. 5th ed. (London: Eyre and Spottiswoode, 1958), pp. 332-42.

more intensive checking can be undertaken as one works further
with the version.

Faithfulness in Rendering

Another major matter which the student of translations has to
consider is faithfulness or accuracy in rendering. A version may be
based on a very good text, but it may translate it in such a way as
to lose much of the meaning and character of the original. Dr.
Oswald T. Allis once said that "the final test of a translation is its
accuracy." He pointed out that "the translator is the custodian or
steward, authorized or self-appointed as the case may be, of that
which is another man's and 'it is required in stewards, that a man
be found faithful.' "[7]

There has, however, been much difference of opinion as to what
faithfulness and accuracy in a translation really are. Should a translator stick very close to the words of the original and produce an
interlinear-type, word-for-word rendering at the expense of English
idiom? Not many would recommend this extremely literal type of
translation. On the other hand, should he content himself with
trying to convey the thoughts of his text with little regard for its
details and even with removal of background elements which reflect
the milieu in which the original was written? At times it is hard to
distinguish the thought-for-thought type of rendering from paraphrase. Although many will grant the value of a paraphrase, few
will be willing to regard it as translation. In between the extremes
of excessive literalness and excessive freedom, of course, there are
all sorts of degrees, stages, and combinations.

The preference of the present writer is for a translation which
sticks close to its basic text and tries to conserve as much as possible
of the details and background of the original, but which does not
lose sight of the thought movement and remembers its responsibilities
to the receptor language to produce a work that is intelligible, idio-
matic, and felicitous. The Autorized Version is an example of re-

---

7. "Dr. Moffatt's 'New Translation' of the Old Testament," *The Princeton Theological Review* 23(1925), 298.

markable success in this respect. In the preparation of the Genevan New Testament of 1557 there was likewise a concern for the faithful rendering of the text "in euery point and worde" and for "proprietie of the wordes," and there was conscientious attention to the sense.[8] Dr. Francis R. Steele has protested against the claims of certain modern versions to be regarded as translations. They do not meet what he regards as a proper definition of a translation: "A translation should convey as much of the original text in as few words as possible, yet preserve the original atmosphere and emphasis. The translator should strive for the nearest approximation in words, concepts, and cadence. He should scrupulously avoid adding words or ideas not demanded by the text. His job is not to expand or explain, but to translate and preserve the spirit and force of the original—even, if need be, at the expense of modern colloquialisms—so long as the resultant translation is intelligible."[9]

The student who wishes to determine what method of translation in general a version is following should note carefully any statements which the translator himself may make about the matter in his preface or elsewhere. It will be useful also to compare the version being studied with the Greek text in several selected passages. Comparison might also be made with the renderings of a number of English versions such as ARV (a close translation), NEB (a free translation), and AV. Such comparisons will give a preliminary impression which can be tested as the student works further with the version.

The student will note that all sorts of specific questions bearing upon faithfulness and accuracy have been considered by translators and have received different answers. Should a thoroughgoing attempt be made to render into English the precise force of the moods and tenses of the Greek verbs? Charles B. Williams has made a determined effort in this direction. For example, he translates Acts 21:21

---

8. *Records of the English Bible,* ed. Alfred W. Pollard (London: Oxford University Press, 1911), pp. 280-81.
9. Francis R. Steele, "Rules for Bible Translators," *"Christianity Today* (September 26, 1960), p. 11.

as follows: "They have been repeatedly told about you that you continuously teach the Jews who live among the heathen to turn their backs on Moses, and that you continue to tell them to stop circumcising their children, and to stop observing the cherished customs." Should a principle of uniformity of rendering be adopted which calls for the translation of the same Greek word wherever possible by the same word in English? AV rejected such a principle, but the Revised Versions adhered to it. Thus the Greek word for "sign" is always translated "sign" in John's Gospel in ERV and ARV, but in AV it comes through sometimes as "sign," but more often as "miracle" (cf. John 2:11 and 20:30). Should background or cultural elements be removed from the text? Phillips, for example, substitutes for the ancient kiss of love (cf. I Peter 5:11) the modern handshake. Again, what should one do about monetary terms and measures? And should a translator seek to convey an impression of the diversities of language and style in the various books of the New Testament?

The student will, of course, wish to test the accuracy of the translation of given words and phrases. He will wish to determine whether the version with which he is dealing has taken account of recent lexical information. He may find it stimulating to see what his version does with some of the questions that Edgar J. Goodspeed mentions in his *Problems of New Testament Translation*.[10]

To translate faithfully and accurately is a task of the most demanding sort. To evaluate accurately a translator's work in this area is hardly less demanding. It is to be feared that, as was said earlier, too many persons commend renderings uncritically. If the way in which Phillips or some other translator puts a text appeals to them, they are willing to cite it in that way and to commend it to others without really determining whether it is an accurate and just representation of the Greek text. In a day when much liberty has been taken in rendering the New Testament, it is essential that students prepare themselves to test thoroughly and fairly the accuracy of the translator's work.

---

10. Chicago: University of Chicago Press, 1945.

Language and Style

A special interest of translators in the period since 1881 has been in the language and style of their versions. Much attention has been given to such matters as clarity, appropriateness, and contemporaneity of expression. Effectiveness, forcefulness, and felicity have been by no means completely ignored; but they have generally fallen outside either the competence or major concern of numerous translators.

In assessing the language and style of a version, it is wise at the start to take notice of what the translators themselves may have said about their aims in these respects. Much has been written by them about the virtue of translating afresh or revising older versions into a contemporary English that should be clear to all. The great tradition of simplicity and intelligibility which flourished in the period from Tyndale to the Authorized Version unquestionably is still influential. Then too the powerful advocacy of the necessity of revision and clarification which produced the English and the American Revised Versions opened the gates for a flood of other versions which hoped to meet the need more adequately than it was felt the Revised Versions had done. Another important influence on translators was the claim made about the close of the nineteenth and the beginning of the twentieth century that the Greek of the New Testament resembled, in large measure at least, the vernacular, informal, popular, nonliterary Greek of its day. It was reasoned that the New Testament was originally written in the language of the people and that therefore it should be translated into modern popular speech. Of course, judgments about the popular nature of the Greek of the New Testament have not always been properly balanced and have failed to take due account of other elements in that Greek,[11] but nevertheless the discovery of some

---

11. On other elements in New Testament Greek, see, for example, J. Gresham Machen, *New Testament Greek for Beginners* (New York: The Macmillan Co., 1959), pp. 4-6, and Nigel Turner, *Grammatical Insights into the New Testament* (Edinburgh: T. & T. Clark, 1965), pp. 182ff., and "The Literary Character of New Testament Greek," *New Testament Studies* 20 (1973-1974), 107-114.

affinity with nonliterary Greek has exercised a large influence on recent translation work.

After considering the objectives expressed by translators, the student might proceed to test the language and style of a version in various ways. He will wish to see whether the translator retains obsolete and archaic expressions. Does he retain old pronominal forms and old verb endings in other than devotional usage, where they are still current English? Does he avoid even established biblical and theological terms, which he thinks might be unclear to his readers (e.g., parables [Matt. 13:3]; justified [Rom. 5:1]; gospel [I Cor. 15:1]; grace [Eph. 2:8]? Does he favor a paratactic style? On this point his work might be checked against the Greek text and other versions at Luke 15:11-20 and at Mark 1:16-28. Does he go in for short sentences? A good place to test this is at Colossians 1:3-8, where the Greek text and AV have only one sentence and the Kleist and Lilly version has nine. Is there monotony in the length and construction of sentences? Have ambiguity and awkwardness been avoided? Is the style terse and the diction clear and simple? Is there an avoidance of harsh sounds, unconscious rhymes, and objectionable alliteration (e.g., "the tiptop turret of the temple," "strengthen the stand of your knocking knees"). Are banal, hackneyed expressions frequently used which are incapable of expressing the vigor and freshness of the original? Is the translator insensitive to the dignity and majesty of the text before him and content to use expressions quite out of tone with the original? Are different grades of diction unnaturally mixed? Is the style marked by aridity and prosiness? Does the version lack music and power? These are some of the questions which must be asked about the language and style of a version. Much can be learned by checking a version at a number of well-selected places; but there is no substitute for reading it all the way through. Then one should be able to report more confidently about the stylistic virtues and defects of the work and assess the general impression that it makes as a whole.

Theological Viewpoint

The theological position of the translator will have an important influence on his work. One who is a stranger to the doctrines of salvation and who does not receive the Bible as the Word of God written may produce a work that will have certain technical values, but which will not be truly responsive to the message of the Scriptures. In many ways the effects of his lack of spiritual understanding may manifest themselves.[12]

To obtain a preliminary impression about the theological position of the translator, one will of course wish to note whatever he may say on this subject and then test his version at various places where his theological position might manifest itself. For example, a translator's viewpoint on the deity of Christ might (though not always necessarily) be indicated by the way in which he handles John 1:1; Romans 9:5; and Titus 2:13. As to how he stands on the doctrine of propitiation, help should be found at Romans 3:25; I John 2:2; 4:10; and Hebrews 2:17. On adoption, see Romans 8:25; Galatians 4:5; and Ephesians 1:5; on justification, Romans 3:26; 5:1; on repentance (or "penance"), Matthew 3:2; on Scripture, II Timothy 3:16; on eternal punishment, Matthew 25:46; on baptism, Matthew 28:19; and on church officers, Acts 14:23 and James 5:14. These are of course a mere scattering of references where a particular theological viewpoint may manifest itself. A more thorough appraisal can be made by checking a version in its rendering of the proof texts contained in a good edition of the Westminster Confession of Faith and by reading a version through, taking note not only of the text itself but also of the annotations and other "helps" provided.

The suggestions given above could, of course, be supplemented and improved. The really important thing is that the student should endeavor to describe and evaluate English versions, whether they are old or new, with accuracy and fairness, and that he arrive at informed conclusions as to what service if any they can perform for himself and for others.

The following survey form is appended with the hope that it may be of some assistance to the student who is trying to develop an orderly procedure in evaluating English versions.

---

12. See Skilton, "The King James Version Today," pp. 95ff.

Survey of English Version of the New Testament

I. Introductory
  1. Title of translation:
  2. Name of translator:
  3. Date of publication:
  4. Number of edition:
  5. Place of publication:
  6. Name of publisher:
  7. If there is a preface or introduction, summarize the information it gives about the nature and the aims of the translation and the viewpoint of the translator:
  8. Evaluation of format (Note particularly size of print and number of columns to a page):

II. The Basic Text
  1. Is the translation made directly from a Greek text?
  2. If it is, on what Greek text is it based?
  3. If it is not made directly from the Greek, what is its textual base?
  4. Check the version at the places of variation listed in Appendix I of Kenyon's *Our Bible and the Ancient Manuscripts.*
  5. What type of text (Alexandrian, Western, etc.) does the version seem to follow in the main?
  6. How would you rate the textual base used by the version?

III. Type of Rendering
  1. Indicate whether the rendering of Matthew 1 and I Thessalonians 1 is close or free.
  2. On the whole, what method of rendering does the translator seem to be employing? Word-for-word? Thought-for-thought? A combination of the two?

IV. Accuracy
  1. Check the accuracy of the rendering at numerous places.
  2. Does the translator try to render the same Greek word by the same English word wherever possible? Make use of a Greek concordance in seeking to answer this question.
  3. Does the translator try to bring out the precise force of Greek verb forms?
  4. How does he deal with monetary and other terms reflecting cultural backgrounds?
  5. How would you rate the version for accuracy?

V. Language and Style
  1. Check the language and style at twenty-five representative places.

2. On the basis of this sampling, state your preliminary impressions of the language and style of the version.
3. Are modern punctuation, spelling, and paragraphing employed?
4. State your impressions of the language and style on the basis of your reading of the version in its entirety.

VI. Theological Viewpoint
1. Check the translation at numerous points where the theological viewpoint of the translator might be indicated.
2. On the basis of this sampling, state your preliminary impressions about the theological position of the translator.
3. State your impression about the theological viewpoint of the translator on the basis of reading the version in its entirety.

VII. Annotations and Other Helps
State what helps are provided for the reader (textual, exegetical, doctrinal, etc.) and briefly evaluate them.

VIII. Summary and Evaluation
1. Summarize your evaluation of the version.
2. Among modern English versions, does it have anything distinctive to offer?
3. Would you recommend it for public reading?
4. Would you recommend it for memorization of texts?
5. Would you recommend it for private reading? If so, to certain readers only?
6. Would you recommend it for study purposes?

Chapter 13

ARTHUR W. KUSCHKE, JR.*

Graduate Theological Research
Identification of Materials and Use of Bibliographies**

A. There are two contiguous footnotes on page 57 of *The Problem of History in Mark*, by James M. Robinson, Naperville, Allenson, 1957 (*Studies in Biblical Theology*, first series, no. 21). They read as follows:

> J. Weiss, *The History of Primitive Christianity*, I, 14ff.
>
> B. Weiss, *Das Marcusevangelium und seine synoptischen Parallelen*, 1872, 54.

Let us suppose that a student wants to locate and use these books. Where can they be found? Are the titles accurate? And especially, who were J. Weiss and B. Weiss? Assuming an inquirer who does not already know the answers to these questions, and assuming that the books are not listed in our own card catalogue, it becomes necessary:

a) to identify the authors, and

b) to verify the titles; and then, and only then,

c) to inquire through our library staff at the Pennsylvania Union Library Catalogue for a location for these books.

---

*Mr. Kuschke is librarian at Westminster Theological Seminary.

**This introduction to bibliography was prepared for the use of students at Westminster Seminary, Philadelphia. It describes materials in the library of that seminary and refers also to local libraries such as that of the Lutheran Theological Seminary, Philadelphia. It has broader implications, however, for other libraries.

The necessary identification and verification, for purposes of inquiry at the PULC, is through a standard major bibliography. Best for the letter W, in 1974, is the British Museum *General Catalogue of Printed Books.* Turning to volume 254 (WAU-WELC) we find listings for the following people named J. Weiss and B. Weiss:

J. Weiss:

    5 different people with first initial J only
    2   "   "   named Jacob Weiss
    1 named Jacques
    1   "   James
    1   "   Jean Jacques
    1   "   Jekuthiel
    1   "   Jiri
    2   "   Joannes
   10   "   Johann
    1   "   Johannes
    4   "   John
    6   "   Josef or Joseph
    1   "   Josua
    1   "   Judith
    1   "   Julius

B. Weiss:

    1 named Benjamin
    3   "   Bernhard
    1   "   Bernhardus
    2   "   Berthold
    1   "   Bruno

It becomes obvious that the footnote on page 57 would have been more helpful if it had given the authors' first names.

Three different people named Rudolf Smend wrote on O.T. subjects. There are at least 2 each of John Knox, Hugh Martin, Friedrich Spanheim, Jacob Trigland, Jonathan Edwards, William Tennent, and Caspar Wistar Hodge; and numerous theologians named John Brown. In such cases an author's dates are necessary for identification.

B. For identification and verification, consult in order the following bibliographies:

1. *National Union Catalog, pre-1956* (not yet complete; for the end of the alphabet use Library of Congress Catalog to 1942, etc.).
2. *National Union Catalog, 1953 to date.*
3. *British Museum Catalogue, and supplements to date.*
4. *Union Theological Seminary Shelf List, to 1960* (red volumes).

Include, in your bibliographical notes, the following:

author's full name, last name first (and if necessary, his dates)
the correct title, as on title page
edition (if specified)
place, publisher, date
volume number or number of volumes (if more than one)
series name and number (if ·in a series)
periodical name, volume and issue (if in a periodical)
page or pages cited
where reference was first found
where title was verified

Write all this down. Make a card file for easiest reference. Don't do the work twice. Don't be in the position of not knowing where you got a reference. If your original source is "hearsay" or "don't know" you can't be sure that your title is more than suppositious. On the same cards enter the page references and other notes from your reading.

Don't turn to others for this bibliographic labor. Do it yourself; this is necessary if you are to become an expert in the literature of your field. Your bibliographic record on cards can be selected and copied off for the bibliography of your thesis. For the arrangement and form of the thesis, see *Form and Style: Theses, Reports, Term Papers,* by William Giles Campbell and Stephen V. Ballou, fourth edition, Boston, Houghton Mifflin, 1974.

C. Special Types of Materials.

Sometimes a book, as described in a footnote, does not exist; the footnoter made a mistake, perhaps by using the spine title rather than the title-page title. But there are other titles which, although incompletely identified, may still be traced. These include:

Articles in periodicals (see periodical indexes)

Articles in Festschriften or symposia (much harder to trace, especially if no index exists to Festschriften articles in your subject: try the card catalogue, watch for other independent references to the same article)

Monographs in series (these are sometimes listed by author and series title only: see our M. in S. red binders described below)

Lectures, pamphlets, tapes, mimeographed materials (inquiry from original authors, publishers, or sources may bring results)

Dissertations (in the U.S., most doctoral theses may be obtained from University Microfilms on microfilm or reprint)

Microforms (some rare books otherwise unobtainable may be available on microfilm, etc.)

D. Use of the Westminster Library.

The card catalogue: Use this first, and give it enough attention and care to make sure that you have followed all its suggestions on subject headings (in CAPITAL LETTERS), all books and articles by important authors, and all its notes about bibliographies. The arrangement is in one alphabet, for authors, subjects, and titles.

"Look before and after." Let us suppose that you wish to find an article in a symposium entitled *The Future of Hope,* published in 1970. You discover such a symposium in the card catalogue, and from the call number given on the upper left corner of the card, locate the book in the stacks. But the book does not contain the article desired. What's wrong? You didn't look at the card before, or the card after: two different symposia were published in 1970 each under the title, *The Future of Hope.* Return to the card catalogue and give it more time to reveal its information.

The classification system (our revision of the system designed for Union Theological Seminary, N.Y.) is efficient for an open-stacks, theological library because it does not require long and complicated call numbers. The short call numbers facilitate use of the library.

Certain parts of the *stacks* are worth extra attention. AA-AT has bibliographies and reference works. Under AY are complete works of important authors (except the fathers, who are upstairs in G) arranged alphabetically by author. Z contains bound periodicals.

Your area of specialization will take you to one or more important sections of stacks, for very thorough familiarity. But it is good also to survey the whole collection from A to Z, with a copy of the classification system in hand.

E. Inter-library Loan.

For books not in the Westminster Library, first verify as described above, then take your full information to our library staff, who will then get in touch with the Pennsylvania Union Library Catalogue to find a location for the book in another library. Don't call the PULC yourself.

Our library staff will fill out an inter-library loan form and request the book from another library. In most cases a book so requested will come within a week.

F. Other Libraries.

Good relationships exist with other theological libraries in our area. Since 1963 the theological librarians of Southeastern Pennsylvania have met twice a year for mutual cooperation. One result has been the *Check List of Periodicals in Nine Theological Libraries of Southeastern Pennsylvania,* fourth edition, 1970, stating in summary form for quick reference the periodical holdings of each library, which are available to member libraries on inter-library loan. Much work has been done to establish a central catalogue for series of monographs. A newsletter *(Teamwork)* is published and information is exchanged whereby unnecessary duplication of materials already in another library may be avoided. In our own card catalogue there are entries for certain important books and reference sets on which, instead of a call number, there appear the symbols "Luth. Sem." and the notation below, IN LUTHERAN LIBRARY, NOT AT WESTMINSTER—indicating that such books are in the library of the Lutheran Theological Seminary, ten minutes away by car. Reciprocal exchange of catalogue cards between the Lutheran library and ours now enables each library to catalogue holdings of the other.

But perhaps the most useful feature of this local library cooperation is the formal agreement whereby a student at any of the cooperating institutions has full borrowing privileges at the library of any of the other seminaries. Besides the Lutheran Library, the most convenient libraries for our use are those of Eastern Baptist and St. Charles Seminaries, which are across the street from each other about half an hour away by car. Everybody is subject to the rules of the lending library but has equal status with students of the lending library.

It will be to the advantage of a graduate student to visit and become familiar with the collections of these other libraries, especially the Lutheran.

As for borrowing books personally at college and university libraries in the area, special arrangements are necessary, often including payment of a fee. But from almost all other libraries most books may be obtained through inter-library loan.

G. Some of the More Useful Bibliographic Tools.

1. *National Union Catalog, pre-1956 Imprints.* This is already, and will continue to be, the largest and most important of all bibliographies in research. Become familiar with it. Begun in 1968, it has now reached the middle of the letter M (volume 349)—except for the volumes on BIBLE, which have been postponed—and will be completed from A to Z in more than 600 volumes. For books published prior to 1956 it includes more authors than any other bibliography and, for most authors, the fullest list of their books and the various editions of their books. It is an authority on an author's correct name and dates. As a "National Union Catalog" it covers the holdings of all major libraries of the U.S. and Canada and also lists libraries where each book may be found.

2. *National Union Catalog, 1953 to date.* Similar to N.U.C. pre-56 but for books printed from 1953 on. There are four major alphabets, as well as many other alphabets in the recent temporary supplements that will later be combined into the fifth major alphabet. For 1953-57, 28 volumes; another alphabet for 1958-1962 in 54; for 1963-67 in 72; and for 1968-72 (in process) more than 100 volumes. (For the *Library of Congress Catalog*—predecessor of N.U.C. and

listing only books in the L.C.—there is one alphabet to 1942 in 167 volumes, another for 1942-47 in 42 volumes, and another for 1948-52 in 24 volumes.)

To save time when using the *N.U.C. 1953-* and the L.C., don't look through all the alphabets. The *date* is the clue. If a book was published in 1966, look first in N.U.C. 1963-67. If you don't know the date of publication but think the book is "recent," start first in the last major alphabet (1968-72) and if your book is not listed there, work through the more recent alphabets in order from the January-March 1973 supplement to the supplement most recently received.

3. *Library of Congress Catalog: Books, Subjects.* While the main L.C.-N.U.C. system covers main entries (usually authors) these *red* volumes list books by *subject* only. They began in 1950, and for books since 1950 they are the fullest subject catalogue. There are four distinct alphabets in 109 volumes for the years 1950-1969, and temporary supplements to date. The first 4 sets together list 16 columns of books about DEAD SEA SCROLLS, 37 columns for THOMAS AQUINAS, 8 columns for BARTH, KARL, 10 columns for CALVIN, JEAN, 244 columns for BIBLE, N.T. (with subdivisions) and 272 columns for BIBLE, O.T. (with subdivisions).

4. *British Museum General Catalogue of Printed Books.* The 263 volumes of this bibliography constituted the largest single publication in history, until it was eclipsed by the N.U.C. pre-56 in over 600 volumes. But the Br. Mus. Catalogue lists hundreds of thousands of books not in N.U.C. at all. It must be approached with respect; it has its own distinct virtues and peculiarities. It does not provide authors' dates and sometimes omits pages or publishers. It lists entries under *author,* and also to a certain extent under *subject,* or *title,* or other headings. The location of subject entries is not always obvious. The Westminster Assembly, Confession of Faith, and Larger and Shorter Catechisms, with texts and commentaries, are to be found in volume 65 under *ENGLAND. CHURCHES AND RELIGIOUS BODIES.—ASSEMBLY OF DIVINES.*) There are 3 volumes which list PERIODICAL PUBLICATIONS not under title, but under place of publication. LITUR-

GIES is a large subject section. On the other hand, under an author's name there usually appear not only books *by* him but also, as cross references, books edited by him or books to which he contributed; and also books *about* him. Do not neglect the Br. Mus. Catalogue. The main alphabet to 1955 is in 263 volumes. There are supplements for 1956-1965 (50 volumes) and 1966-1970 (26 volumes).

5. *Union Theological Seminary Shelf List.* Union Theological Seminary in New York has probably the largest special theological library in the U.S. This is a catalogue of their collection through 1960, only. Note that there is an important difference between the 10 red volumes and the 10 black volumes. The 10 red volumes list books alphabetically by *author,* and like N.U.C. and Br. Mus. are of very great importance as an author bibliography. The 10 black volumes, however, list the same books, completely re-sorted by *subject.*

Thus the black volumes are a theological subject bibliography, following the Union Seminary classification system. The index to this system is found in the green classification volume (AE/Un3a). To find material on a subject look up the subject first in the classification volume to find the classification numbers which cover the subject desired. Thus commentaries on Hebrews are listed under FP90-FP99. A feature of this classification worth noting is that section G (Christian Literature) presents, in chronological groups, many theologians from the apostolic fathers to recent times: not only books *by* them, but also books about them. Thus Origen will be found at GM3/069; Augustine under GN3; Luther under GT2 to GT8; Bultmann at GW28/B939.

6. *Periodical Indexes.* Since it began in 1949 the *Index to Religious Periodical Literature* has made it possible to locate articles in periodicals, and now indexes 150 theological journals by author and by subject. There is also (after the black-edged page) an index of authors of books reviewed in these journals. Volume 10 (for 1971-72) lists Greek and Hebrew words, and useful articles under such headings as ROMANS (under BIBLE. NEW TESTAMENT), KÜNG, MISSIONS, MOLTMANN, PAUL, REFORMATION, TRINITY.

The *Check List of Periodicals in Nine Theological Libraries of Southeastern Pennsylvania,* referred to above, will give *locations* in nearby libraries for many periodical volumes not in our own library.

The *Internationale Zeitschriftenschau für Bibelwissenschaft und Grenzgebiete* (since 1951) classifies, under large subject groups, only selected articles from about 400 journals, but then briefly summarizes each article. There are also author indexes at the end of each part.

Articles on New Testament subjects are similarly classified and summarized in the annual volumes of *New Testament Abstracts* (since 1956).

7. Monographs in Series: A monograph in a series is any scholarly work, small or large, which appears in a sequence of similar monographs, all under one general series title. The monographs are usually numbered. Thus number 9 of *Ecumenical Studies in Worship* is Moule, Charles F. D.: *Worship in the New Testament,* and number 19 in the same series is Allmen, Jean-Jacques: *The Lord's Supper.* Red-bound loose-leaf binders in the library office, in 16 volumes, record the names of the more important series of monographs in biblical and theological research, and also identify all the monographs in each series by number, author, title, and date.

Some examples of series of monographs:

Analecta Biblica
Beihefte zur Zeitschrift für die alttestamentliche Wissenschaft
Beiträge zur Förderung christlicher Theologie, II. Reihe
Beiträge zur Geschichte und Lehre der reformierten Kirche
Études bibliques
Studies in the History of Christian Thought

Sometimes there are series within series, or monographs that appear in more than one series. All monographs in our library are entered in the card catalogue by series name and number, as well as by author, title, and subject for each monograph. The red binders referred to above become useful when you wish to identify, in an especially useful series, other numbers which our library does not have. The red binders are often the only source for the *authors* and *titles* of such numbers.

8. *Union List of Serials* (3rd ed.) and *New Serial Titles, 1950-1970* give the most comprehensive list of both periodicals and series of monographs. They are the best source for *identifying* and *verifying* periodicals and series. They also give *locations* in various libraries. But they do not provide the analytical descriptions of each number, of monographs in series, that are available in the red binders.

9. *Biblica: Elenchus Bibliographicus Biblicus.* Starting in 1920, this has become the most helpful annual bibliography of biblical studies. Each year the latest important contributions are listed: articles in periodicals, books, and book reviews. In O.T. and N.T. studies, familiarity with Biblica: E.B.B. is essential. It is usually the best source for verifying an elusive biblical monograph or symposium.

Comparable, in the field of historical theology, is the annual *Bibliographie* of the *Revue d'histoire ecclésiastique.*

For the years 1921-1939 (only) the great *Bibliographisches Beiblatt der theologischen Literaturzeitung* covers *all* branches of theology. See *Theologischer Jahresbericht* for the years 1881-1916.

10. *Dictionnaire de la Bible.* As an example of Bible encyclopedias consider this, which has been called "by far the most valuable Bible dictionary available." It is also much more than a Bible dictionary; it contains massive articles, with bibliographies, on such subjects as EXPIATION, KÉNOSE, KYRIOS, LOGOS, PAROUSIE; and articles on scholars such as Bousset, Gunkel, Mowinckel. This *Dictionnaire* was begun under the editorship of F. Vigouroux. There are two alphabets: the main work in volumes 1-10, the supplements in the following volumes. Consult the *Supplément* first; articles are more thorough and more recent.

11. *Schaff-Herzog.* This dependable encyclopedia covers church history, theologians, and the literature on theological topics. It is old but still one of the most useful reference books. There is a two-volume supplement, under the title *Twentieth Century Encyclopedia of Religious Knowledge* (1955). Also very good is McClintock & Strong: *Cyclopaedia of Biblical, Theological and Ecclesiastical Literature* (with supplements).

12. *Die Religion in Geschichte und Gegenwart.* The three different editions (1909-13, 1927-32, and 1957-65) display the trends of German scholarship. The second edition has full treatment of 19th and 20th century figures, while the third has cut down on these to provide more space for large topical articles.

13. *Dictionary of National Biography.* National means British. For our purposes this best of all biographical dictionaries might be considered as a "Dictionary of British Theologians, with a Bibliography of their Writings." To move to Britain may be to become British: see *Acontius, Bucer.*

For the U.S., the *Dictionary of American Biography.* For Dutch theologians: die Bie, and Glasius. For the Huguenots: Haag.

14. *Society for Old Testament Study.* Since 1946 this Society has published a yearly *Book List* of recent books on O.T. subjects. Each book is critically *reviewed.* The first eleven years of these book lists were edited by H. H. Rowley and are bound together under his name; the next decade was edited by G. W. Anderson.

15. *Missionary Research Library: Dictionary Catalog.* These fifteen volumes on Missions enter authors, titles, and subjects in one "dictionary," or alphabet, as is done in our card catalogue. *Bibliotheca Missionum* (31 volumes, and continuing) must be used through its indexes because the cleavages of its arrangement are first geographical, and then chronological.

16. *McAlpin Catalogue.* One of the greatest collections of the *British Puritans* in the world, apart from the British Museum and the Folger and Huntingdon libraries, is at Union Seminary, N. Y. (These books are not included in their *Shelf List*). Volume 5, the index volume, lists the titles for each author; volumes 1-4 reproduce the entire *title-page* for each book. This is informative, since a title-page of a seventeenth-century book often describes the contents in a wealth of polemic detail.

The *Short-title Catalogue* (Pollard and Redgrave, and Wing) seeks to list all books printed in the British Isles, as well as books in English printed elsewhere, from 1475 to 1700. A project to microfilm many S.T.C. titles is under way, and from these microfilms xerographic reprints in book form are available. These include early

English translations of Latin works of the Reformation period which are otherwise not readily accessible in either Latin or English.

The vast world of Renaissance and Reformation times should also be explored in *Bibliographie Internationale de l'Humanisme et de la Renaissance* (since 1965), *Bibliographie de la Réforme* (since 1940), the Literature Review Supplement of *Archive for Reformation History* (since 1972), and Schottenloher: *Bibliographie zur deutschen Geschichte im Zeitalter der Glaubensspaltung*.

17. *American Bibliography*. The more than 68,000 books and pamphlets printed in America from 1639 to 1813 are listed in 49 volumes. A third or more of these are of theological interest. The complete texts of all these books and pamphlets have been fully reproduced on microprint cards. Westminster shares with nine other Philadelphia libraries in the purchase and in the use of these microprint cards, which are kept at the Free Library of Philadelphia, but which will be sent to us on interlibrary loan at our request.

18. Winchell, Constance M.: *Guide to Reference Books,* 8th edition, Chicago, American Library Association, 1967, is a comprehensive list of reference works basic for research in all areas. The scope, merits, and peculiarities of each are described. The explanations of how to use each work are well worth noting. Winchell may also be consulted with a specific reference question in mind, to find quickly the most likely bibliographic coverage of that question.

CHECK LIST OF REFERENCE WORKS

A list of some more important bibliographies, encyclopedias, etc., for identification. Locate each; enter the call number on the left margin; on the right enter your notes on scope, arrangement, and the value of the work to you.

I. *General Bibliographies*

National Union Catalog, pre-1956.
National Union Catalog, 1953–.
Library of Congress Catalog, to 1952.
Library of Congress Catalog—Books: Subjects.
British Museum Catalogue of Printed Books.
Deutsche Bibliographie.

Verzeichnis lieferbarer Bücher.
Le Catalogue de l'Edition Française.
Cumulative Book Index.
Books in Print.
Subject Guide to Books in Print.
Publishers' Trade List Annual.
British Books in Print.
Besterman: World Bibliography of Bibliographies.
Winchell: Guide to Reference Books.
Evans, Shaw, and Shoemaker: American Bibliography.
Ulrich's Periodicals Directory.
Union List of Serials in Libraries of the U.S. and Canada.
New Serial Titles.
The Times Atlas of the World.
Atlas of Israel.

II. *Theological Bibliographies*

Union Theological Seminary Shelf List.
Biblica: Elenchus Bibliographicus Biblicus.
Bibliographisches Beiblatt der theologischen Literaturzeitung.
Theologischer Jahresbericht.
Darling: Cyclopaedia Bibliographica.
Ephemerides Theologicae Lovanienses.
Revue d'Histoire Ecclésiastique: Bibliographie.
Missionary Research Library Catalog.
Bibliotheca Missionum.
Barrow, John G.: A Bibliography of Bibliographies in Religion.
(SPECIAL SUBJECTS)
A Baptist Bibliography.
McAlpin Catalogue (for British Puritans).
Dr. Williams's Library Catalogue: Early Nonconformity, 1566-1800.
Short-title Catalogue (Pollard, Redgrave, and Wing).
International Bibliography of the History of Religions.
Thomsen, P.: Palästina-Literatur.
Darlow and Moule: Printed Editions of Holy Scripture.
Bibliographie de l'Assyriologie.

Society for O.T. Study: Book List (Rowley, etc.)
Bibliography of N.T. Literature, 1900-1950.
Hurd: A Bibliography of N.T. Bibliographies, 1966.
Mattill: A Classified Bibliography . . . on Acts, 1966.
Metzger: Index of Articles on the N.T. . . . in Festschriften, 1951.
Metzger: Index to Periodical Literature on the Apostle Paul, 1951.
Metzger: Index to Periodical Literature on Christ and the Gospels, 1966.
New Testament Abstracts.
American Historical Association: Guide to Historical Literature.
Bibliographia Patristica.
Augustine Bibliography.
Chevalier, U.: Répertoire des Sources . . . (4 vols.).
Bibliographie de la Réforme.
Bibliographie Internationale de l'Humanisme et de la Renaissance.
Schottenloher: Bibliographie zur deutschen Geschichte.
Burr: A Critical Bibliography of Religion in America.
Anderson, Gerald H.: Bibliography of the Theology of Missions.
Anderson, Gerald H.: Mission Research, Writing, and Publishing (in The Future of the Christian World Mission, PA/B836).
World Council of Churches: Catalog of the Ecumenical Movement.

III. *General Encyclopedias*

Enciclopedia Italiana.
Encyclopaedia Britannica.
Encyclopedia Americana.
Der grosse Brockhaus.
Meyers Enzyklopädisches Lexikon.
Larousse: La Grande Encyclopédie.
(SPECIAL SUBJECTS)
Pauly-Wissowa: Realencyclopädie der classischen Altertumswissenschaft.
International Encyclopedia of the Social Sciences.
The Encyclopedia of Education.
The Encyclopedia of Philosophy.
Eisler: Wörterbuch der philosophischen Begriffe.

Ritter: Historisches Wörterbuch der Philosophie.
Bibliography of Philosophy.
Lalande: Vocabulaire Technique et Critique de la Philosophie.
Dictionary of the History of Ideas.

IV. *Theological Encyclopedias*

Dictionnaire Apologétique de la Foi Catholique (d'Alès).
Dictionnaire d'Histoire et de Géographie Ecclésiastiques (Baudrillart).
Encyclopaedia Judaica.
Encyclopedia Biblica (in Hebrew).
Dictionnaire d'Archéologie Chrétienne et Liturgie (Cabrol).
New Catholic Encyclopedia.
Enciclopedia Cattolica.
Christelijke Encyclopedie.
The Encyclopedia of Christianity (Palmer, Cohen, Hughes).
Evangelisches Kirchenlexikon.
Hastings: Encyclopaedia of Religion and Ethics.
Dictionary of Christ and the Gospels.
Dictionary of the Apostolic Church.
Hauck: Realencyklopädie für protestantische Theologie und Kirche.
International Standard Bible Encyclopaedia.
Encyclopaedia of Islam.
Jewish Encyclopedia.
Reallexikon für Antike und Christentum.
Lexikon für Theologie und Kirche.
McClintock and Strong: Cyclopaedia of Religious Literature (be sure
   to check the two supplementary volumes).
Oxford Dictionary of the Christian Church (second edition).
Die Religion in Geschichte und Gegenwart (three editions).
Sacramentum Mundi.
Sacramentum Verbi.
Schaff-Herzog Encyclopedia of Religious Knowledge.
Dictionnaire de Théologie Catholique (Vacant).
Dictionnaire de la Bible (Vigouroux).
Julian: Dictionary of Hymnology.

V. *Indexes to Periodical Literature*

A.T.L.A. Index to Religious Periodical Literature.
Biblica: Elenchus Bibliographicus Biblicus.
Christian Periodical Index.
Religious and Theological Abstracts.
Bibliographie Biblique.
Internationale Zeitschriftenschau für Bibelwissenschaft. . . .
International Index to Periodicals.
New Testament Abstracts.

VI. *Biographical Dictionaries*

Dictionary of American Biography.
Dictionary of National Biography.
Biographische Woordenboek van Protestantsche Godgeleerden in
Nederland.
Fasti Ecclesiae Scoticanae.
La France Protestante.
Niceron: Mémoires . . . des Hommes Illustres.
Dictionary of Christian Biography (Wm. Smith).
Who's Who.
Who's Who in America.

Chapter 14

The Graduate Student at Work: Digests of Th.M. Theses

a. Papyrus Bodmer II and the Text of John's Gospel

H. Wilbur Aulie[*]

The publication of Papyrus 66 in 1956 was hailed by Kurt Aland as an event in New Testament textual criticism of great importance. Chapter one of the thesis deals with the significance of this manuscript. Consisting of sixty-eight percent of the Gospel of John, it contains more than any other papyrus fragment of comparable date. The famous John Rylands fragment, which is dated somewhat earlier, consists only of five verses of chapter eighteen, of which three are incomplete. The Chester Beatty Papyrus (P45) offers somewhat less than two chapters. P66 has been given the date of A.D. 200, which is fifty years earlier than the dating of P45. P66 stands as one of the earliest and best preserved manuscripts of John which offer an extensive text for study.

Chapter two presents a description of the manuscript, discussing history and form, date, orthographical variations, additions, significant omissions, scratchings, and transpositions. Chapter three is a collation of the manuscript against the twenty-third edition of the Nestle text. In Chapter four the variants are analyzed by the multiple variant method which calls for the study of all those passages where there are at least three variants, each of which has one or

---

*Th.M. degree received from Westminster Theological Seminary in 1960. Mr. Aulie is a missionary translator with Wycliffe Bible Translators.

more important witnesses. None of the witnesses which were compared with P66 supported P66 in a majority of the multiple variants, but there was a clear gradation of relationship. Vaticanus holds the top place in relationship to P66. Then follow ℵ , L, Θ, D, and 33 somewhat farther behind and in that order. From the standpoint of text types, it is significant to observe that P66 gets most support from the Alexandrian text type. However, there are enough witnesses from other text types to keep P66 out of a single text class. Mixture is indicated by the presence of Θ and A representing Byzantine, D representing early Western, and W Western. Chapter five discusses the relation of P66 with selected witnesses: the Caesarean text, the Alexandrian text, the Byzantine text, and with certain groups of documents. Chapter six, on the relation between P66 and the text of John's Gospel, deals with four classes of passages: (1) cases where a reconsideration of the text of our printed testaments is called for; (2) those which confirm the text of Nestle and the best tradition; (3) those which confirm the text of Nestle but which remain in doubt; (4) those which clearly follow inferior readings.

Conclusion: (1) Corruptions entered the major textual tradition at an early date. (2) P66 is a mixed text. (3) A mixed text was current in Egypt early in the second century. (4) The data of P66 do not give enough information to make any statement about the origin of the "Neutral" text.

b. Healing in the New Testament   Kenneth Brown*

This thesis has been developed around the usage of the words *therapeuo* and *iaomai*. On the one hand the former incorporates the concept of therapy or some type of care or nursing. It normally involves process, development, or means. On the other hand the latter has been reserved for the miraculous, and necessitates immediate, spontaneous, and permanent health without the function of natural laws. God can and does heal, though some of the physical relief and cures affecting the body may not be considered healing in the sense of this thesis.

---

*Th.M. received from Westminster Theological Seminary in 1960.

Healing, as a divine gift to men in the early church, does not function today, since the canon of Scripture is closed. The passage in the book of James relates to medical care in association with prayer rather than a unique ministry of the Holy Spirit. It is permissible for Christians to consult physicians, and the use of medical and surgical care does not conflict with prayer. Some consideration is given to the role of physicians in history and their absence in Israel. In view of the fact that health is relative, and the body of each individual will ultimately need repair or some kind of cure, it is concluded that one should do three things when illness strikes: first, self-examination lest God should be employing this method of divine discipline; second, prayer; third, should the Lord not be pleased to restore health, quiet resignation and submission to bear the affliction as a testimony to the grace of God, who said, "My grace is sufficient for thee."

c. The Relationship of Christ's Sonship and Priesthood in the Book of Hebrews   David G. Dunbar*

This thesis is a biblical-theological exposition of an important aspect of the theology of the book of Hebrews—the correlation of Christ's sonship and priesthood. That the writer of Hebrews was conscious of such a correlation is suggested by the opening verses of the Epistle, where the priestly work of "purification of sins" is attributed to the *Son*. This judgment is confirmed by Hebrews 5:5, 6, where quotations from Psalm 2:7 and Psalm 110:4 are combined, and by Hebrews 7:1-3, where Melchizedek supplies a type both of Christ's priesthood and sonship.

Chapter 1 is given over to delimiting the problem and establishing a method of approach to the data. While it was not the intention to give a full treatment of either the sonship or priesthood doctrines, some preliminary understanding was needed particularly in the area of sonship. It was found that the New Testament in general presents two aspects of Christ's sonship—the ontological aspect and the mediatorial aspect. It was necessary, therefore, to consider both aspects in their relationship to the priesthood of Christ in Hebrews.

*Th.M. received from Westminster Theological Seminary in 1974.

In accord with a biblical-theological treatment of the data it was important to examine the epochal development of the sonship-priesthood teaching. Three revelatory epochs seemed to be in view in Hebrews: first, the Old Testament period as suggested by the quotations from Psalm 2:7, Psalm 110:4, and Genesis 14:18-20 (chap. 2); second, the period of Christ's earthly ministry (chap. 3); third, the period of Christ's heavenly ministry since the resurrection-ascension (chap. 4).

In chapter 2 attention is given to the important place of Melchizedek in the theology of Hebrews. Since our Lord did not trace His descent from the tribe of Levi (7:14), the priestly order of Melchizedek is the only one to which he may lay claim. It is with this unique order of priesthood that the writer of Hebrews links the sonship of Christ. In 7:1-3 the characteristics of Melchizedek are given which lie at the basis of his priesthood. Typologically these may be summed up in the idea of sonship: "made like the Son of God" (vs. 3). The parallel between Melchizedek and Christ would then suggest that our Lord's priesthood is likewise grounded in His sonship. Further, this sonship is to be understood in the ontological sense as suggested by the "eternity aspect" of verse 3: "having neither beginning of days nor end of life." The quotations in 5:5, 6 also connect sonship and priesthood, but here the mediatorial sonship is in view (unless one interprets "this day" in Ps. 2:7 to refer to God's eternal day).

Chapter 3 treats the period of our Lord's earthly ministry. It was necessary to examine the question first raised in the controversies between the Reformers and the Socinians: Was Christ a priest on earth? It was found that the data in Hebrews are paradoxical—at times Christ is presented as acting in a priestly capacity during His earthly ministry, at other times the priesthood seems to find its inception at His entrance into the heavenly sanctuary. A proposed resolution of the data is reserved for the following chapter; however, since the writer does certainly consider Christ a priest on earth, it was necessary to consider the connection of the priesthood with the sonship. The link between the earthly priestly ministry and the ontological sonship is found in 9:13, 14, where the Savior is said to offer himself (the priestly function) "through eternal spirit." Here the ontological sonship is the basis of the value and efficacy of the atonement. The mediatorial sonship and the priesthood are joined in 2:10-18; 5:7-10; and 7:28, where this sonship is seen to provide the identification of nature and experience which is required between sinful men and the priest who represents them to God.

The final section of the thesis deals with the heavenly ministry of Christ. Support for the idea of a heavenly offering is found to be lacking in the Epistle, and the main aspect of the heavenly ministry is simply "intercession" (7:26; cf. 2:16; 4:16; 9:24). With this heavenly work the ontological sonship is intimately connected as it indicates the source of power by which Christ acquires and administers His priesthood (7:16; 4:14-16), while the mediatorial aspect of the sonship relates to His sympathy with His people (2:17, 18; 4:14-16).

In this chapter also the problem of the exegesis of 5:5, 6 and the inception of Christ's priesthood is resumed. Good support is found for identifying the day of Christ's begetting with the day of the resurrection. Likewise, the oracle of Psalm 110:4—"you are a priest forever"—is fulfilled at the resurrection. Thus, Jesus must in some sense become both son and priest at the resurrection. However, since He was a son-priest even during His earthly ministry, the passage in 5:5, 6 must refer to a new investiture and exercise of power and authority which surpassed anything which could be ascribed to Him before the resurrection.

d. The Authorship of the   George W. Knight III*
Pastoral Epistles

The Pastoral Epistles, I and II Timothy and Titus, specifically claim to be written by the Apostle Paul (I Tim. 1:1; II Tim. 1:1; Titus 1:1). This self-testimony is corroborated by various personal references throughout the letters.

This self-testimony has been called in question and two alternative theories have been proposed. The Fictional Approach, advocated by H. J. Holtzmann and M. Dibelius, regards the epistles as

*Th.M. received at Westminster Theological Seminary in 1957. Dr. Knight is at present a member of the faculty of Covenant Theological Seminary.

entirely pseudonymous. The Fragment Approach, advocated in a most able way by P. N. Harrison, admits the use of genuine Pauline fragments by an admirer of Paul.

The thesis examines the arguments urged against the Pauline authorship and offers answers to those arguments. First, there are sufficient data to establish a release from his first imprisonment and a second imprisonment for Paul. Thus there is no conflict between this historical situation reflected in the Pastorals and the rest of the New Testament. Second, the situation and teaching presented in the Pastorals are shown to be in accord with Paul's teaching and to fit this period in the history of revelation and the history of the church, i.e., the ecclesiastical organization reflected or taught, the false teaching and false teachers, the doctrine taught by Paul, and the personal and circumstantial details. Last of all, the linguistic and stylistic features, contra Harrison particularly, are shown to be in accord with Paul's usage when one takes into account the appropriate variable factors which influence and affect linguistic and stylistic features, i.e., different recipients, relation of recipients to writer, specific subject matter, effect on writer of change of locale, age, etc., and different or unique amanuensis.

The last chapter confronts the Fragment Approach in particular, but also the Fictional Approach, with the ethical question involved for the presumed writer in writing in Paul's name and also for the Christian community in recognizing these letters as part of the canon.

The final conclusion is "that all the lines of evidence converge upon the thesis of this paper which is the self-testimony of these epistles, namely that their author is none other than the Apostle Paul."

e. Gospel and Commandment: A Study of the Apostolic Kerygma and Didache   W. L. Lane*

A comprehensive investigation of the apostolic kerygma and didache was undertaken in order to provide a better understanding of the witness of the primitive church.

*Th.M. received at Westminster Theological Seminary in 1956. Dr. Lane is at present Visiting Professor in Philosophy and Religion at Western Kentucky University.

Kerygma signifies the apostolic proclamation of the gospel. Four postulates were deemed essential, for they are present in every illustration of the mission proclamation to those for whom Scripture was a point of reference. These are (1) the assertion that the age of fulfillment has been inaugurated since the Messiah has fulfilled the Scriptures, (2) the declaration of the redemptive facts concerning Jesus of Nazareth, who is the Messiah, (3) the call to repentance and the offer of forgiveness of sins, and (4) the affirmation that the apostles are witnesses to the truth announced. When Gentiles were addressed, to whom Scripture was unfamiliar, appeal was made to God's natural revelation which declared him to be Creator and Sustainer. The other three postulates would then follow.

Didache signifies the apostolic instruction taught catechetically to those who responded to the gospel. The didache explained more fully the content of the kerygma, developing and illustrating its implications, applying evangelical principles to the practical concerns of the new disciple. The content of the didache was thus theological, apologetic, and parenetic in character. Facts concerning Jesus and His sayings were an integral part of this catechesis, and from the beginning the teaching of Jesus furnished an authoritative standard alongside Old Testament revelation.

The apostolic kerygma and didache are integrally related under the rubric of the sovereign disposition of God. God initiates the sovereign and gracious redemptive acts which constitute the content of the proclamation. He imposes His righteous law upon those who receive the blessings of redemption, and the didache declares this law. Thus kerygma and didache are thoroughly God-centered concepts. They declare what God has done for man and how man must respond to God's gracious action. For this reason the kerygma and didache are situated by the apostles within the larger context of the covenant and the kingdom, both manifestations of the sovereign disposition of God.

The New Testament documents significantly reflect the content of the primitive kerygma and didache. While to a considerable extent they have the character of didache, they appeal to the kerygma and presuppose that its message is accepted by the readers. When the documents speak of the gospel proclamation, they do so in terms of the postulates of the kerygma. They recall the reader to the kerygma and the didache he has received. They continue the apostolic instruction by addressing themselves to new problems, applying the tenets of the didache to the situation of the Christian in a non-Christian environment. The continuity with the apostolic kerygma and didache accounts in part for the remarkable unity which characterizes the New Testament writings.

The origin of the apostolic kerygma and didache must be traced directly to Jesus Himself. While the mission and message of Jesus prior to His crucifixion furnished much of the content of the kerygma and didache, the formal origin of these related aspects of early Christian witness must be traced to Jesus' post-resurrection ministry. The commission of the disciples recorded in Luke 24:44-48 is expressed in terms of proclamation, and the essential postulates of the kerygma are clearly enunciated. The commission preserved by Matthew 28:18-20, however, is expressed in terms of instruction and is sufficiently broad in scope to account for the character of the didache. The forty-day period of instruction for the disciples by the risen Lord provides an adequate explanation for the unity of emphasis and perspective which marks the apostolic presentation of the kerygma and the didache.

f. The Kingdom of God Has Come   J. Ramsey Michaels*

A survey of those passages in the synoptic Gospels which seem to view the kingdom of God as a present reality in the ministry of Jesus (e.g., Matt. 11:11-12; 12:28; Luke 17:21). These were studied within the framework of the Old Testament background of the kingdom idea and of Jesus' proclamation of an imminent *future* kingdom.

The conclusion was that the "present kingdom" passages cannot be separated from the "imminent future kingdom" passages; that is, it was Jesus' very act of proclaiming the imminent *future* kingdom

---

*Th.M. received at Westminster Theological Seminary in 1956. Dr. Michaels is at present a member of the faculty of the Gordon-Conwell Theological Seminary.

which made this kingdom in some sense *present* and within the reach of his hearers. In this sense his proclamation of the kingdom is self-authenticating; it is not simply the announcement of a prophet, but belongs to Jesus' distinctly messianic work.

g. Peter's and Paul's Common Use   Erwin Penner*
of Old Testament Quotations

The concern of this thesis was to examine the NT's use of the OT by focusing on the OT quotations common to Peter and Paul from two basic perspectives: (1) the origin of the quotations, and (2) the hermeneutical questions raised by the quotations. The specific passages under study were I Peter 2:6-8, 10, and Romans 9:25, 33, in which Isaiah 8:14, 28:16, and parts of Hosea 1-3 are quoted.

With respect to the origin of the quotations, the following conclusions were reached. First, the LXX text represented by the A codex lies behind the apostles' use of the OT, although a definite influence from the Hebrew text is present in Isaiah 8:14. Second, Peter's and Paul's common differences with the LXX and MT can best be explained in terms of their use of a strong, primarily oral, Christian tradition. For example, (1) the source of their use of Isaiah 8:14 and 28:16 is a common stone-tradition that can be traced back to certain *Verba Christi;* and (2) their use of Hosea 1-3 arises from the practice of contextual quotation, which was common in the Church and developed around certain "favorite" Scripture passages. Finally, the apostles' differences from one another are best explained in terms of a primarily *independent* use of Christian oral tradition.

Many hermeneutical problems arise in these few verses, but their solution lies in four basic considerations. First, the apostles do not allegorize the OT texts, but understand them in their original grammatical-historical sense. Second, in applying these texts the apostles do not err or do violence to the original meaning by adding their interpretive notes, but give a legitimate interpretation. It must be recognized, however, that the apostles give further revelation in their interpretive writings. Third, Peter and Paul follow a thor-

---

*Th.M. received at Westminster Theological Seminary in 1969. Mr. Penner is at present a member of the faculty of Winkler Bible Institute.

oughly biblical-theological approach in quoting the OT, seeing the fulfillment of the OT in Christ. Christ is their interpretive principle of the OT. Fourth, it is in terms of this approach (the biblical-theological method based on sound grammatical-historical exegesis) that the NT hermeneutic must be seen as normative for modern interpretation of the OT; the only discontinuity being that the modern interpreter cannot add further revelation as did the apostles.

The study of the NT's use of OT is, then, of tremendous importance to understand God's whole revelation, particularly the unity of His redemptive work. This study also teaches us *how* to understand God's revelation, it provides a hermeneutic by which the revelation of the past can be made relevant to the present.

h. The Sound of Koine Greek Roger F. H. Pugsley*

In a century replete with discoveries of a lasting and depth nature, Professor W. B. Stanford's work *The Sound of Greek*[1] appears as a dynamic and powerful contribution to our understanding of ancient Greek culture.

Stanford emphasizes that the system of writing used in Greek was that of symbols which acted as memory aids for sound. He demonstrates conclusively that the Greeks were in fact "ear-readers" and not "eye-readers."

The purpose of this thesis is to apply the discoveries propounded by Professor Stanford to the Koine Greek.

It may be truly said that the impact of *The Sound of Greek* on the study of the Greek New Testament is indeed revolutionary and calls for a sober re-evaluation of the New Testament language. This thesis represents only a beginning with respect to the need for the exploration in depth of the sound aspects of New Testament Greek.

The Importance of Sound as Implicit
in Ancient Greek Language and Communication

It is now of importance to seek to explain exactly and specifically the significance of sound with respect to ancient Greek communica-

---

*Th.M. received at Westminster Theological Seminary in 1971.

1. W. B. Stanford, *The Sound of Greek* (Berkeley & Los Angeles: University of California Press, 1967).

tion. How did the sound value affect the ancient Greek language?

It is doubtless superfluous to say that in the beginning the written word or book merely preserved a record of that which had once been spoken.

For the words and sentences of this record to recover life and meaning, it was necessary that they be reanimated by the voice of someone who understood the significance of the written characters.

The Continuity of the Greek Language

The Greek used at the time of the writing of the New Testament is called Koine Greek, and is originally a derivative chiefly from the ancient Attic Greek. One can trace a historical development and progressive emergence of Koine from the Attic Greek. The very essence of the Koine biblical Greek and that of its predecessors encompass the same elements, which enable one to apply to them common principles of linguistic study.

Application of W. B. Stanford's Thesis of the Value of Sound to the New Testament Koine Greek

The factors noticed about the oral nature of ancient Greek society certainly were characteristic of New Testament times. Such was the nature of the New Testament writings that they were written to be read aloud to groups of people.

These early documents of the New Testament were written for the ear-reader not for the eye-reader, as is commonly assumed.

So, to the student of the Koine Greek the following is important: that the substance of the physical material which the historian like Luke and the Apostles Paul and Peter used to convey their thoughts and feelings was primarily and essentially vocal sound, and the writings should be studied and interpreted in view of the ancients' conception of communication and writing.

When exhaustive consideration is given to the sound aspects of the New Testament Greek in the context of the essentially oral nature of ancient society and the general practice of oral reading, it presents the writings of the New Testament in a new dimension.

One must first appreciate the significance and purpose of ancient writing and then fully grasp the new perspective and implications of this as it is applied to the Greek of the New Testament.

It requires the same kind of sensitivity to sound and musical qualities which the ancients possessed and which was inherent in their educational system.

It is now possible truly to understand the essential nature of the text of the New Testament in the light of the perspective of language and communication in the historical period from which it was derived.

i. Bultmann's Methods of Formgeschichte
Ronald C. Scharfe*

The purpose of this thesis is to examine critically some of the assumptions and principles involved in Bultmann's methods of Formgeschichte, especially as they are apparent in his study of the synoptic Gospels. Chapter one traces historically the background and growth of the Formgeschichte movement in New Testament studies up to the time of Bultmann. Chapter two attempts to examine Bultmann's analysis of the synoptic Gospels from as objective a standpoint as possible. Chapter three in conclusion provides an evaluation of Bultmann's historical skepticism as evidenced in his principles of gospel criticism.

The conclusion reached is that his methods of Formgeschichte are largely negative and thus severely limited in their usefulness for a study of the Gospels which is true to the self-testimony of the Scriptures. Moreover, his methods are damaging to any attempt to build a constructive biblical theology which rests faithfully upon the authenticity of the New Testament records.

j. The Study of Words in New Testament Interpretation
Moisés Silva**

The first chapter, which serves as an introduction, reviews the work of James Barr on biblical semantics, advocates the use of

---

*Th.M. received at Westminster Theological Seminary in 1967. Mr. Scharfe is at present head librarian and a member of the faculty of Fort Wayne Bible College.

**Th.M. received at Westminster Theological Seminary in 1971. He is a member of the faculty of Westmont College.

modern linguistic studies for the purpose of N.T. exegesis, and exposes the dangers of too much concentration on word studies. However, since lexical work remains a necessity, the rest of the thesis seeks to apply sound linguistic principles—both historical and descriptive—to the study of N.T. words.

Chapter two, "The History of Words," insists on Ferdinand de Saussure's distinction between diachronic linguistics (which studies the evolution of languages) and synchronic linguistics (which studies one state in the evolution of a language). The rest of the chapter, devoted to the first of these approaches, deals primarily with the dangers of etymological studies; the root of a word, however, can be of value if it has played a role in the consciousness of the writer. A few words on semantic change—and the value of the Septuagint for this type of study—conclude the historical discussion.

Descriptive semantics is the concern of the final chapter, "The Meaning of Words." The notion of structuralism is discussed and the possibility of studying semantic structure is defended. Relying heavily on the work of John Lyons, most of the chapter is devoted to the various semantic relations to be found in a given language. In the end, however, absolute primacy must be given to contextual considerations when we try to determine the meaning of a word.

A few concluding remarks—including some thoughts on language instruction and exegetical method—end the thesis.